Enhancing Teaching and Learning

Enhancing Teaching and Learning

A Leadership Guide for School Librarians

THIRD EDITION

Jean Donham

Neal-Schuman

An imprint of the American Library Association

Chicago   2013

JEAN DONHAM is a professor in the School Library Studies graduate program at the University of Northern Iowa. Previously she was library director at Cornell College in Mount Vernon, Iowa. Prior to her appointment there, she was a tenured member of the faculty in the School of Library and Information Science at the University of Iowa. She served as district coordinator for library and technology programs in the Iowa City Community School District for 13 years. Author of numerous professional articles, Dr. Donham has been a presenter at national, regional, and state conferences. Active in the Iowa Association of School Librarians, she was the first recipient of that organization's Media Professional of the Year. In addition, she served as a member of the board for the American Association of School Librarians. She holds a master's degree in library and information studies from the University of Maryland and a PhD in educational administration from the University of Iowa. Dr. Donham is married to Kelley Donham and has two sons, Andrew and Joel.

Printed in the United States of America

17 16 15 14 13   5 4 3 2 1

Extensive effort has gone into ensuring the reliability of the information in this book; however, the publisher makes no warranty, express or implied, with respect to the material contained herein.

ISBNs: 978-1-55570-887-0 (paper); 978-1-55570-893-1 (PDF). For more information on digital formats, visit the ALA Store at alastore.ala.org and select eEditions.

Library of Congress Cataloging-in-Publication Data

Donham, Jean.
  Enhancing teaching and learning : a leadership guide for school librarians /
Jean Donham. — Third edition.
    pages   cm
  Includes bibliographical references and indexes.
  ISBN 978-1-55570-887-0
  1. School libraries—United States. 2. Instructional materials centers—United States.
  I. Title.
Z675.S3D65 2013
027.80973—dc23   2013006365

Book design in Melior and Din typefaces.
Cover design by Kimberly Thornton. Images ©Shutterstock, Inc.

♾ This paper meets the requirements of ANSI/NISO Z39.48–1992 (Permanence of Paper).

Contents

Figures

Preface

This book updates and expands previous editions, but its overall purpose—to help school library professionals effect change in their library programs by integrating these programs into the school's overall instructional plan—remains unchanged. Leadership requires a delicate balance between being simultaneously proactive and responsive. On the one hand, the library professional has an agenda for leading inquiry-based learning, advocating for reading, supporting professional principles of intellectual freedom and equity of access, and facilitating effective uses of information technologies. Advancement of this agenda demands leadership. On the other hand, that agenda can be fully accomplished only when it is integrated into the school culture and curriculum, and such integration requires collaboration between the library professional, school administrators, and the teaching staff. The result of the interaction between the library program and the other components of the students' school experience is a synergy in which the effect is greater than the sum of the parts. These interactions serve to increase its impact on students. However, when the parts work in isolation, the potential for their effectiveness is diminished.

All professions have an inclination to become egocentric and to see their specialty as the center of the universe. In medicine, the primary care physician sees his or her role as central to patient care, while the surgeon sees himself or herself taking the lead in case decisions. In education, a school administrator is often perceived as the pivotal instructional leader of the school. Language arts and reading teachers are often seen as central to student success because reading and writing are foundations for success. The school librarian likes to perceive his or her program as central to education because it relates to all curricular areas and all grade levels in the school and therefore influences the school administration and the community. Yet, it is important for school librarians to consider respectfully the expertise of classroom teachers, the position of school administrators, and the beliefs and values of the community at large. Striking the balance between collaboration and leadership is a key to successful implementation of an effective library program. My hope is that this book helps its readers find the appropriate balance. Finding this middle ground means that the library program is at once affected by and affects its surroundings.

During my 13 years as a district-level library and technology coordinator, I observed a variety of implementations of the fundamental principles of effective school librarianship. No two schools in my district had identical library programs, yet each was effective in meeting local needs. There is not just one right way to carry out a successful library program. Certainly the school library profession has nonnegotiable elements: an inquiry curriculum; teachers and school librarians who collaborate; an adequate collection of resources to meet the needs of students and teachers; facilities that accommodate a variety of simultaneous activities; and students' access to resources at their point of need. The school librarian must advocate for all of these. Yet the implementation in any given school must be adapted to suit the local school culture, which means that what works in a multiage, continuous-progress setting may not fit a more traditional school. Where to draw the line of acceptability is the key decision for library professionals.

This edition is expanded to reflect changes—professional, theoretical, legal, and political—in the library field and in education. As you read, you will encounter the role of standards; the influence of the media, including the web; the educational needs of millennials (those born since 1983); changing reading habits, including nonfiction, discussion groups, and reward-based reading programs; and so on. Scenarios for Discussion at the end of each chapter are intended to provide opportunities to apply the ideas presented to practical challenges and situations that call for leadership.

This book is divided into two parts. Part I, "The Environment," addresses the components of the school environment—the students, the content area curricula, the principal, the school district, the local community, and the library's virtual environment.

Part II, "The School Library Program," provides specific tactics for establishing the library program as an active player in teaching and learning. This section examines strategies for collaborating with teachers, policies and practices to maximize students' access to physical and virtual resources, the important contributions of the library to literacy efforts, the unique characteristics of inquiry-based learning, the school library's responsibilities for leadership in technology planning and implementation, student assessments, strategies for continuous improvement of the library program, and finally the importance of leadership. The overarching message of this book is that school librarians must overcome the lack of high expectations for them and their program through a proactive stance that is called leadership.

Acknowledgments

This book grew out of years of experience and study, both of which were influenced and aided by many people. Two important mentors for me have been David Loertscher and Al Azinger. David gave me a vision for school library programs and has continued to reinvent that vision as times and schools have changed. Al taught me the meaning of leadership.

The librarians in the Iowa City Community School District invested energy and talent to bring a vision to life in schools where they have made important differences in teaching and learning. I am especially grateful to Denise Rehmke, Cindy Kunde, Lynn Myers, Victoria Walton, Ann Holton, Anne Marie Kraus, Barbara Stein, Deb Dorzweiler, Mary Jo Langhorne, and Deb McAlister for their ideas.

This project required that someone believe that I had something to offer the profession. June Gross brainstormed with me, read versions of every chapter, and gave me advice. She helped ensure that the book reflected excellence in school library practice. Michaela Seeman did background research for me. Sherry Crow, Nancy Everhart, and Donna Shannon read all chapters and provided valuable feedback. Charles Harmon supported the work from beginning to end. My family tolerated the imposition on their time for me to complete this work.

The text includes a quotation from Robert Reich: "Rarely do even Big Ideas emerge any longer from the solitary labors of genius." This book, like the other work in my life, is the product of collaboration. The synergy that comes from many people sharing ideas and working together is what produced this book, and that is its topic as well.

PART I

The
Environment

Students

This chapter:

- describes conditions of youth attending American schools and how school library programs can improve equity of opportunity;
- discusses the ever-growing demands for meeting the needs of exceptional students;
- describes the nature of motivation and its effect on learning;
- examines the importance of today's students becoming lifelong learners and the role of the library program to support them; and
- identifies leadership strategies for working with students.

Students represent the diversity of our culture and are unique individuals. Denise is ambitious and hard-working, hopes to become an engineer, and is eager to please her teachers. Jana is popular and chatty, and wants to be liked. Kate is angry, outspoken, and sometimes hostile. Michael is on the quiet side, shy, tense, and anxious. John is bright, inquisitive, and success-oriented. And so it goes, with each student as individual as his or her name: Peter, Tom, Angelique, Joel, Manuel, Kerri, and Andrew.

A chapter about students is an appropriate beginning for a book about the school library program. While the library has many constituencies—teachers, parents, and the community at large—its primary goal is to help students become effective users of information. To accomplish that goal, the library program must be sensitive to young people's cognitive and affective needs.

The relationship between adults and youth can be fragile. Power and authority, levels of self-confidence, and implied and explicit expectations complicate the relationship. An adult's unintended cue can direct a less-than-confident student away from the library. Young people's assumptions regarding authority figures or their desire for independence can prevent them from seeking help. Many students see the school librarian as different from the teacher—perhaps less threatening. However, some may find the librarian more intimidating because they have relatively few interactions. Each interaction with a student determines whether that student will want to return to the library. An adage in business customer service says that dissatisfied customers often will not express their complaints—they will just never return. An encounter with a salesperson in a retail store will determine the likelihood that the customer will return. Effective customer relations requires understanding and appreciating the nature as well as the needs and wants of the customer. This chapter focuses on the most important library program customers—students.

Students entering school libraries seek help and resources for a variety of reasons, and each student brings a different level of confidence. They hope to find what they need and have access to friendly, knowledgeable, and sincere help. The library staff is in a unique position for building relationships with students. Teachers set expectations for student performance, and school librarians help students meet those expectations. Librarians can enjoy a special partnership with students. Those students who feel disenfranchised from the school culture may benefit particularly from the special nature of that relationship. The librarian shares the student goal of "getting the assignment done" or "finding the answer," as compared to the teacher's role of "giving the assignment" or "posing the question." The librarian has an unusual opportunity to facilitate learning.

Conditions of American Youth

The conditions of American young people vary dramatically. In affluent families, children have their own computers, mobile phones, and other devices. Other students have none of these resources in their homes. In each school, considering students' economic and family conditions is a first step toward being responsive to their needs. Often such data on economic and family conditions of students are available at the state department of education website. It is also helpful to understand the conditions of young people in the nation; this knowledge helps educators relate the condition of local youth to others. Schools tend to be insular, but in many situations student conditions are transient.

Poverty

In 2011, over 15 million American children were living in families with incomes below the federal poverty level of $22,050 per year for a family of four, according to the National Center for Children in Poverty (Wight, Chau, and Aratani, 2011). National Center for Education Statistics (NCES) 2009 high school data indicated the proportion of 18- to 24-year-olds who have earned a high school diploma or an equivalent credential. The overall completion rate was 91.9 percent and varied significantly by racial group—96.6 percent for Asians, 94.8 percent for whites, 90.7 percent for blacks, 82.4 percent for Hispanics, and 86.8 percent for Native Americans (NCES, 2011). Among various reports that provide evidence of the relationship between poverty and student achievement, the NCES 2010 Condition of Education report stated that approximately 68 percent of twelfth-graders in high-poverty schools and 91 percent of twelfth-graders in low-poverty schools graduated with a diploma (NCES, 2010a). High-poverty schools are those where more than 76 percent of students are eligible for free or reduced lunch programs, and low-poverty schools are those where fewer than 25 percent of students are eligible. These data reveal that significant poverty and racial factors create differences in degrees of success among students. While school librarians, like all educators, have concerns about young people, the realities of some of these students lie beyond the library program. Still, the library program can try to encourage a student to stay in school. Sometimes, a library can be a haven for the student who feels disenfranchised elsewhere in school.

Language

NCES data for 2009 revealed that 21 percent of students spoke a language other than English at home (NCES, 2010b). Immigrant children newly arriving in the United States do not all face the same issues. Some face language barriers, some face poverty, and others are affected emotionally or psychologically by their life experiences. For a large proportion of them, English language acquisition is an immediate challenge. Their potential to acquire English language skills depends on a variety of factors, such as age, length of time in this country, socioeconomic status, parental education, and residence location (Rong and Preissle, 1998). Some of these students arrive here having been first-hand witnesses to the horrors of war and other inhumanities. The learning challenges for these children are intensified by the emotional complications their experiences may have created. Some have left family behind and may no longer have an adequate social network to support them. These added emotional and social circumstances hinder their attempts to learn a new language. The school librarian may be in a particularly strong position to offer consolation and support to these students. In a 2009 survey of school librarians, 36 percent reported they used no special strategies to serve their English language learner (ELL) student populations (AASL, 2009). This situation seems at the least unfortunate and at the worst a dismissal of the ALA Library Bill of Rights, which ensures access to resources and services for all users. Adams (2010) suggests that school libraries have the opportunity to assist newly immigrated children in a variety of ways, including providing resources in native languages, learning to welcome students in their native languages, and reaching out to students through ELL classes and teachers.

Exceptional Learners

NCES data for 2008–2009 indicated that 13.2 percent of public school students received services from federally funded special education programs (NCES, 2010b). The landmark Individuals with Disabilities Education Act (IDEA) Amendments of 1997 stipulates that differently abled students are entitled to participation and progress within the general education curriculum (Yell and Shriner, 1997). With IDEA came a call for alternative media for both accessing information and communicating information (Hitchcock, Meyer, Rose, and Jackson, 2002). These alternatives create an essential role for school librarians to provide resources, to make available assistive software and hardware for improving visual or auditory access to information, and to recommend and teach a variety of Web 2.0 communication tools (e.g., graphic organizing tools like Bubbl.us or Kidspiration and speech-text tools like Write:OutLoud or WordQ) to assist these learners (Smith and Okolo, 2010).

In addition to resources, physical access is an important consideration in the library. Examples include workstations and space between shelving ranges that accommodate wheelchairs, adjustments of screen displays to accommodate visual needs, and provision of audiobooks. School librarians can help special needs students become more confident and independent by helping them develop skills in accessing information in the library. Cooperation with public libraries provides an opportunity to acquaint these students with a resource that will be valuable to them beyond their school years (Murray, 2000).

Another group of exceptional learners deserving special consideration in the library are those students identified as gifted and talented. Research suggests that from 2000 to 2007 achievement for the highest performing students (as measured by the National Assessment of Educational Progress) stagnated, while the lowest performing students made significant gains (Duffett, Farkas, and Loveless, 2008). With regard to gifted learners and the impact of No Child Left Behind, Jolly and Makel (2010) cite various studies as they assert:

> Research shows that gifted students learn differently than their classroom peers. These differences include being able to process more information over a shorter period of time, thinking in an abstract and complex manner, learning information the first time (making re-teaching and repetition unnecessary), liking and seeking intellectual challenge, and already knowing 50 to 60% of the curriculum at the beginning of the school year (Bleske-Rechek, Lubinski, & Benbow, 2004; Reis & Purcell, 1993; Rogers, 2004).

Jolly and Makel then question whether the effect on accountability under No Child Left Behind causes these students to be overlooked in the effort to bring all students to a minimum level of proficiency. Analyzing growth measures of student achievement in both reading and mathematics, Theaker and colleagues (2010) surmised that many high-achieving students struggle to maintain their elite performance over the years and often fail to improve their reading ability at the same rate as their average and below-average classmates. Their findings raise questions regarding how well schools have sustained attention to gifted learners under educational accountability policies of the past ten years. Clearly, the library program has potential to support gifted learners. Supporting gifted learners requires that the library be accessible to these students individually and for classes, that the library provide resources aimed to both pique and satisfy independent curiosity and exploration, and that the library program include teaching these exceptional students advanced information-seeking strategies. (Note: It is inaccurate to assume that just because these students are gifted, they already know how and where to search for authoritative information and how to evaluate it critically for bias, scope, purpose, and accuracy.) The library program can have an impact by improving access and helping increase opportunities for learning by considering level of difficulty and ethnic representation in collection development, by teaching information skills, by initiating participation of the library program in learning opportunities for gifted/talented programs and individual students, and by responding to the impact of out-of-school influences.

Improving Access

According to the report *America's Children: Key National Indicators of Well-Being, 2011* (Federal Interagency Forum on Child and Family Statistics, 2011), more than 10 percent of children ages 9–11 are on their own after school, and over 35 percent of children ages 12–14 take care of themselves once they leave school each day. The gap between parents' work schedules and their children's school schedules can amount to 20–25 hours per week. In many settings, before- and after-school programs are sponsored by parent and community groups as well as school districts to keep children at school longer hours. The library ought to be accessible to children whenever they are at the school. This may require school librarians to give up some control of the facility. Providing some operations training to after-school program staff and having them run the center before and after school can extend access if library staff contracts would otherwise limit access. If there is no existing before- or after-school program, the librarian might advocate extending the library hours to accommodate children who have essentially no safe place to go otherwise.

While it is tempting to say that is not the responsibility of school librarians, children need a safe and productive way to use the hours from the end of the school day until the time their parents come home from work. Library resources offer opportunities for making those hours safe and productive. Collaboration with other community agencies, especially the public library, may pave the way for homework help or arts activities in the library media center as well. The library should no longer be seen as a facility that operates for children only during school hours from 8:30 a.m. to 3:00 p.m.

School libraries need to forge close alliances with local public libraries. Bringing public library staff to school library facilities for "rush hours" or adjusting the work hours of school library staff to include early morning, late afternoon, or early evening hours may be solutions. Online access assists those students who have computers at home. Neighborhood centers or other facilities where students can do homework also offer means for providing access to information resources with the cooperation of the school library program. Cooperative grant seeking may be a path to added resources to meet these needs.

The needs of secondary school students call for careful policy making for both school hours and after-school hours. Extended hours increase access for some secondary school students. However, in 2010 16 percent of high school students were working (Child Trends, 2011b). Open access to the library during the school day may be the only opportunity for these students because their jobs may fill their after-school hours. After-school time is also heavily booked for students involved in extracurricular activities such as music, drama, and athletics. For example, data from 2008 indicate that at least half of secondary school students are involved in school sports (Child Trends, 2011a).

Access to the library is a two-way concern. While the library must have an open-access policy, teachers must also have a policy of open access; that is, they must allow students to leave their classrooms and study halls to go to the library. Although it is common for high school teachers to allow students some time in class to work on assignments, it is sometimes difficult for students to move to the library to access resources or assistance they might need. Concerns for orderliness in the halls and accountability for students' whereabouts can conflict with providing school-day open access. Solutions to that conflict require the systemic rethinking of teachers, administrators, and the school librarian. Librarians must advocate for open access and encourage school policies that facilitate it. As secondary schools investigate block scheduling or initiatives to expand the length of class periods, eliminate study halls, and make other modifications in the schedule, librarians must be alert and assertive in protecting student access to the library when they need it.

Access to the library can help alleviate concerns about equity among students in terms of computer use. NCES data indicate that the United States still experiences pronounced gaps in Internet use along several demographic lines (NCES, 2010a). Minorities are less connected than whites, and those with modest income and education are less wired than those with college educations and household incomes over $75,000. These differences in access at home underscore the role of the school—and especially the school—as a force for equity. Differences in access also serve as a stark reminder that not all schools can assume students will have high-speed Internet at home for completing schoolwork. A study by Celano and Neuman (2008) indicates that pointing those less privileged toward the public library may not be the solution either. They reported seeing young children in low-income neighborhood libraries floundering in their attempts to use technology:

> Left to their own devices, children from lower-income families will not use information sources in the same way as their middle class peers. Children in middle class neighborhoods are exposed to more print in books, use more educational applications on computers and get more support from adults. Low income children, often left on their own, read less and spend more time playing games, activities that limit their knowledge growth. (p. 262)

Such an assertion suggests that children in poverty need access not only to the resources but also to adults who can provide the support they may not receive in their families to take advantage of the resources provided. In an information-based environment—and that is what school is—both access and skill in using the computer as an information and communication tool are highly advantageous.

Disconcerting are the findings of a study of school libraries' incidental closures for hours or days during the school year (Dickinson, Gavigan, and Pribesh, 2008). Findings in this study revealed a relationship between the poverty of the school and the numbers of days that students were unable to access the school library. The implication is that school libraries in the poorest schools are closed the most, thus denying access to marginalized children who have the greatest need for accessing resources. School libraries have the potential to bridge the achievement gap for these students by providing access to books and other resources. They can also bridge the digital divide by providing free access to computers and electronic information. Closing a school library has significant implications for these students, whereas students in wealthier schools may have multiple avenues to seek access to both print and electronic resources.

Socioeconomic Status and Student Achievement

The relationship between socioeconomic status (SES) and student achievement is well documented. Some researchers have found that low SES negatively affects student achievement because of limited access to resources. For example, children's initial reading competence is correlated with the home literacy environment, including the number of books owned (Aikens and Barbarin, 2008). Parents from low-SES communities may be unable to afford resources such as books, computers, or tutors to create a positive literacy environment (Orr, 2003).

Pribesh and Gavigan (2009) undertook a study to examine whether school libraries are indeed leveling the playing field for students living in poverty. Their findings were disappointing in that school libraries that serve poor populations were found to be less well staffed, open fewer hours per week, and less well resourced than those serving middle income children. When children come from homes less likely to have learning resources or high-speed Internet access, the school library should be an opportunity for them to compensate. However, it appears that school librarians will need to advocate for these children and their needs. Yet, librarians cannot solve these problems alone. Social policy decisions create inequities—policies related to housing, school districting, busing, and employment. Nevertheless, school librarians who are aware of the needs of students in their own schools can seek opportunities to provide access to learning resources and can advocate for them at the local building level. One step is to know students and their needs.

Millennials

The students populating high schools today are members of the generation dubbed "millennials" by Neil Howe and William Strauss (2000). These authors have been profiling generations for a couple of decades, and the portrayal of the millennials is one of optimism and great promise. This generation has benefited from careful attentiveness by their parents. Attributes like confident, sheltered, pressured, achieving, and team-oriented fit the profile of the millennials. Howe and Strauss portray this as a generation that trusts authority more than recent generations. If this characterization is accurate, the value of libraries and information literacy should not be a difficult "sell." School librarians may find that this generation of students will exhibit interest in developing lifelong learning skills that will help them succeed. Their academic ambition is likely to bring them to the library. It will be important to adopt positive assumptions about these students and create programming that feeds their academic appetites—book discussions, book talks, increasingly sophisticated technologies, guest speakers, and opportunities for problem solving come to mind as possibilities that may suit this age group.

Prensky (2010) dubbed this generation "digital natives"—born and raised in a digitally connected world. Black (2010: 99) asserts that these digital natives approach learning as a "plug and play" experience. She describes today's student body as:

- often unprepared for the level of work expected because it lacks basic quantitative and literacy skills;
- preferring collaborative to individual work;
- assertive and confident (perhaps more confident than competent);
- supported by "helicopter parents"; and
- dependent on technology as a tool for learning and socializing.

Kruger-Ross and Holcomb (2011: 4) remind us to be cautious about overgeneralizations concerning the technological adeptness of today's students:

> While it may seem that students already "get it," it is also possible that this apparent technical expertise is actually just eagerness and a willingness to give the technology a try. Still others assume that because students can use the Internet, YouTube, and a cellular telephone, that they will automatically know how to properly format a Word document or cite a picture on a blog. Students need to learn how to appropriately and effectively use the technology that you use in the classroom. That learning can happen as a result of direct instruction, through group work, online tutorials and resources, or through any number of other avenues. It is vital that this learning takes place, regardless of the specific avenue.

The potential for a deepening digital divide between students immersed in their technology and those who lack access or skills signals the need for watchfulness and attention in school libraries and the larger school context. The enthusiasm for BYOD (bring your own device) approaches to technology in schools, wherein students bring their own tablets, cell phones, and other mobile devices, requires caution lest this practice also intensify the digital divide.

Media Influence

One pervasive source of information and entertainment is television—a significant influence on today's students. According to a study conducted by Roberts and Foehr (2008), 68 percent of children ages 8–18 have televisions in their bedrooms. Even more sobering is the finding from a Common Sense Media (2011) study reporting that 42 percent of children under eight years old have a television in their bedroom. Roberts and Foehr report that young people spend an average of 5.48 hours per day with all media, including computers, video games, radio, and MP3 players. In at least two ways, time spent with potentially intellectually empty media can be detrimental, because it is time not spent doing something more intellectual like reading and may involve violence or misinformation or other content that may be inherently detrimental. In a review of the research on the relationship between television viewing and academic achievement over a 25-year period, Thompson and Austin (2003) surmised that:

- moderate levels of viewing are better than high levels or no viewing at all;
- the type of programming is more critical than the intrinsic qualities of the medium itself (i.e., informational versus noninformational);
- high informational viewing generally correlates positively with achievement, while low informational viewing correlates negatively;
- once IQ, SES, and other mediating factors are accounted for, the relationship between television viewing and academic achievement weakens; and
- it is not clear at this time whether negative television viewing causes or is caused by low levels of achievement.

The crux of the issue may be what programming children are watching and how it is used to advance learning. Television has valuable programming to offer. Concerns are often raised about how inappropriate televised material affects young minds. Heintz (1994) described an interesting study of teenagers having "massive" exposure (three hours per night for five consecutive nights) to prime-time, sexually oriented programming. Such viewing was found to influence the moral judgment of 13- and 14-year-olds. Specifically, the teens who had been exposed to such programming in the experiment rated a series of sexual indiscretions and improprieties as "less bad" and described the victim as "less wronged" than did teens who had not seen the programs. The power of the medium is evident, but it needs to be channeled into productive uses, especially for youthful audiences. A more recent study reveals a statistically significant relationship in preschool children who watched violent content and verbal aggression (Daly and Perez, 2009). Overall, Murray (2008) asserts that the accumulation of research on the effect of TV violence on children leads to the inescapable conclusion that viewing media violence is related to increases in aggressive attitudes, values, and behaviors.

A significant body of research indicates that parents can influence the effects of television programming on their children by intervening or even by watching with them. Research (Abelman, 1984) suggests that parents can inoculate children against possible negative consequences and amplify positive effects in the following ways:

- Perceived reality. If parents explain the unreal nature of televised presentations, the effects should be minimized.
- Consequences. If parents associate consequences with acts portrayed on television, the impact of behaviors associated with positive consequences is strengthened, while acts associated with negative consequences should minimize their attraction.
- Motives. If parents interpret the reasons for an action as principled, more learning should occur.
- Evaluation. If parents express approval or disapproval, this should increase or decrease performance because it cues the child to parental attitudes.

Yet, even though parents can use television for teaching, research clearly indicates that few parents involve themselves in their children's consumption of media. A 2010 study by Rideout, Foehr, and Roberts found that, for example, 66 percent of parents have rules about which shows eight- to ten-year-olds may watch, and 47 percent have rules about how much time those children may spend in front of the television. This suggests room for more parental intervention in many homes and may signal the need for schools to develop students' skills as critical, thoughtful consumers of television. In most communities, instruction for media literacy exists only due to the energy and initiative of a single teacher, not because of a coordinated, community-wide programmatic plan of implementation. School librarians can be advocates for media literacy education. Developing critical viewing skills is parallel to developing critical reading skills; in this media age, such skills need to be taught with equal or greater emphasis. To begin, students need to be aware that media developers make many conscious decisions that will affect their audience's perception and interpretation of a message. One analytical approach to media study is to apply a strategy referred to as MAPS (mode, audience, purpose, and situation) to the study of a film, television clip, or other mediated communication (Rodesiler, 2010):

- Mode. Speech, music, and pictures that involve attention to the details of style, tone, perspective, and other features such as nonverbal cues
- Audience. Identifying who the intended audience seems to be based on the mode as well as language, pacing, personalities featured, and other details
- Purpose. Determining whether the intent of the communication is to inform, persuade, influence, entertain, and so on
- Situation. Considering the context in which the communication was created and the situation in which it is shown

This example serves only to point out that media literacy is the intentional study of media to afford students the skills to assess messages with critical analysis of media technique. Often, producing media messages in a variety of formats is a teaching strategy that can help students experience the decision-making process of a producer so that as consumers of multimedia they develop sensitivity to the effects of those decisions on them as audience.

Besides television, other media constitute important intrusions on time for young people. Highly ranked among these would be video and computer games. While there has been considerable discussion about the effects of violence in video games, in a substantial meta-analysis of research on relationships between behavior and participation in violent video games, Anderson and colleagues (2010: 151) conclude that "exposure to violent video games is a causal risk factor for increased aggressive behavior, aggressive cognition, and aggressive affect and for decreased empathy and prosocial behavior." Yet,

Rideout, Foehr, and Roberts (2010) found that only 30 percent of parents of 8- to 18-year-olds set rules about what video games were allowed to be played. Hence, the impact of this activity raises concern about students as they participate in their learning and living communities.

In summary, many environmental conditions affect students. Educators cannot simply throw up their hands in dismay and say, "I can't fix all that is wrong with society." Granted that the library cannot resolve all the difficulties in young people's lives, some actions may improve students' opportunities to succeed. The hard task is determining what can be done within the school to address equity, attention, or involvement in learning. Advocacy and sensitivity are dispositions an effective school librarian can use to create a student-friendly environment, acquire materials that match students' needs and interests, and attempt to increase opportunities for all students. Many factors have significant influence on students' disposition toward school and learning. These factors intensify the need for educators to focus attention on motivating students to want to be learners. Understanding theory of motivation in the context of the lives of today's students is exceedingly important in creating in all students a readiness to learn.

Motivation for Learning

Motivation Theory

A classic work in motivation is Maslow's (1971) hierarchy of needs. He theorized that human needs fall into a hierarchy and that the higher needs arise only after lower needs have been met. At the lowest level are physical and organizational needs, the basic needs for security and survival. Above these basic needs are social needs, the need for esteem and for a sense of belonging. As social needs are met, intellectual needs such as the need for knowledge and understanding emerge. Above these are the aesthetic needs met by the appreciation for life's order, beauty, and balance. At the top of Maslow's hierarchy is self-actualization. He described the self-actualized person as one motivated by needs to be open, to love others and self, to act ethically, and to express autonomy and curiosity.

Students need approval, affiliation, and achievement. Some students are approval-dependent; they conform because they need the assurance from others that their performance is at an acceptable standard. Other students have less need for approval and are motivated by their own need for achievement or affiliation. A corollary to the achievement need is the need to avoid failure. Motive will affect the risks one is willing to take; for example, often students who are driven by a fear of failure will be less willing to take risks, to try new strategies or tasks. Similarly, students high in the need for affiliation perform in ways that they perceive to be respected by their peers.

Individuals who generally attribute their successes and failures to their own behavior are said to have an internal locus of control, while those who generally attribute their success and failure to luck, task difficulty, or an action by others are said to have an external locus of control. Self-concept as a learner also appears to affect a student's achievement motivation. The student with an internal locus of control for success and a positive self-concept as a learner ("I can succeed because I have the ability and I can exert the effort") has a better chance for high achievement than the student with an external locus of control ("I can't succeed because the teacher doesn't like me").

Extending beyond the concept of locus of control, self-determination theory contends that need for competence (to be effective), autonomy (to have choice and personal control), and relatedness (to feel connected) are essential to psychological growth and well-being (Arnone, Reynolds, and Marshall, 2009). These aspects provide a valuable set of directives for the school library program: to develop students' competence, to provide opportunity to pursue questions of personal interest, and to create an environment that affords students a feeling of belonging.

Motivation Strategies

A substantial body of research exists related to intrinsic and extrinsic motivation. Intrinsic motivation refers to the perception that one engages in an activity because it is rewarding or gratifying. Extrinsic motivation, on the other hand, is the perception that one engages in an activity for some external reward (e.g., students read a set number of books to win a special prize, such as a pizza). The research literature contains more than 100 studies that conclude that extrinsic rewards are often ineffective, and in fact can be detrimental in the long run. In one typical experiment, Lepper, Greene, and Nisbett (1973) observed three- to five-year-old preschool children coloring with felt-tip markers. The researchers observed that the children enjoyed playing with the markers. Next they asked the children to draw with the markers. The researchers promised some children a "Good Player Award" for drawing pictures. Other children drew pictures without the promise of a reward. Two weeks later, the researchers returned and observed the children's inclination to draw with the markers. Those children who had been promised a reward spent only half as much time drawing as they had originally. Those who did not receive rewards showed no decline in interest. Many studies follow this pattern with similar outcomes—ultimately a decline in motivation to do the task is associated with external rewards.

The literature identifies three types of reward contingencies (Dickinson, 1989). Task-contingent rewards recognize participation; in the preschool coloring activity, for example, the children were rewarded just for participating in the task. Performance-contingent rewards are provided only when the student completes a task. In such studies, rewarded students were less inclined to perform the task later than were the students who had not been paid (Deci, 1971). Every parent who has paid a son or daughter for sidewalk shoveling knows how likely it is that sidewalk shoveling will be done voluntarily in the future. Success-contingent rewards are given for good performance. Dickinson (1989) maintains that extrinsic rewards can be effective when they are contingent upon successful performance and when the standard for success is attainable. Chance (1992) offers some suggestions for judicious use of rewards, and urges that educators remain aware that extrinsic rewards can have adverse effects on student motivation:

- When possible, avoid using rewards as incentives. For example, don't say, "If you do X, I'll give you Y." Instead, ask the student to perform a task and then provide the reward for having completed it.
- Remember that what is an effective reward for one student may not work for another. Effective rewards are things that students seek—positive feedback, praise, approval, recognition; they relate to the needs of each student.
- Reward success and set standards so that success is within the student's reach. To accommodate differences among students, reward improvement or progress.

DeCharms (1968) designed a program to change motivation in children from external to internal with favorable results in their achievement. The students learned their own strengths and weaknesses, chose realistic goals, and assessed their own progress toward their goals. The program stressed personal responsibility. DeCharms reported that children in the study improved in both their achievement motivation and their actual achievement. In a follow-up study (DeCharms, 1970) found that the improvements had persisted and indicated that the participants showed evidence of being likely to graduate from high school.

Educators want students to believe that they have some internal control over their own prospects for success. What teachers and other school adults say and do influences the attribution patterns that students develop, and ultimately influences their achievement (Bal-Tar, Raviv, and Bal-Tar, 1982). One important aspect of DeCharms's work was the effort to help students assess their own strengths; within the body of research on intrinsic and extrinsic motivation, many studies emphasize the difference that self-concept makes in motivation. Children with a high self-concept tend to attribute their success to their own ability and are less dependent on extrinsic motivation—they are self-rewarding (Ames, 1978).

Kohn (1993) has studied motivation extensively. He states that internalization of motivation is crucial to developing enduring habits and behaviors. To that end, he declares that extrinsic reward and punishment systems are counterproductive. In an interview he states:

> In general, the more kids are induced to do something for a reward, whether tangible or verbal, the more you see a diminution of interest the next time they do it. That can be explained partly by the fact that praise, like other rewards, is ultimately an instrument of control, but also by the fact that if I praise or reward a student for doing something, the message the child infers is, "This must be something I wouldn't want to do; otherwise, they wouldn't have to bribe me to do it." (Brandt, 1995: 15)

Kohn recommends, instead, three ways to motivate students. First he suggests that the work must interest students. He poses the question, "Has the child been given something to do worth learning?" His second recommendation has to do with the school community. Do students feel part of a safe environment in which they feel free to ask for help? Finally, he raises the issue of choice. He urges teachers to give students opportunities to choose what they will do, how, and with whom.

Curiosity

Libraries should stimulate, nourish, and satisfy students' curiosities if they are indeed aiming to develop behaviors of lifelong learning. For how can self-activated learning—learning that will occur beyond school—occur without curiosity to initiate it? Carter (1999: 61) recalls the curiosity that young children bring to school as kindergarteners. She challenges educators to reflect on these questions:

> Do I teach children to read so that they can test well? Or do I teach them to read so that they can have direct lines to the thoughts, hopes and dreams of thousands of writers? Do I teach children to write so that they can have a nice piece of writing in their portfolios for next year's teacher? Or, do I teach them to write in order to help them sprout wings and access new avenues for self-expression? Question the reasons why you teach the things you teach.

According to Reio (2009), cognitive curiosity stimulates new information-seeking and exploratory behavior. This finding suggests that a key to engaging children with information seeking in the library is to raise curiosity. One strategy related to curiosity is to provide incomplete or contradictory information that compels the student to explore information resources. Another way to pique curiosity is to suggest topics for research that relate to students' personal lives. Giving students choices in deciding what they will investigate also supports curiosity. The need for self-expression calls for students to have a variety of media available for projects and activities in response to assignments. Developing multimedia, designing print publications, or producing dramatic productions are examples of ways to build creativity into students' work that will increase motivation with appeals to their desire to be original. Another strategy to respond to the need for creativity is to expand the audience for student work—use local cable television to send student work out into the local community, use the web as a publication forum, or identify interest groups or other classes within the school as audiences for student work.

In her study of intrinsic motivation in children, Crow (2009) identified factors that can support intrinsic motivation:

> *"Anchor relationships"*—relationships with adults who show interest and provide support for information seeking. Such relationships can be with parents, teachers, or librarians. Crow reminds us of authors

who recall that it was a librarian who excited them about reading and exploring for information.

Mentoring—connecting children with experts or other people interested in the same questions

Point-of-passion experiences—seminal events that trigger a genuine focused interest

Her work offers suggestions for school librarians to consider how they might manufacture opportunities for such experiences or relationships to create intrinsic interest.

Given the research on intrinsic and extrinsic motivation, at the heart of the work of school librarians is nurturing curiosity so that students seek information and ideas from self-generated interests and questions. Today's environment characterized by intense accountability challenges educators to adhere to the basic understanding that learning for life begins with intrinsic interest and motive to find out something, to solve a problem, or to make a decision. As librarians work with teachers to design library research projects and activities, creating a sense of purposefulness and wonder may result in a more intrinsically motivated student—and as a consequence, perhaps a more engaged and more successful student.

The Library as Learning Commons

What is a learning commons? Recall the notion of a commons—a central resource shared by all in a community or a virtual or physical place where community members come together to collaborate, find resources used by all in the community, and share their work with others. The atmosphere is one of busy productivity. In a learning commons, teacher, librarian, and student all engage actively in exploring resources to solve information problems. Frequent consultation, conversation, clarification, and brainstorming occur amid an environment that supports inquiry.

The library program can be a valuable asset to the teacher and everyone else in the school who is seeking to cultivate motivation through success, curiosity, originality, and relationships. As a learning commons, the library becomes the ideal space to pique and satisfy curiosity with its resources, to

Imagine . . .

A high school social studies teacher perceives the library as a learning commons for his American Studies classes. Students work as teams on a weeklong project in which they spend each class period in the library. Each team has responsibility for studying a dimension of American life in the 1920s (such as sports, politics, prohibition, entertainment, transportation, economics, or religion). The goal is to investigate and work as if each team were a department of a magazine staff. The final product will be an e-magazine that brings together the work of all teams. The library offers a collection of resources that will respond to these students' needs, ensuring they will be successful in their search for information. They have access to the necessary resources for web publishing. The library staff provide the support to students as they work in this productive atmosphere. Curiosity is the key to this project; the students generate their own questions and have control over their work. The end product allows for originality as students design the magazine. They count on each other. The time the project takes allows group members to develop meaningful relationships and identify the substantive contributions that each member can make.

encourage learning relationships with its ambiance, and to support creativity with its technology and expertise. Stedman and Carroll (2010) describe their implementation of such a philosophy around a case in point centering on a study of plant life. The learning commons at their school became something of a hands-on learning center with interactive displays and exhibits, a wiki space for participative learning, and a variety of available learning resources—physical, virtual, and human. High schools too can adopt a learning commons model. Cicchetti (2010) describes a metamorphosis of a traditional high school library to a learning commons. The transition called for reassessing staff positions to align responsibilities toward more teaching and more technology integration, reorganization and reduction of the print collection to afford more "people space," introduction of new technologies and opening up availability of social learning web resources, professional development for faculty to help them take advantage of the new potential, and outreach to teachers one-by-one with a library teaching agenda driven by the AASL (2007) *Standards for the 21st-Century Learner.* Results of this transformation are evident in reported data on increased library use. While it is easy to emphasize the physical and technical aspects, the learning commons begins with dispositions that favor open exploration; deep investigation; collaborative learning in person and online; creative production; and standards of excellence.

Conclusion

Students are the ultimate customers for the school library. While collaboration with teachers, communication with parents, and support from administrators are all important for the library program, student learning is the bottom line. The fundamental principles of librarianship call for librarians to be advocates for the rights of learners to have access to information resources and to attain skills to be efficient and effective users of those resources. Attention to all kinds of learners is a hallmark of a school library program. School libraries have a role to play in leveling the playing field and improving equity of opportunity for all students. Ultimately, school libraries can be places for information quests that nurture dispositions of curiosity and encourage self-directed inquiry and learning.

Leadership Strategies

Teacher and Partner

Enlist at-risk students with the aptitude for technology as student aides.

Beyond providing access, teach students how to use electronic resources. For example, offer voluntary "short courses" outside the school day focusing on specific technology applications or coordinate with teachers to teach use of resources for specific assignments during class time.

Support teachers who engage their students in creative work—promote the center as a learning commons.

Information Specialist

Provide materials at various levels of difficulty to meet assignment demands, especially in core courses.

Cooperate with such agencies as neighborhood centers to seek funding for online access to school and public library resources.

Provide leisure reading, especially magazines, on topics of high interest—if necessary, seek local business funding to support subscriptions.

Provide Internet access with bookmarks or use LibGuides (www.spring share.com/libguides) for topics that match local students' interests. In this way, students begin to explore how to locate and evaluate information about topics of personal interest to them.

Invite a public librarian to introduce ELL students to public library services and facilitate their obtaining library cards.

Maintain open hours in the library media center before and after school for students. This schedule may require adjusting work hours or seeking after-school volunteers.

Offer space to community groups who provide after-school tutoring.

Market resources at various levels and in languages appropriate to the student population to teachers so that students with special learning needs can access information with less frustration.

Program Administrator

Emphasize the importance of relevance as a motivational consideration for instruction in the library. Encourage teachers and administrators to schedule instruction accordingly.

Scenarios for Discussion

Scenario 1

Some students who attend an elementary school are living at a neighborhood shelter until their families find housing. The shelter is crowded, and little space is allocated for families. It proves difficult for many students to take care of their books or return them on time. Books frequently are lost. Often students' families leave without notice, taking their books with them. Many overwhelming family issues present obstacles. The librarian wants to support students in developing an interest in reading, and he wants to help them develop responsibility for taking materials home, returning materials on time, and returning materials before moving. He is also committed to the value of helping them develop basic literacy skills of daily reading at home. He wants these children to have opportunities equal to those of the more privileged children in the school. How can he accomplish these goals?

Scenario 2

Jane Dillard is the school librarian in an elementary school where a behavior management system has been adopted so that students receive tickets when they are "caught behaving properly." The principal encourages Jane to use tickets to reward students for being quiet in the library. Jane has two thoughts about this: (1) She is trying to create a learning commons environment in the library where students work collaboratively and wants to hear that productive buzz of activity that says minds are at work. Therefore, she is not seeking a "quiet" library. (2) She would rather have students experience the reward of seeing the outcome of their productive work than receiving tickets for their good work. What does she do? What does she say?

REFERENCES

AASL (American Association of School Librarians). 2007. *Standards for the 21st-Century Learner.* American Library Association. www.ala.org/aasl/ guidelinesandstandards/learningstandards/standards.

———. 2009. *School Libraries Count! Supplementary Report on English Language Learners.* American Library Association. www.ala.org/ala/mgrps/ divs/aasl/researchandstatistics/slcsurvey/2009/ell2009.pdf.

Abelman, R. 1984. "Children and TV: The ABCs of TV Literacy." *Childhood Education* 60, no. 3: 200–205.

Adams, H. 2010. "Welcoming America's Newest Immigrants: Providing Access to Resources and Services for English Language Learners." *School Library Monthly* 27, no. 1: 50–51.

Aikens, N. L., and Barbarin, O. 2008. "Socioeconomic Differences in Reading Trajectories: The Contribution of Family, Neighborhood, and School Contexts." *Journal of Educational Psychology* 100, no. 2: 235–251.

Ames, C. 1978. "Children's Achievement Attributions and Self-Reinforcement: Effects of Self-Concept and Competitive Reward Structure." *Journal of Educational Psychology* 70, no. 3: 345–355.

Anderson, C. A., A. Shibuya, N. Ivory, E. L. Swing, B. J. Bushman, A. Sakamoto, H. R. Rothstein, and M. Saleem. 2010. "Violent Video Game Effects on Aggression, Empathy, and Prosocial Behavior in Eastern and Western Countries: A Meta-Analytic Review." *Psychological Bulletin* 136, no. 2: 151–173.

Arnone, M. P., R. Reynolds, and T. Marshall. 2009. "The Effect of Early Adolescents' Psychological Needs Satisfaction upon Their Perceived Competence in Information Skills and Intrinsic Motivation for Research." *School Libraries Worldwide* 15, no. 2: 115–134.

Bal-Tar, D., A. Raviv, and Y. Bal-Tar. 1982. "Consistency of Pupils' Attributions Regarding Success and Failure." *Journal of Educational Psychology* 74, no. 1: 104–110.

Black, A. 2010. "Gen Y: Who They Are and How They Learn." *Educational Horizons* 88, no. 2: 92–101.

Brandt, R. 1995. "Punished by Rewards? A Conversation with Alfie Kohn." *Educational Leadership* 53, no. 1: 13–16.

Carter, Paula. 1999. "Their Sense of Wonder Still Intact." *Teaching Pre K–8* 30, no. 1: 60–61.

Celano, D., and S. Neuman. 2008. "When Schools Close." *Phi Delta Kappan* 90, no. 4: 256–262.

Chance, P. 1992. "The Rewards of Learning." *Phi Delta Kappan* 73, no. 3: 200–207.

Child Trends. 2011a. "Participation in School Athletics." Child Trends Data Bank. Accessed September 26. www.childtrendsdatabank.org/?q=node/367.

———. 2011b. "Youth Employment." Child Trends Data Bank. Accessed September 26. www.childtrendsdatabank.org/?q=node/374.

Cicchetti, R. 2010. "Concord-Carlisle Transitions to a Learning Commons." *Teacher Librarian* 37, no. 3: 52–58.

Common Sense Media. 2011. *Zero to Eight: Children's Media Use in America: A Common Sense Media Research Study.* Common Sense Media. October 25.

www.commonsensemedia.org/researchzero-eight-childrens-media-use
-america.

Crow, S. R. 2009. "Relationships That Foster Intrinsic Motivation for Information Seeking." *School Libraries Worldwide* 15, no. 2: 91–112.

Daly, L. A., and L. M. Perez. 2009. "Exposure to Media Violence and Other Correlates of Aggressive Behavior in Preschool Children." *Early Childhood Research and Practice (ECRP)* 11, no. 2.

DeCharms, R. 1968. *Personal Causation: The Internal Effective Determinants of Behavior.* New York: Academic Press.

———. 1970. "Motivation Changes in Low-Income Black Children." Paper presented to the American Educational Research Association. Minneapolis, MN.

Deci, E. 1971. "Effects of Externally Mediated Rewards on Intrinsic Motivation." *Journal of Personality and Social Psychology* 18, no. 1: 105–115.

Dickinson, A. 1989. "The Detrimental Effects of Extrinsic Reinforcement on 'Intrinsic Motivation.'" *Behavior Analyst* 12, no. 1: 1–15.

Dickinson, G., K. Gavigan, and S. Pribesh. 2008. "Open and Accessible: The Relationship between Closures and Circulation in School Library Media Centers." *School Library Media Research* 11. www.ala.org/aasl/aaslpubsandjournals/slmrb/slmrcontents/volume11/dickinson.

Duffett, A., S. Farkas, and T. Loveless. 2008. *High-Achieving Students in the Era of NCLB.* Washington, DC: Thomas B. Fordham Institute. www.edexcellence.net/publications-issues/publications/high-achieving-students-in.html.

Federal Interagency Forum on Child and Family Statistics. 2011. *America's Children: Key National Indicators of Well-Being, 2011.* Washington, DC: US Government Printing Office. www.childstats.gov/pdf/ac2011/ac_11.pdf.

Heintz, K. 1994. "Smarter Than We Think—Kids, Passivity, and the Media." *Media Studies Journal* 8, no. 4: 205–219.

Hitchcock, C., A. Meyer, D. Rose, and R. Jackson. 2002. "Providing Access to the General Curriculum: Universal Design for Learning." *Teaching Exceptional Children* 15, no. 2: 8–17.

Howe, N., and W. Strauss. 2000. *Millennials Rising: The Next Great Generation.* New York: Vintage Books.

Jolly, J., and M. Makel, 2010. "No Child Left Behind: The Inadvertent Costs for High-Achieving and Gifted Students." *Childhood Education* 87, no. 1: 35–40.

Kohn, A. 1993. *Punished by Rewards.* Boston: Houghton Mifflin.

Kruger-Ross, M., and L. B. Holcomb. 2011. "Toward a Set of Theoretical Best Practices for Web 2.0 and Web-Based Technologies." *Meridian: A Kindergarten through High School Information and Communication Technologies Journal* 13, no. 2. www.ncsu.edu/meridian/winter2011/krugerross.

Lepper, M. R., D. Greene, and R. E. Nisbett. 1973. "Undermining Children's Intrinsic Interest: A Test of the 'Overjustification' Hypothesis." *Journal of Personality and Social Psychology* 28, no. 1: 129–137.

Maslow, A. H. 1971. *The Farther Reaches of Human Nature.* New York: Viking Press.

Murray, J. 2000. "How School Librarians Can Contribute to the Personal Growth of Students with Disabilities." *Orana* 36, no. 2: 5–11.

Murray, J. P. 2008. "Media Violence: The Effects Are Both Real and Strong." *American Behavioral Scientist* 51, no. 8: 1212–1230.

NCES (National Center for Education Statistics). 2010a. "Closer Look 2010." *The Condition of Education.* National Center for Education Statistics. http://nces.ed.gov/programs/coe/analysis/2010-index.asp.

———. 2010b. "Elementary and Secondary Education." Chapter 2 in *Digest of Educational Statistics: 2010.* National Center for Education Statistics. http://nces.ed.gov/programs/digest/d10/ch_2.asp.

———. 2011. "Fast Facts: Dropout Rates." National Center for Education Statistics. Accessed September 26. http://nces.ed.gov/fastfacts/display.asp?id=16.

Orr, A. J. 2003. "Black-White Differences in Achievement: The Importance of Wealth." *Sociology of Education* 76, no. 4: 281–304.

Prensky, M. 2010. *Teaching Digital Natives: Partnering for Real Learning.* Thousand Oaks, CA: Corwin.

Pribesh, S., and K. Gavigan. 2009. "Linworth/ALISE 2009 Youth Services Paper: Equal Opportunity? Poverty and Characteristics of School Library Media Centers." *Library Media Connection* 27, no. 5: 20–22.

Reio, T. G. Jr. 2009. "Where Does the Curiosity Go?" *New Horizons in Adult Education and Human Resource Development* 23, no. 2: 3–5.

Rideout, V. J., U. G. Foehr, and D. F. Roberts. 2010. *Generation M2: Media in the Lives of 8- to 18-Year-Olds.* Menlo Park, CA: Kaiser Family Foundation.

Roberts, D. F., and U. G. Foehr. 2008. "Trends in Media Use." *The Future of Children: Future Child* 18, no. 1: 11–37.

Rodesiler, L. 2010. "Empowering Students Through Critical Media Literacy: This Means War." *The Clearing House* 83, no. 5: 164–167.

Rong, X. L., and J. Preissle. 1998. *Educating Immigrant Students: What We Need to Know to Meet the Challenges.* Thousand Oaks, CA: Corwin.

Smith, S. J., and C. Okolo. 2010. "Response to Intervention and Evidence-Based Practices: Where Does Technology Fit?" *Learning Disabilities Quarterly* 33, no. 4: 257–272.

Stedman, P., and G. Carroll. 2010. "The Learning Commons is Alive in New Zealand." *Teacher Librarian* 37, no. 3: 59–62.

Theaker, R., Y. Xiang, M. Dahlin, J. Cronin, and S. Durant. 2011. "Do High Flyers Maintain Their Altitude? Performance Trends of Top Students." Thomas R. Fordham Institute. September 20. www.edexcellence.net/publications-issues/publications/high-flyers.html.

Thompson, F. T., and W. P. Austin. 2003. "Television Viewing and Academic Achievement Revisited." *Education* 124, no. 1: 194–202.

Wight, V. R., M. Chau, and Y. Aratani. 2011. *Who Are America's Poor Children? The Official Story.* National Center for Children in Poverty. www.nccp.org/publications/pub_1001.html.

Yell, M., and J. Shriner. 1997. "The IDEA Amendments of 1997: Implications for Special and General Education Teachers, Administrators, and Teacher Trainers." *Focus on Exceptional Children* 30, no. 1: 1–19.

2

Curriculum

This chapter:

- describes major influences on curriculum;
- examines how the school librarian contributes to the curriculum development process; and
- identifies leadership strategies for working within the context of curriculum.

Curriculum can be considered the substance of the experiences teachers intend for students to have in school—the content and how students interact with that content. A typical curriculum includes the disciplinary content standards with indicators that describe what students should know and be able to do at particular grade levels or grade spans. District-developed curriculum guides often contain recommended textbooks and other resources, and sometimes they will include exemplary lesson designs and learning activities as well as assessments to measure student achievement in the discipline.

A number of influences on curriculum are particularly relevant for the library program, because they change either the nature of assistance teachers and students seek or the design of classroom instruction, or because they affect what students need to know. Examples of these influences include the cognitive theory of constructivism; acknowledgment of the importance of learner dispositions; adoption of the Common Core Curriculum Standards; increased emphasis on accountability, especially based on standardized testing, as a result of federal or state legislation; and expanded availability of technology.

Constructivism

Constructivism is a theory that emerges from two lines of research: cognitive constructivism grounded in Piaget's developmental theory and Vygotsky's social constructivism (Powell, 2009). Piaget posited that humans cannot simply be given information but must construct their own knowledge (Piaget, 1953). Vygotsky's theory is based on the social nature of learning; essentially, learners construct understanding based on their prior knowledge, the integration of new information gathered from experts, and social interactions into existing schema (Powell, 2009).

Authentic intellectual work (AIW) is an initiative that values constructivism as a central component for effective teaching. The AIW model is designed around the notion that schools must educate students to be learners beyond school in a world where change is constant and where adults must be ready to accept the responsibility of continuous learning. AIW proponents state:

> Skilled adults in diverse occupations and participating in civic life face the challenge of applying skills and knowledge to complex problems that are often novel or unique. To reach an adequate solution to new problems, the competent adult has to "construct" knowledge because these problems cannot be solved by routine use of information or skills previously learned. Such construction of knowledge involves organizing, interpreting, evaluating, or synthesizing prior knowledge to solve new problems. (Carmichael, King, and Newmann, 2009: 43)

To that end, AIW calls for classroom instruction to be designed so that students are not merely recalling factual information but are instead applying their knowledge to problem solving. Clearly, this constructivist approach integrates well with the school library program and its goals to develop in students a critical stance toward information as well as the skills to locate, interpret, and evaluate information. Learning activities in a constructivist setting are characterized by active engagement, inquiry, problem solving, and collaboration with others (Cannella and Reiff, 1994). A constructivist curriculum needs to "recognize the child as an active constructor of his/her own meaning within a community of others who provide a forum for the social negotiation of shared meanings" (Blaik-Hourani, 2011: 232). Constructivism pervades all content areas; however, mathematics and science educators particularly tend to be committed to constructivism where students work with

manipulatives and perform hands-on experiments to create their own understanding of numeracy and scientific phenomena.

In a library, students engage in inquiry—a constructive task. Following the
national standards set by AASL (2007), learners use skills, resources, and
tools to do the following:

- Inquire, think critically, and gain knowledge.
- Draw conclusions, make informed decisions, apply knowledge to new
  situations, and create new knowledge.
- Share knowledge and practice ethically and productively as members
  of our democratic society.
- Pursue personal and aesthetic growth.

For example, if students are challenged to envision what the major social
issues of the twenty-first century will be, they might begin by collecting demographic data, such as population projections for the next 50 years. Using
these data, they begin to relate population projections to other projections,
such as land-use trends. Similarly, they might investigate scientific advance-
ments in medicine, transportation, or energy. Once these data are collected and
discussed, students can begin to construct a picture of the future and envision social problems that may result from these physical, social, and scientific trends. On a much simpler scale, young children can construct their own
understanding of community by investigating examples of communities around
the world and developing generalizations about what those various communities
have in common. They then construct for themselves the concept of community.

Such constructive tasks are substantially different from traditional written reports about a country or a historical event, because these accounts of
fact finding do not create meaning. Meaning making occurs in a constructivist
learning environment. School librarians must be creative in designing learning experiences with teachers that challenge students to construct meaning as
they solve problems or make decisions.

A tension exists between teaching to content standards and adhering to constructivist principles of learning. It is in effect the tension between teaching
factual content and teaching learning processes. Those favoring fact learning
support the idea that a canon of learning should constitute the K–12 curriculum. Further, this sector tends to believe that students can and should
be tested on the canon in a high-stakes testing system where school funding,

student progression from grade to grade, and teacher pay or advancement are examples of the stakes at issue. Sometimes, the commitment to the canon or the pressure of high-stakes testing leads to rote learning. Embracing constructivism does not deny that students ought to gain fundamental knowledge. As Brooks and Brooks (1999: 23) assert: "State and local curriculums address what students learn. Constructivism, as an approach to education, addresses how students learn."

Constructivism supports the engagement of students in inquiry, and that engagement in inquiry creates the need for information that brings students to the library. In their inquiry, students ask themselves, "What do I already know? What questions do I have? How do I find out? What did I learn?" (Donham et al., 2001: 1). Through this process, students are active participants in their learning, rather than passive recipients of knowledge. The end result can be the same factual content as a more didactic approach to learning, but constructivists contend that the potential for deeper understanding is greater when students are active learners constructing meaning by integrating prior knowledge with new information. Moreover, students develop the skills and dispositions to learn independently beyond school. The school librarian must make explicit to all stakeholders this connection between inquiry in the library and the constructivist classroom. When students engage in inquiry, they seek answers to questions they pose, they gather information from various sources, they interpret and integrate information, and they ultimately make meaning out of the information they have found. This meaning making is a constructivist process. School librarians need to be ready to describe inquiry using constructivist language in order for teachers to see that students are doing more than gathering facts when they engage in inquiry—it is a sense-making process.

Learner Dispositions

The term *disposition* carries a variety of connotations across disciplines, but for educators it is perhaps best expressed as a habit of the mind, an attitude, a tendency to engage in a certain kind of thinking (Ritchhart, 2001). Integrating a variety of thinking disposition lists, Ritchhart has synthesized ideas about dispositions of learners into three categories:

- Looking out (creative thinking)
    Open-mindedness
    Curiosity
- Looking in (reflective thinking)
    Metacognition
    Truth seeking
- Looking at (critical thinking)
    Strategic thinking
    Healthy skepticism

Clearly, these are dispositions that school librarians seek to encourage when students engage in inquiry, and they are dispositions that are nurtured in the constructivist classroom. Perhaps most significantly, these are the dispositions that sustain lifelong learning. Without open-mindedness and curiosity, where do we gain the motivation to continue to learn and to explore new ideas? Without metacognition—reflecting on our own learning processes—how do we improve our abilities as learners? Without healthy skepticism, how do we avoid being taken in by the glut of misinformation in today's unjuried information universe?

A crucial consideration for educators is the extent to which learning activities are aimed at developing these dispositions or habits of minds. Awareness of dispositions requires that school librarians take proactive and intentional steps to develop and support learning dispositions; these might include the following:

Modeling learning dispositions (looking out). Thinking aloud is one strategy for modeling curiosity or open-minded dispositions. For example, a school librarian might be heard saying: "That makes me wonder . . ." Or, "What might be the argument on the opposing side of this question?" Or, "What evidence supports that assertion?" Or, "How strong is the evidence on the other side of the argument?"

Encouraging metacognitive behavior (looking in). Students may be required to keep a reflective research journal where they record their perceptions about their progress. Or, students might write a reflective self-assessment describing what they might do differently if they were to approach an assignment anew.

Encouraging a critical stance (looking at). Students may be required to seek confirming sources to verify information they find or to provide support for the authority of the sources they cite. Or, students may be required to state explicitly their assumptions before beginning a research activity.

Intentionality is important. It is not enough to mention or expect that students will develop dispositions of learning as by-products of their school experiences. Developing the disposition of a learner occurs by design. Collaboration between school librarians and classroom teachers can result in assignments and activities that aim intentionally at authentic inquiry and at developing dispositions that will result in graduates who are skillful, creative, reflective, and critical learners. In the AASL (2007) *Standards for the 21st-Century Learner,* dispositions are included as a strand. While it is difficult to imagine how these learner dispositions can be directly taught, they can indeed be nurtured, particularly in an inquiry-based learning environment. Key dispositions to be supported in students according to those standards are as follows:

- Initiative
- Self-direction/motivation
- Creativity
- Critical stance
- Adaptability/flexibility
- Resilience
- Confidence
- Productivity
- Social responsibility
- Curiosity
- Openness (open-mindedness)
- Appreciation for literature

While the specific language in this list may differ from Ritchhart (2001), the overall view of dispositions of a learner is certainly similar. That said, teacher-librarians can point to their own standards to support their efforts to provide inquiry-based learning experiences within the school curriculum that afford opportunities to nurture these dispositions.

The Common Core Curriculum

The Common Core Curriculum Standards (Common Core) released in 2010 represent an unprecedented shift away from disparate content guidelines across individual states in the areas of English language arts and mathematics. The standards establish consensus on expectations for student knowledge and skills that should be developed in grades K–12 (Porter et al., 2011). Examination of the Common Core reveals a number of potential links to the school library program. The English Language Arts Standards specify that students should develop cognitively complex skills. The following examples have readily apparent connections to the instructional goals of the school library program (Common Core State Standards Initiative, 2012).

K–5 Reading

- Analyze how and why individuals, events, and ideas develop and interact over the course of a text.
- Integrate and evaluate content presented in diverse formats and media, including visually and quantitatively, as well as in words.
- Read and comprehend complex literary and informational texts independently and proficiently.

6–12 Reading

- Read closely to determine what the text says explicitly and to make logical inferences from it; cite specific textual evidence when writing or speaking to support conclusions drawn from the text.
- Integrate and evaluate content presented in diverse formats and media, including visually and quantitatively, as well as in words.
- Delineate and evaluate the argument and specific claims in a text, including the validity of the reasoning as well as the relevance and sufficiency of the evidence.
- Analyze how two or more texts address similar themes or topics in order to build knowledge or to compare approaches the author takes.
- Read and comprehend complex literary and informational texts independently and proficiently.

K–12 Writing

- Write informative/explanatory texts to examine and convey complex ideas and information clearly and accurately through the effective selection, organization, and analysis of content.
- Use technology, including the Internet, to produce and publish writing and to interact and collaborate with others.
- Conduct short as well as more sustained research projects based on focused questions, demonstrating understanding of the subject under investigation.
- Gather relevant information from multiple print and digital sources, assess the credibility and accuracy of each source, and integrate the information while avoiding plagiarism.
- Draw evidence from literary or informational text to support analysis, reflection, and research.

School librarians can readily align their instructional programs with these standards and assert their role in several ways:

- Teaching the inquiry process
- Teaching students to adopt a critical stance as they gather and select information on which to base arguments
- Teaching students to use technologies for gathering information, collaborating with peers, and creating presentations to highlight their insights
- Providing diverse collections of digital and print texts

In addition to these standards, the Common Core proposes a definition of complex text that warrants consideration, particularly in today's reading environment often guarded by Lexile scores. In the Common Core, three dimensions define text complexity:

Qualitative evaluation of the text—Levels of meaning, structure, language conventionality and clarity, and knowledge demands

Quantitative evaluation of the text—Readability measures and other scores of text complexity

Matching reader to text and task—Reader variables such as motivation, knowledge, and experiences, and task variables such as purpose and the complexity generated by the task assigned and the questions posed (Common Core State Standards Initiative, 2012: 57)

Such a definition of complexity in text challenges educational settings where children are denied the opportunity to have books that are above their Lexile level. In a well-meaning effort to support reading fluency, some educators urge school librarians to limit children's selections in the library to texts "at their level." This approach fails to acknowledge certain aspects of the reading experience, such as the benefit of browsing a book that piques the child's interest or the potential for children to exceed their level when the motivation or background knowledge supports their understanding. Hence, this more sophisticated notion of complexity is a welcome relief from the strictly quantitative measure in place in many schools.

While nearly all states and the District of Columbia have adopted the Common Core State Standards, not all educators agree that standardization of curriculum across the nation is warranted:

> To think that every student in this country should be made to learn the same things is illogical on its face—it lacks face validity. The United States is just too large and too diverse to even want to engage in such folly. We all should have learned from the Soviet Union that central planning just does not work in the long run. The diversity of the United States is its greatest strength. The U.S. economy is able to adapt to change because of the diversity of the workforce. China is trying desperately to crawl out from under the rock of standardization in terms of curriculum and testing. Chinese officials recognize the negative impacts a standardized system has on intellectual creativity. Less than 10 percent of Chinese workers are able to function in multinational corporations. Chinese winners of Nobel Prizes are scarce, and China does not hold many scientific patents. (Tienken, 2011: 60)

Nevertheless, such standardization seems to fit the political tenor of the nation today where accountability is key and the emphasis is on facilitating national measures of student achievement. A society that tends to be more mobile also views such standardization as a benefit to consistent expectations for children transitioning from school to school. Further, the pressure for international competitiveness compels policy makers to define high standards for American schools.

Accountability

Perhaps one of the most influential pieces of federal legislation to affect schools in recent times was the No Child Left Behind Act of 2001—Title I, Improving the Academic Achievement of the Disadvantaged (2002). The act, scheduled for enforcement until 2014, contains four basic principles:

- Increased accountability
- Increased local flexibility in use of federal education funds
- Emphasis on research-supported teaching methods
- Expanded options for parents

This legislation has had particular impact on curriculum because of its first principle—increased accountability. To comply, states have established standards and standards-based assessments in reading, mathematics, science, and English-language proficiency. The call for standardized testing to document progress has dictated the curriculum. With potential sanctions such as transfer of students and their funding, the pressure for students to succeed on these high-stakes tests forced teaching to the tests. A test-driven curriculum led educators toward a canon of factual learning in K–12 education, and the authors of the tests have defined that canon. The potential impact on curriculum has not only included narrowing the curriculum to what is tested but also lessening the emphasis on process learning (e.g., information literacy and critical thinking skills). The areas of the curriculum not measured suffered as schools started to preclude or reduce their focus in those areas, including history, art, civics, music, physical education, health, and other cultural areas (Ravitch, 2010). Robert Linn of the University of Colorado has been engaged in educational testing and assessment since 1965. Bracey (2000: 137) quotes Linn on the efficacy of standardized tests:

> As someone who has spent his entire career doing research, writing, and thinking about educational testing and assessment issues, I would like to conclude by summarizing a compelling case showing that the major uses

of tests for student and school accountability during the last 50 years have improved education and student learning in dramatic ways. Unfortunately, that is not my conclusion. Instead, I am led to conclude that in most cases the instruments and technology have not been up to the demands that have been placed on them by high-stakes accountability. Assessment systems that are useful monitors lose much of their dependability and credibility for that purpose when high stakes are attached to them. The unintended negative effects of the high-stakes accountability uses often outweigh the intended positive effects.

Striving to make the required adequate yearly progress (AYP) has forced schools to be more concerned about teaching students to perform well on the tests than teaching what might be appropriate to develop skills and dispositions as lifelong learners. In this high-stakes legislation, states are advised to have a process in place to take at least some of the following actions against a school district that is unsuccessful at meeting the expected AYP:

- Defer programmatic funds or reduce administrative funds.
- Institute and implement a new curriculum.
- Replace personnel.
- Remove particular district schools and establish alternative governance.
- Appoint a trustee in place of the superintendent and school board.
- Abolish or restructure a school district.
- Authorize students to transfer to a higher-performing school and provide transportation.

These sanctions placed substantial pressure on school districts to see that students performed well on tests in order to demonstrate their yearly progress. In such a context, school librarians have had a challenge to affirm the importance of teaching not only content but also processes that will result in students learning to learn and learning to think critically.

While new legislation will inevitably come along, there is little reason to believe that the climate of accountability will change. Indeed, the call for accountability today focuses on teacher performance as related to student performance. This climate of measured performance leaves school librarians in an unsettling position because, though not accountable as teachers, they have the potential to influence student learning. The concern persists nevertheless that accountability will continue to discount students' mastering of the processes of lifelong learning or developing the dispositions of lifelong learners.

Technology Access

Ready access to the web offers extensive possibilities for inquiry-driven curricula, but the test anxiety created in today's educational policy climate may limit how readily teachers avail students of this opportunity. Nevertheless, in many classrooms the web will influence how teachers expect their students to acquire information, how students communicate with one another about the content of their curriculum, and how they publish their findings.

The wide availability of the web also raises concern about the ethics of Internet use. Topics such as plagiarism, intellectual property, evaluation of web-delivered information, and copyright violations need to find a place in the curriculum and must be taught explicitly if students are to really understand the nature of being responsible citizens on the web (Kruger, 2003). These are not concepts likely to appear on high-stakes tests, but they are important in developing good citizenship in the information-rich world dominated by the Internet. School librarians have responsibility for being both advocates and experts in the area of information ethics.

Further, school librarians can promote constructivist activities with Web 2.0 tools. For example, Haefner and Friedman (2008: 295) describe a history unit on World War II in which students developed wikis to communicate their constructed understandings of events of that time period:

> Wikis provided a learning environment that enabled students to individually explore battles, images, events, and people, such as the changing role of African Americans and women, in more depth than the traditional teacher-directed approach. Students used textbook readings as foundational knowledge and contextual information to build the content framework for their wiki. Then students spent class time watching digital videos on trench warfare, viewing images of "Wreaths" in Poland, sifting through graphic photos of Holocaust victims, and reading journals of African American soldiers and letters from women on the home front. . . . Students used wikis to make links, both literally and figuratively, to the events of World War II and to how these events impacted the lives of

Americans as well as citizens of all countries involved. As an example, students developed separate pages evaluating the war in Europe, the war in the Pacific, and the "war" on the American home front.

By encouraging creations of this sort, the school librarian can support integration of ideas and information from a variety of sources and construction of understandings and insights not likely to develop through textbook reading alone.

A number of elements are at work today influencing curriculum. The school librarian can either be overlooked as a mere bystander supporting curriculum or be perceived as playing a crucial role in developing and teaching a curriculum that will prepare students for life in this century. To be a participant, today's school librarian must be conversant on the trends in curriculum and be articulate in expressing the crucial ways the library program is an essential component. Unfortunately, there is currently no place at the table reserved for a professional whose role is little understood by many educators. Yet, when the school librarian's role is understood, these learning professionals can make a substantial contribution to a school's efforts to both set and meet high standards for students.

The School Librarian's Expertise

Teachers have obvious roles in curriculum and instruction. Far subtler is the role of the school librarian. However, school librarians can bring important assets to enhance the curriculum because of their unique perspective and skill set.

Uniqueness

Situated with a cross-grade-level and cross-discipline perspective, a school librarian knows the curriculum content and the teaching strategies in each classroom. While the principal and the guidance counselor are also in touch with each teacher, their relationships to classrooms usually focus on managerial issues or individual students' personal concerns. The librarian's connection with each teacher focuses on what is being taught and how it is taught. Such a relationship may place the librarian in the position of knowing more than any other professional in the building about the total curriculum. Such knowledge can then be valuable for curriculum articulation.

Curriculum mapping is a valuable strategy for librarians to implement. This process essentially charts the curriculum across grade levels to show what students are expected to learn at each grade level in the school within each discipline. A curriculum map is best created in collaboration with teachers—perhaps grade-level teams at the elementary level and disciplinary departments at the secondary level. Along with content, the map should include major projects that will require the library's resources. Given such a map, the school librarian can then align the library curriculum with the disciplinary content. For example, when a second-grade social studies class is studying the concept of community, the school librarian can identify skills related to locating nonfiction books about community helpers for an investigative activity included in the teacher's plans. Or, when the eighth-grade science curriculum calls for students to create presentations on questions related to energy, the library curriculum might include instruction related to awareness and acknowledgment of special-interest information sources. Additionally, the curriculum map is a guide for collection development for the school librarian. The curriculum map reveals content for which library resources, physical and virtual, can complement classroom instructional materials. By developing such a curriculum map, the school librarian becomes the expert on the overall curriculum in the school and simultaneously develops a way to integrate library collection and instruction with content area curriculum.

Knowledge Base

Some educators may be naive about the expertise of school librarians. In the history of American education, the school library field is relatively young, and many teachers today may not have had experience with school librarians when they attended school. Also, colleges of education do not teach about collaboration with school librarians. Many people who teach expect that their work will be relatively isolated to the classroom. Unfortunately, many teachers do not even know that in nearly all states school librarians must also be trained as teachers (Jesseman, Page, and Underwood, 2011). What more do school librarians bring to the conversation? Some key examples of specialized knowledge include the following:

- Information technologies and strategies for using these technologies powerfully and efficiently

- Learning resources in the form of trade books, software, and websites
- Design and production skills in a variety of media formats
- Planning and management skills and knowledge
- Curriculum and instructional design
- Information ethics
- Computer systems

This set of knowledge and competencies is added value that school librarians bring to the curriculum planning process, but only if they can articulate clearly how the school library program can enhance curricular offerings and classrooms instruction.

Coaching

A reference librarian seeks as much information as necessary in order to provide the client with exactly the needed information. The reference questioning strategy proceeds from identifying the topic, to refining the question, analyzing the question to formulate a search strategy, and evaluating the information found to ensure that it meets the client's need. A good reference interview accomplishes two objectives: first, to understand and subsequently meet the actual information need of the client, and second—perhaps not intentional—to help the client clarify what he or she is actually seeking. Working with teachers, librarians apply similar strategies, with similar results. The reference interview questioning strategy of the librarian is similar to the strategy of cognitive coaching (Costa and Garmston, 1994). In the cognitive coaching model, the coach assists teachers in reflection. The intent is to foster collegiality and deepen reflective skills.

In a case study, coaching was identified as one important way for the school librarian to work with teachers (Donham van Deusen, 1996). In one example from this case, a teacher approached the school librarian about teaching information location skills. Through the reference interview strategy, the librarian pursued what the teacher really wanted children to learn. Her questioning revealed that the teacher wanted to improve children's skills in reading nonfiction. The librarian then offered to locate articles so that the children spent their time on the reading skills that the teacher wanted to address rather than on locating the texts to be read. Together, they team-taught strategies for extracting information from articles. Interaction with the librarian caused the teacher to refocus the lesson so that instructional time was used to the best advantage.

A coaching model emphasizes the importance of reflection on teaching and learning. The coach uses questioning to help the teacher evaluate information that will lead to decisions on future teaching. The model is not that of an expert providing direction to the teacher, but rather as a colleague encouraging another colleague's thought and reflection. In this case, the librarian knew that these students already had attained the needed location skills, and rather than declare this fact she instead raised relevant questions so that the decision was collaborative. Those questions followed a pattern that proceeded from "What is your lesson about?" (describing) to "What exactly will the students be doing?" (translating) to "What will be the order of activities in the unit?" (sequencing) to "How will you know that students have been successful?" (operationalizing criteria). By posing such questions, the librarian encourages teachers to think through plans, clarify them for themselves, and communicate them to the librarian, who can then assist in their implementation. In similar ways, the school librarian can influence implementation of curriculum by participating in teaching the inquiry process, the skills of critical evaluation, and the technical skills for presentation, and by engaging students as they analyze complex ideas and construct new knowledge.

Conclusion

Participation in curriculum involves not only being a part of the planning process but also being part of the implementation. Each example described in this chapter has some common features. Most important, the librarian works with teachers—not in isolation. Also, the expertise that the librarian offers is different from the classroom teacher's—it is the expertise of a specialist. Finally, the school librarian takes initiative. The worst-case scenario is for the school librarian to be included in curriculum planning meetings but failing to contribute in unique and useful ways. Being on committees is not enough. The challenge is to improve instruction. The question for every librarian after every curriculum planning meeting and after every interchange about curriculum must be, "In what ways did my contribution improve the content and delivery of the curriculum?"

Leadership Strategies

Teacher

Map local content area curriculum to the library curriculum and design instruction in collaboration with teachers accordingly.

Refer to the AASL crosswalk between the Common Core Curriculum and the AASL *Standards for the 21st-Century Learner* (accessible at www.ala.org/ala/mgrps/divs/aasl/guidelinesandstandards/common corecrosswalk).

Join, encourage, or initiate professional learning communities on cross-disciplinary study topics such as multiage grouping, student performance assessment, block scheduling, or instructional technology.

Embrace the role of technology advocate, facilitator, and staff developer.

Collaborate with teaching colleagues to develop a written library curriculum with connections to classroom curriculum.

Information Specialist

Share interesting curriculum-oriented articles with staff either one-on-one or at staff meetings.

Participate in curriculum development projects. Raise the principal's awareness of your potential to contribute and promote the idea of becoming a part of the team.

- Provide literature searches on the topics of interest.
- Locate instructional materials to consider.
- Exploit your knowledge of children's or young adult literature to help teachers identify specific titles for developing units that challenge students to engage with complex texts.

Program Administrator

Maintain current awareness of trends in the content areas.

- Read (or at least skim) articles (i.e., not just materials reviews) in journals from curriculum areas, such as the following:

Social Education

Social Studies and the Young Learner

English Journal

Language Arts

The Reading Teacher

Science and Children

Teaching Children Mathematics

- Attend a professional conference outside the library profession.
- Become familiar with national standards and guidelines from various disciplines.

Participate in long-range curriculum planning and evaluation.

Scenarios for Discussion

Scenario 1

A middle school faculty is reviewing its policy on homework. The next two faculty meetings will be devoted to this topic as faculty members consider these questions:

- How much homework should we give students?
- What is the parents' role in homework?
- Should there be homework-free nights to support family time?
- What kind of homework should we give students, and what assumptions should we make about access to resources for doing homework?

What is the role of the school librarian in the discussion of these issues?

Scenario 2

Ben is the school librarian at Ford Middle School, where the district has encouraged schools to begin incorporating the Common Core Standards. Sitting at lunch with the seventh-grade team he learns that they are struggling to figure out ways to design assignments that incorporate reading informational texts in the content areas. The English language arts teachers are very familiar with narrative (fiction) texts that they want to use but cannot offer suggestions to their colleagues in science and social studies. What should Ben say?

REFERENCES

AASL (American Association of School Librarians). 2007. *Standards for the 21st-Century Learner.* American Library Association. www.ala.org/aasl/ guidelinesandstandards/learningstandards/standards.

Blaik-Hourani, R. 2011. "Constructivism and Revitalizing Social Studies." *History Teacher* 44, no. 2: 227–249.

Bracey, G. 2000. "The 10th Bracey Report on the Condition of Public Education." *Phi Delta Kappan* 82, no. 2: 133–144.

Brooks, M. G., and J. G. Brooks. 1999. "The Courage to Be Constructivist." *Educational Leadership* 57, no. 3: 18–24.

Cannella, G. S., and J. C. Reiff. 1994. "Individual Constructivist Teacher Education: Teachers as Empowered Learners." *Teacher Education Quarterly* 21, no. 3: 31–35.

Carmichael, D. L., M. B. King, and F. M. Newmann. 2009. "Authentic Intellectual Work: Common Standards for Teaching Social Studies." *Social Education,* 73, no. 1: 43–49.

Common Core State Standards Initiative. 2012. Common Core State Standards: For English Language Arts and Literacy in History/Social Studies, Science, and Technical Subjects. Common Core State Standards Initiative. www.corestandards.org/assets/CCSSI_ELA%20Standards.pdf.

Costa A., and R. Garmston. 1994. *Cognitive Coaching: A Foundation for Renaissance Schools.* Norwood, MA: Christopher-Gordon.

Donham, J., K. Bishop, C. C. Kuhlthau, and D. Oberg. 2001. *Inquiry-Based Learning: Lessons from Library Power.* Worthington, OH: Linworth.

Donham van Deusen, J. 1996. "The School Library Media Specialist as a Member of the Teaching Team: 'Insider' and 'Outsider.'" *Journal of Curriculum and Instruction* 11, no. 3: 229–248.

Haefner, T. L., and A. M. Friedman. 2008. "Wikis and Constructivism in Secondary Social Studies: Fostering a Deeper Understanding." *Computers in the Schools* 25, no. 3–4: 288–302.

Jesseman, D. J., S. M. Page, and L. Underwood. 2011. School Library Media Certification by State. Accessed November 6. www.schoollibrarymonthly .com/cert.

Kruger, R. 2003. "Discussing Cyber Ethics with Students Is Critical." *Social Studies* 94, no. 4: 188–189.

No Child Left Behind Act of 2001, Pub. L. No. 107-110, 115 Stat. 1425 (2002).

Piaget, J. 1953. The Origins of Intelligence in Children. New York: Basic Books.

Porter, A., J. McMaken, J. Hwang, and R. Yang. 2011. "Common Core Standards: The New U.S. Intended Curriculum." *Educational Researcher* 40, no. 3: 103–116.

Powell, K. 2009. "Cognitive and Social Constructivism: Developing Tools for an Effective Classroom." *Education* 130, no. 2: 241–250.

Ravitch, D. 2010. *The Death and Life of the Great American School System: How Testing and Choice Are Undermining Education.* New York: Basic Books.

Ritchhart, R. 2001. "From IQ to IC: A Dispositional View of Intelligence." *Roeper Review* 23, no. 3: 144–150.

Tienken, C. H. 2011. "Common Core Standards: The Emperor Has No Clothes, or Evidence." *Kappa Delta Pi Record* 47, no. 2: 58–62.

3

The Principal

This chapter:

- outlines standards for school administrators;
- describes the role of the principal as leader and manager;
- relates the principal's role to the school librarian's role;
- describes the impact of the principal on the library program;
- considers the relationship between the school library program and the pressures for accountability in a data-driven environment; and
- identifies leadership strategies for working with the principal.

Standards for School Administrators

Just as school library professionals are guided by the expectations in *Empowering Learners* (AASL, 2007) and by the National Board for Professional Teaching Standards (www.nbpts.org), so principals are guided by standardized expectations. For example, the Interstate School Leaders Licensure Consortium has defined six standards for school administrators as education leaders (Council of Chief State School Officers, 2008: 14–15):

> STANDARD 1: An education leader promotes the success of every student by facilitating the development, articulation, implementation, and stewardship of a vision of learning that is shared and supported by all stakeholders.
>
> - Collaboratively develop and implement a shared vision and mission
> - Collect and use data to identify goals, assess organizational effectiveness, and promote organizational learning
> - Create and implement plans to achieve goals

- Promote continuous and sustainable improvement
- Monitor and evaluate progress and revise plans

STANDARD 2: An education leader promotes the success of every student by advocating, nurturing, and sustaining a school culture and instructional program conducive to student learning and staff professional growth.

- Nurture and sustain a culture of collaboration, trust, learning, and high expectations
- Create a comprehensive, rigorous, and coherent curricular program
- Create a personalized and motivating learning environment for students
- Supervise instruction
- Develop assessment and accountability systems to monitor student progress
- Develop the instructional and leadership capacity of staff
- Maximize time spent on quality instruction
- Promote the use of the most effective and appropriate technologies to support teaching and learning
- Monitor and evaluate the impact of the instructional program

STANDARD 3: An education leader promotes the success of every student by ensuring management of the organization, operation, and resources for a safe, efficient, and effective learning environment.

- Monitor and evaluate the management and operational systems
- Obtain, allocate, align, and efficiently utilize human, fiscal, and technological resources
- Promote and protect the welfare and safety of students and staff
- Develop the capacity for distributed leadership
- Ensure teacher and organizational time is focused to support quality instruction and student learning

STANDARD 4: An education leader promotes the success of every student by collaborating with faculty and community members, responding to diverse community interests and needs, and mobilizing community resources.

- Collect and analyze data and information pertinent to the educational environment
- Promote understanding, appreciation, and use of the community's diverse cultural, social, and intellectual resources
- Build and sustain positive relationships with families and caregivers
- Build and sustain productive relationships with community partners

STANDARD 5: An education leader promotes the success of every student by acting with integrity and fairness, and in an ethical manner.

- Ensure a system of accountability for every student's academic and social success
- Model principles of self-awareness, reflective practice, transparency, and ethical behavior
- Safeguard the values of democracy, equity, and diversity
- Consider and evaluate the potential moral and legal consequences of decision-making
- Promote social justice and ensure that individual student needs inform all aspects of schooling

STANDARD 6: An education leader promotes the success of every student by understanding, responding to, and influencing the political, social, economic, legal, and cultural context.

- Advocate for children, families, and caregivers
- Act to influence local, district, state, and national decisions affecting student learning
- Assess, analyze, and anticipate emerging trends and initiatives in order to adapt leadership strategies

Two significant conclusions emerge from reviewing this list of expectations for the principal. First, principals have many demands on them and are accountable to a variety of stakeholders. Second, these standards reveal that the librarian and the principal have much in common.

Many of these standards for school administrators relate directly to the work of the school librarian. In the language of the stage, in some areas the librarian may perform in a supporting role and in some areas he or she may costar. For example, the first standard involves the articulation and implementation of a vision of learning that is shared by the school community. The roles for the school librarian are immediately evident. As costar, he or she can help shape that vision so that it incorporates the notion of learning to learn that is so fundamental to information literacy. In a supporting role, the school librarian then advocates within the school community for buy-in. Similarly for the second standard, one expectation is that the principal promote the most effective and appropriate technologies to support learning. The school librarian's expertise is highly valuable in this area of responsibility. Likewise, school librarians should position themselves to be likely candidates as the principal seeks to "develop the instructional and leadership capacity of staff"—both as potential leaders and as facilitators in the instructional development of the professional staff, particularly in the area of technology. Each of the remaining four standards suggests roles for the school librarian to work cooperatively with school administrators. A school librarian will do well to determine how the library program can support and enhance the work of the principal as defined by these standards.

Principal as Leader and Manager

The school principal experiences a constant tension between two distinct expectations: to be a leader and to be a manager. A considerable body of research confirms this role ambiguity (Manasse, 1985). Horng, Klasik, and Loeb (2010) conducted an intensive study of the ways in which school principals used their time. The study was conducted in the Miami-Dade School District—a diverse district where data were collected from principals at high school, middle school, and elementary school levels. Somewhat surprisingly, they discovered little difference across grade levels in the time distribution of activities. They organized tasks into five categories: administrative tasks, internal relationships, external relationships, instructional tasks, and personal tasks. The findings indicated the following distribution of time:

- Administrative tasks such as managing budgets and staff and hiring personnel as well as managing discipline and fulfilling compliance requirements represented just over 50 percent of their time.

- Internal relationships such as interacting to develop relationships with students and staff took up approximately 15 percent of their time.
- External relationships such as fund-raising accounted for approximately 5 percent of their time.
- Instructional tasks such as classroom visits and observations, informally coaching teachers, curriculum, and professional development together accounted for less than 15 percent of their time.
- The remainder of time was allocated to personal tasks such as lunch and restroom breaks or transition from one task or location to another.

Similarly, a 2007 Illinois survey of principals examined several aspects of the principalship in practice (White et al., 2011). The survey results draw from 877 respondents representing school administrators in the state. While principals ranked instructional tasks as most important in the survey, their report of time use showed that this category represented just over a quarter of their time (p. 18). Only 30 percent of principals rated themselves as "very effective" in tasks related to instruction.

While the professional literature indicates and the public expects the principal to be an instructional leader, these studies suggest that the balance between instructional leader and operations manager weighs heavily in favor of manager. The ever-increasing demands for accountability may provide one explanation for the heavy burden of managerial tasks for today's school principal.

In their examination of how principals spend their time, Camburn, Spillane, and Sebastian (2010) found considerable managerial demands take time away from instructional leadership by principals. These authors propose, "A growing body of evidence suggests schools can work against these constraints by giving responsibility for instructional leadership to other leaders, particularly teacher leaders" (p. 720). Meanwhile, the professional literature speaks to a burgeoning concept of teacher leadership and schools as learning organizations. Lieberman and Miller (2004: 28) define teacher leadership to include the roles of "teacher as researcher, teacher as scholar, and teacher as mentor." Such teacher leaders could certainly be found among the ranks of school librarians willing to step into teacher-leader roles by asserting their special expertise in such areas as teaching with technology, critical reading, evaluation of information, and inquiry-based learning. Such leadership may take the form of collaborating with colleagues in action research to investigate pedagogical practices in the school. Or, it might take the form of mentoring teachers for inquiry-based learning.

School librarians face a dilemma similar to principals in determining how best to allocate time. The tension between the operational demands and the educational demands of the library mirror the tensions of principals as they address administrative and managerial tasks that compete for their time with instructional tasks. And just as the balance between leader and manager is a key to success for the principal, so is the balance between two competing sets of priorities a key to success for the school librarian. Figure 3.1 shows parallel lists of tasks for both principal as leader and manager and school librarian as educator and manager.

FIGURE 3.1

Comparison of Dual Roles of Principal and School Librarian

Principal	School Librarian
LEADER	**EDUCATOR**
Goal setting	Goal setting
Modeling	Teaching
Decision making	Collaborating with teachers
Coaching	Providing staff development
Interacting with parents about school vision	Communicating with teachers, administrators, and parents about the library program
Monitoring programs	Monitoring programs
MANAGER	**MANAGER**
Scheduling	Scheduling
Supervising	Supervising
Purchasing	Purchasing
Budgeting	Budgeting
Accountability/compliance	Data collection
Maintaining the physical plant	Maintaining the facility
Writing policies	Writing policies
Responding to parental concerns	Troubleshooting

Acknowledging the analogous tension between roles, the school librarian can empathize and enter into dialogue with the principal, conscious of whether the topic at hand deals with management or leadership.

Aligning the School Library Agenda with the Principal's Agenda

Yetter (1994) found that the librarian's leadership ability is crucial to the success of a library program. By recognizing the nature of the principal's work, the school librarian can learn to interact with the principal to marry their goals. Consider first the principal as leader. What is the principal's vision for the school and how does the library program facilitate bringing that vision into reality? By fitting the library program's agenda to that of the principal, the librarian communicates important messages. Hartzell (2003) aptly describes this strategy as WIIFM—what's in it for me? The savvy school librarian can advance the library program by thinking about the principal's aims. In the school library profession, it is common to read of the isolation of the librarian as one-of-a-kind in the school. This same separateness characterizes the principal. The two are a natural team since both must be concerned with all the teachers and students in the school. Both share an across-grade-level and across-discipline view of the school. To make the alliance work, however, it is necessary for the librarian to embrace the principal's vision as the guiding light for the school. While affirmations like "The library is the hub of the school" are common in library advocacy literature, the reality is that though the library program may be a comprehensive support system, it is not the driving force of the school's educational agenda. That driving force is the school's mission statement. So, the librarian does well to align his or her program explicitly with the school's mission.

Another message sent when the librarian aligns the library program with the principal's vision is that the library program itself is part of the implementation of the vision. Making the role of the library program explicit and highly visible is crucial to gaining support for successful library programming. Opening up the library to the community for technology training for parents, for example, may garner support from the community for technology expenditures. More important, however, it can engender parental support for the instructional work that the library program represents in teaching students to be effective users of electronic information resources. When parents support the school library's instructional efforts, the ultimate winners are the students.

Data-Driven Decision Making

The high level of accountability in schools today requires principals to make data-driven decisions. This trend has important implications for the school librarian. Of particular concern to the school librarian is collecting and reporting to the principal data related to student learning, funding for resources, staffing, and scheduling in the library.

Perhaps first it is important to acknowledge where principals develop their initial expectations for school libraries and school librarians. In a 1996 survey of NCATE programs that offer principal licensure, only 18 percent included information about the school library in coursework (Wilson and MacNeil, 1998). Church (2010) investigated principals' sources of knowledge of the instructional role of the school librarian and reported that 60 percent of respondents indicated that they formed their views from interactions with school librarians during their administrative careers, while 32 percent indicated they formed their views from interactions with school librarians during their teaching careers. This potential naiveté is cause for concern. It seems difficult to imagine that a principal can effectively hire personnel for a library program without understanding the program's role and relationship to the overall school program. Further, it indicates the important responsibility of school librarians to teach administrators what to expect of them. Unfortunately, principals' expectations often are too low as a result of their firsthand observations, whether from their classroom days or from their administrative posts.

In a data-driven climate, a principal's naiveté about the school library can be particularly problematic. Performance evaluation cannot be effective without fundamental knowledge about library programming. The intent of evaluation is the improvement of professional practice, yet such guidance cannot occur without awareness of what constitutes effective practice.

There is a continuing tendency to use a teacher model for performance appraisal of school librarians (Bryant, 2002). Principals typically observe the librarian following criteria designed for classroom teachers without regard to the unique aspects of teaching in the library. These unique aspects include the reality that the school librarian sees each group of students less frequently than the classroom teacher, and therefore has less relationship with each group of students. Also, the instruction often is isolated from other instruction in settings where the library class schedule is a fixed cycle or weekly time period. Student assessment in library instruction tends to be more formative and often, from the student perspective, "doesn't count." Yet both formative and summative assessments are important criteria in classroom teacher evaluation. The authority in the class belongs to the classroom teacher, and the librarian can easily be perceived as a "guest." These and other aspects of library teaching make the standard evaluation instrument less relevant. Instead, the librarian's teaching evaluation needs to consider how well the teacher and librarian collaborate, how effectively the librarian relates the library instruction to the classroom and/or to real-world application, how well the librarian maximizes limited time, and/or how well the librarian relates prior learning to help students see connections between instructional sessions that may be days or weeks apart. More important, however, is the fact that the teaching role is only one aspect of the librarian's work, and principals tend to be naive as to other aspects of the school librarian's role. For example, organizing resources for ready access—whether those resources sit on a shelf or a server—is a significant part of the library professional's work. Similarly, collaborating with teachers for instructional planning and collection development is a crucial responsibility of the position. Still, the "data" collected about the librarian's performance tend to be nothing more than the formal teaching observation.

"Rounds" (Black, 2007) or "walk-throughs" (Downey et al., 2004) have become a popular way for principals to gather data about their schools. Downey's walk-through is a structured process that suggests a cursory glance to notice "attending behavior" (whether or not students are engaged); to determine the actual curricular objectives and content being taught; to determine the alignment of the taught curriculum with the prescribed curriculum; to note the context or "mode of student response"; and to note the cognitive level of questioning/learning activities (p. 27). Some principals use a PDA-compatible tool for their classroom "walkabouts" (Lovely, 2006). This checklist reminds the principal to look for a variety of categories related primarily to teaching practices. The checklist includes looking for the following:

- Depth of student activity (e.g., recall, skill development)
- Teaching practice (e.g., learning groups, advance organizers)
- Differentiation of instruction
- Standards-based models (e.g., standards-based rubrics)

"Walking the walls" is another dimension of the walk-through model wherein principals attend to student work on the walls or around the room or other artifacts that inform the principal about the teaching and learning experiences of the classroom. These walk-throughs are followed by conferences or conversations with teachers to reflect on observations and to celebrate successes or propose alternatives or strategies for improvement. This practice holds promise for school libraries as well—if the school library is on the "rounds" route. In fact, wherever principals are "managing by walking around," the school librarian is wise to nudge the principal to include the library in order for the principal to see firsthand the level of active engagement in learning that is likely to be occurring there.

Everhart (2006) studied what data principals in New York gathered to evaluate school librarians and discovered that one overwhelming source of information about the library was the informal visit, followed by word-of-mouth reports from students and teachers. Everhart followed up the survey with interviews to determine what the informal visits yielded. She asked participants to list observed activities that led them to believe that appropriate activities were happening. She listed these observations:

- Students are actively engaged with books or technology.
- The librarian is interacting with teachers and students.
- There is an organized, clean, inviting environment.
- A variety of materials is available.
- There are relevant displays.
- Students are borrowing books.

These findings offer a straightforward guide for teacher librarians to take stock of the library in which they work and ask themselves what their principal will observe at any point throughout the day. After all, the principal's perception of the library is crucial to its development. Resources—human and fiscal—are often determined at building-level administration, especially in small school districts. Hence, school librarians do well to ensure that when principals visit, they see activities that indicate student learning and engagement in the library.

Besides observation, other forms of evidence can inform administrative decision making. Data on student performance are perhaps the most important category for consideration. The accountability culture today focuses heavily on student achievement. Todd (2009: 88–89) asserts:

> Aligned with the student outcomes focus of many international educational systems, an integral component of evidence-based school librarianship is the systematic collection, integration and dissemination of evidence of the tangible impacts, and outcomes of school library practices, with organizational goals and objectives including student achievement and the development of deep knowledge, deep understanding, and competencies and skills for thinking, living and working. . . . At a local school level, evidence-based practice of school librarianship seeks to demonstrate the value-added role of a school library to the life and work of a school—outcomes that center on learning, literacy and living and the development of students personally, socially, culturally, and globally.

So, the school librarian does well to gather evidence of the impact of the library on student achievement. Using a standardized—and free—online testing program like TRAILS (Tools for Real-time Assessment of Information Literacy Skills, available at www.trails-9.org) is one way of demonstrating the impact of the library instruction program on student learning or the need to expand and improve library instruction. Also, working with teachers to include assessment of students' information-seeking behaviors can provide data on the impact of the library instruction program; for example, teachers can include quality of resources as a factor in evaluating students' research assignments. The school librarian can design and carry out action research to compare the quality of resources with the quality of student work. Gathering evidence to measure the library program's effectiveness is key, and the closer the evidence is to measures of student achievement and student engagement, the better.

Monthly reporting on the use of the library and its resources is also a way to keep the library program within the viewing range of the principal. In a data-driven environment it is important to remember that only the school librarian has the data to portray the activity in the library media center. Whether a principal values a data-rich report will vary from principal to principal. Figure 3.2 shows an example of a spreadsheet that can be maintained monthly to record traffic in the library and the number of classes taking advantage of the library and the school librarian.

The data collected here can then be summarized into a brief form as shown in Figure 3.3. Notice the emphasis on students individually and in classes using the library space.

Even more helpful, however, are reports that succinctly describe the activity of the library program to demonstrate its relationship to classroom

FIGURE 3.2

Monthly Data Recording

MONTHLY STATS		FEBRUARY									
		Individual Students Library (open hour or from study hall)									
Date	Library Classes	Before School	Per.1	Per.2	Per.3	Per.4	Per.5	Per.6	Per.7	After School	Total
1	5	54	25	61	20	31	31	53	40	42	357
2	5	42	20	11	19	11	43	11	2	39	198
3	0	39	30	12	24	25	51	41	31	30	283
4	4	25	12	20	31	14	10	12	8	20	152
5	3	40	32	14	19	10	17	15	13	9	169
8	6	12	14	17	8	20	10	7	9	7	104
9	4	15	21	18	45	15	21	10	19	21	185
10	4	12	19	11	13	11	5	17	3	23	114
11	3	16	31	14	9	19	11	43	32	30	205
12	3	17	25	41	20	31	41	2	8	21	206
15	3	14	19	11	10	11	6	4	9	34	118
16	4	22	9	5	10	25	42	20	31	41	205
17	4	29	19	11	14	51	6	5	9	35	179
18	0	18	5	19	11	43	11	9	5	22	143
19	0	15	4	8	9	4	20	22	25	29	136
22	2	31	22	31	25	41	20	8	6	19	203
23	2	34	19	11	30	31	7	21	5	23	181

teaching. The report in Figure 3.4 is an example of such a descriptive report. It shows what classes in the library required direct instruction by the librarian. A brief description of the activities shows the curriculum connection. The information literacy column lists the skill areas taught. The levels of instructional support reveal the degree of collaboration with the classroom teacher. This single page conveys considerable information about the nature as well as the amount of teaching and learning activity occurring in the library program.

Even if a principal simply files this document away, the school librarian should meet annually with the principal to review the year's accomplishments in the library program and to review needs for resources or staffing or space. At that time, these data can be used effectively and efficiently to help describe needs. Also, in the face of any question from a parent, central office administrator, or teacher, the principal has available documentation to characterize the library program.

Some principals may respond with greater enthusiasm to media productions showing activity in the library. In those situations, the school librarian

FIGURE 3.3
Monthly Statistics Report to Principal

HIGH SCHOOL LIBRARY FEBRUARY STATISTICS

Books and print materials circulated	3,189
Nonprint materials circulated	75
Total circulation	3,264

Attendance in Library and Lab	Computer Lab	Library
Classes scheduled	61	64
Study hall/open hour	1,964	3,608
Individual student/day average	98	180

MONTHLY SUMMARY USE OF LIBRARY AND COMPUTER LAB

Total classes scheduled	125
Average classes per day in seven available periods per day	6
School enrollment	1,250

FIGURE 3.4

Instructional Support Monthly Data Summary

This report summarizes support to teachers in preparation for classes. It stresses those areas where the media program enables resource-based teaching and the areas of the information skills curriculum addressed.

Key to levels of instructional support:

1. Gathering materials in response to teacher requests
2. Working with students on a small group or individual basis during a teacher-planned activity
3. Teaching classes in support of a teacher-planned activity
4. Sharing equal responsibility with the teacher to plan and teach

Keys to areas of information literacy curriculum:

1. Task definition
2. Information-seeking strategies
3. Location and access
4. Use of information
5. Creation and communication
6. Evaluation and self-assessment

Date	Teacher	Periods	Level	Activities	Info. Lit.
April 1,2	Cochran	1,2,3	2	English 11 Research papers	3,4
April 1,3,5	Smith	4,5	4	English 9 Shakespeare and his times	2,3,4,5
April 1,4	Routh	1,2,3,5,6	2	European history research	3
April 2,3,4,5,8,9,10	Warner	7	3	Futures careers research	3,4,5
April 4,5,8	Cooper	3	3	Environmental analysis research	3,4
April 5,10,12,15,17	Brown	3,4,6,7	2	Humanities decades research	3
April 15	Franks	1,3,4	3	China/Japan fiction book selection	3
April 16,17,18,19	Franks	6,7	3	Global studies change agent research	2,3,4
April 17,18	Brothers	5	3	Personal history collages	3
April 18,19,22	Phipps	1,3,6	2	US Lit research	1,3
April 19	Castor	1,3,6,7	3	English 10 research	3
April 22,23	Brown	3,4,6,7	2	Humanities	1,3
April 24	Robbins	1,2,3,5,6	2	European history research post-WW II	3,4
April 24,25,26	Becker	7	2	Panel discussion research	3,4
April 24,25	Flynn	6,7	3	Global studies change agent research	3,4
April 26,29,30	Cohn	6	2	Government panel discussion research	3,4

might create a short video of activity in the library, perhaps highlighted with a brief student or teacher interview, to post on the library website. Simply advising the principal to view the video on the website may be all that is needed to give the administration a media-based look; such glimpses at library activity can become effective public relations resources for the principal to use in parent communiqués.

A Principal's Workday

Manasse (1985) summarized several portrayals of the principal's workday as fragmented days composed of as many as 400 short, unplanned verbal interactions regarding 50 to over 100 separate events. More recently, Camburn, Spillane, and Sebastian (2010) studied daily time logs to describe the work of a principal. They report the following example of a one-hour snapshot of a principal's time log:

12:08   On the phone. Interviewing a prospective Latin language instructor to help children with vocabulary

12:28   Composing a memo on energy management

12:38   Conference with a counselor to discuss a student who is failing

12:48   Continuing work on energy management memo, interrupted by phone call

12:58   Meeting with a fourth-grade teacher about air conditioning in her classroom

1:08   Meeting with a social worker to discuss student with 15 school absences

Consider a stream of events that includes dealing with a potential child-abuse situation, a clogged toilet, a teacher in need of more mathematics textbooks, a parent seeking advice about homeschooling a child, or a student sent in with chewing tobacco in his pocket—all unrelated events requiring prompt attention. This is the school principal's day.

The school librarian must keep in mind the nature of the principal's day. The characterization of the day as a bombardment of as many as 400 separate interactions stands as a reminder that getting the undivided attention of the principal for extended development of ideas requires some advance notice and planning. Sensitivity to the nature of the principal's work can help the school librarian work as a teammate rather than as one more interruption. Considering the time constraints of the principal, the librarian does well to provide critical information efficiently.

Impact of the Principal on the School Library Program

Perhaps the greatest impact the principal can have is on integrating the library program into the school program. A study of the occurrence of consulting between librarians and classroom teachers revealed the influence of the principal's expectations (Donham van Deusen and Tallman, 1994). In that study, school librarians reported whether they perceived that their principals held expectations for them to collaborate with teachers. Those who perceived that their principals expected them to collaborate with classroom teachers reported significantly more instances of consultative work with teachers than those whose principals were not perceived as holding that expectation. In the same study, librarians reported the occurrences of their teaching information skills in association with classroom instruction. Again, the principal's expectation that such collaboration occur made a significant positive difference in the amount of collaboration. Likewise, Campbell (1994) found that support from the principal is essential for library programs to succeed, regardless of the professional level of the librarian.

Farmer (2007) identifies several ways in which principals can influence and largely determine the success of the school library program. In summary, she states that principals:

- appoint committee and task force members,
- mandate collaborative efforts as part of teacher retention,
- allocate resources for collaborative efforts,
- schedule time for collaboration and class access,
- create professional development opportunities that foster collaboration,

- develop and encourage policies for library use and collaboration, and
- recognize and award collaborative efforts.

No doubt, these actions have substantial influence on how the school library operates and what the school librarian can accomplish. Given that principals are not generally educated about the competencies of school librarians, the values of the school library profession, the standards for school library programs, or the curriculum to be taught in the school library, a heavy responsibility rests on the school librarian to help the principal gain insight into how the school library program can improve student achievement and the school climate.

Research suggests that the degree to which principals share decision making with staff members develops over time as a result of specific factors. Yukl and Fu (1999) found that competence, job level, goal congruence, and time together with the principal were determinants in the level of participation in decision making. The influence-seeking librarian can make particular effort toward two of these: goal congruence and time together with the principal. Aligning the goals of the library program with those of the principal is an obvious step toward greater influence. Equally important is communicating that alignment explicitly so that the principal recognizes and appreciates the sense of common purpose between the librarian and himself or herself. Similarly, these findings suggest that time spent with the principal can yield greater influence. This is not to say "hanging out" in the principal's office is a good idea, but it does suggest that frequent, substantive communication with the principal leads to greater influence than "hiding out" in the library.

Conclusion

Two facts are clear with regard to the principal and the school librarian. First, it is unlikely that the principal will have a comprehensive view of the potential of a library program and a school librarian to impact student learning and enhance a collaborative climate. Second, the principal makes decisions that will impact the potential of the library. Hence, it is incumbent on the school librarian to ensure that the principal expands his or her expectations.

The school librarian needs to inform the principal so that decisions made about resources, schedules, staff development, and collaborative endeavors are well-informed decisions that reflect high expectations for the library program.

Leadership Strategies

Teacher and Partner

Assess students' knowledge and skills in information literacy and provide data on results of those assessments to the principal as acknowledgment of the accomplishments in the library program or as indicators of the need for a more comprehensive instructional program in the library.

Information Specialist

Help the principal maintain current awareness of innovations, such as new technologies for instruction or management. Be selective and focus on that which is locally relevant.

Arrange with the principal for opportunities to appear as a "regular" on staff meeting agendas to share information that relates directly to concerns of teachers. Use this opportunity well by preparing thoroughly and presenting clearly and concisely.

Program Administrator

Educate the principal on the role of the librarian. Remember what the workday of the principal can be and that providing the principal with an unsolicited deluge of articles and books to read is not necessarily helpful. Instead, explain your work to the principal in terms of your profession. Use terms from the AASL guidelines, such as *instructional partner* and *teacher,* to identify your roles.

Create opportunities for meaningful communication with the principal. Given the nature of the principal's day, it makes sense to schedule a weekly or monthly 20-minute session with the principal to review issues related to the library program. These must not be complaint sessions but productive meetings of give-and-take, advice seeking, brainstorming, and activity reporting. Provide documentation that shows what is occurring in the library. Use e-mail for updates, but don't overload the principal's mailbox. Choose your medium for communication based on your principal's preferred style.

Read the same journals your principal reads (e.g., *Bulletin of the NASSP*, *Principal*, and *Educational Leadership*). This practice will increase your familiarity with "principal vocabulary."

Be attuned to the vision the principal holds for the school and seek ways to communicate the relationship of the library program to that vision.

Help make the principal and the school look good by showcasing the library program to constituents—parents, community members, school board members, and school district officials.

Scenarios for Discussion

Scenario 1

The principal at Smith Memorial Middle School takes her role as an instructional leader very seriously. She is determined to focus staff meetings on professional growth issues. At the end-of-the-year meeting, she announces her goal for the coming year: a series of staff development meetings focused on how to improve student performance on standardized tests. Mr. Brown, the library media specialist, is worried that this emphasis on tests means that the library program will be completely written out of staff meetings for the coming year. He recalls that research studies indicate a positive correlation between library programs and student achievement. He also has concerns regarding test items about information literacy. Should he approach the principal to ensure that the library program is part of the year's staff development agenda? If so, how should he approach the topic with the principal?

Scenario 2

Dr. Hibbs is the principal where Mark serves as the school librarian. Dr. Hibbs is quite infatuated with his PDA-facilitated practice of doing rounds to gather data about what is going on in his school. At the beginning of the year, Mark heard in the teachers' lounge that Dr. Hibbs visited virtually all classrooms in the first six weeks of class—and in fact, he had visited some classrooms more than once. However, Dr. Hibbs has never come into the library during his rounds. In his monthly meeting with Dr. Hibbs, Mark encourages the principal to add the library to his rounds. Before long, Dr. Hibbs has made two visits to the library. Once, there were no students in the library at all. On his second visit soon after, Dr. Hibbs observed three students reading magazines, two students surfing the web, and a student looking for a book among the display of new fiction. It just seems that he never shows up when the library is packed with students and Mark is teaching. Mark is very worried that Dr. Hibbs is developing the wrong impression of activity in the library; in fact, he is regretting ever mentioning that Dr. Hibbs should include the library in his rounds. What should Mark do? What should he say to Dr. Hibbs?

REFERENCES

AASL (American Association of School Librarians). 2007. *Empowering Learners: Guidelines for School Library Programs.* Chicago: American Library Association.

Black, S. 2007. "Making the Rounds." *American School Board Journal* 194, no. 12: 40–45.

Blase, J., and J. Blase. 2002. "The Dark Side of Leadership: Teacher Perspectives of Principal Mistreatment." *Educational Administration Quarterly* 38, no. 5: 671–728.

Bryant, M. 2002. "The Role of the Principal in the Evaluation of the School's Library Media Specialist." *School Libraries Worldwide* 8, no. 1: 85–91.

Camburn, E., J. Spillane, and J. Sebastian. 2010. "Assessing the Utility of a Daily Log for Measuring Principal Leadership Practice." *Educational Administration Quarterly* 46, no. 5: 707–737. doi: 10.1177/0013161X10377345.

Campbell, B. 1994. "High School Principal Roles and Implementation Themes for Mainstreaming Information Literacy Instruction." PhD dissertation, University of Connecticut.

Church, A. 2010. "Secondary School Principals' Perceptions of the School Librarian's Instructional Role." *School Library Media Research* 13. www.ala.org/aasl/slmr.

Council of Chief State School Officers. 2008. *Educational Leadership Policy Standards: ISLLC 2008.* Council of Chief State School Officers. www.ccsso .org/Documents/2008/Educational_Leadership_PolicyStandards_2008.pdf.

Donham van Deusen, J., and J. Tallman. 1994. "The Impact of Scheduling on Curriculum Consultation and Information Skills Instruction." *School Library Media Quarterly* 23, no. 1: 17–25.

Downey, C. J., B. E. Steffy, F. W. English, L.E. Frase, and W. K. Poston Jr. 2004. *The Three-Minute Classroom Walk-through: Changing School Supervisory Practice One Teacher at a Time.* Thousand Oaks, CA: Corwin.

Everhart, N. 2006. "Principals' Evaluation of School Librarians: A Study of Strategic and Nonstrategic Evidence-based Approaches." *School Libraries Worldwide* 12, no. 2: 38–51.

Farmer, L. 2007. "Principals: Catalysts for Collaboration." *School Libraries Worldwide* 13, no. 1: 56–65.

Hartzell, G. 2003. "The Power of Audience: Effective Communication with Your Principal." *Library Media Connection* 22, no. 2: 20–22.

Horng, E., D. Klasik, and S. Loeb. 2010. "Principal's Time Use and School Effectiveness." *American Journal of Education* 116, no. 4: 491–523.

Lieberman, A., and L. Miller. 2004. *Teacher Leadership.* San Francisco: Jossey-Bass.

Lovely, S. 2006. *Setting Leadership Priorities: What's Necessary, What's Nice, and What's Got to Go.* Thousand Oaks, CA: Corwin.

Manasse, A. L. 1985. "Improving Conditions for Principal Effectiveness: Policy Implications of Research." *Elementary School Journal* 85, no. 3: 439–463.

Todd, R. 2009. "Evidence-Based Library and Information Practice." *Evidence Based Library and Information Practice* 4, no. 2: 78–96.

White, B. R., K. S. Brown, E. Hunt, and B. K. Klostermann. 2011. *The View from the Principal's Office: Results from the IERC Principals Survey.* Illinois Education Research Council 2011-2. www.siue.edu/ierc/publications/ pdf/2011-2_Principal_Survey.pdf.

Wilson, P. P., and A. J. MacNeil. 1998. "In the Dark." *School Library Journal* 44, no. 9: 114–116.

Yetter, C. 1994. "Resource-Based Learning in the Information Age School: The Intersection of Roles and Relationships of the School Library Media Specialist, Teachers, and Principals." EdD dissertation. Seattle University.

Yukl, G., and P. P. Fu. 1999. "Determinants of Delegation and Consultation by Managers." *Journal of Organizational Behavior* 20, no. 2: 219–232.

4

The School District

This chapter:

- describes the school district's influence on the school library program;
- discusses specific contributions that a library media specialist can make to district planning and policy;
- suggests approaches to the library budget proposal process;
- outlines board-approved policies that affect the school library; and
- identifies leadership strategies for working within the school district context.

School districts vary in size, number of schools, and number of students. Some districts cover expansive countywide areas, and others govern a single K–12 school. Some districts have an extensive hierarchy of central-office administrators, specialists, and support staff, while others have a single chief officer and a small support staff. While some large districts continue to have a library director or coordinator at the central office, many districts assign oversight for the library program to a central-office administrator (e.g., a curriculum director or an assistant superintendent), and many have no central-office representative for the library program at all. In each setting, the person who takes responsibility for relating the library program to the district's direction and policy varies, and in many small districts it is the building-level librarian. Whoever acts as liaison between the district's central decision-making authority and the school library program must contend with four major organizational issues: funding, personnel, curriculum, and technology.

Funding

Funding is allocated in different ways in different school districts, but trends seem to be moving toward centralization because of the call for greater efficiency and accountability to state and federal agencies, greater equity, and smaller budgets overall. Often, centralized districts allocate a per-pupil amount earmarked specifically for library resources. Many librarians appreciate this automatic allocation to their program for its reliability and equity across the district. Still, some districts allow building-level discretion on budget allocation, so the school librarian needs to learn the local process for budget allocation and proposals.

Building-Level Budget

Even when the library budget is governed at the district level, classroom teachers and the school librarian should work together to make decisions about resource spending. Faculty buy-in and support for the library requires opportunities for teacher input. This support may be important when district-level budget discussions occur; teachers tend to have credibility when questions are raised about how resources are allocated. Whether curriculum changes are occurring or not, school librarians are wise to involve teachers in understanding the library's budget and the ways in which resources are allocated. Figure 4.1 shows an example of a proposal presented at a staff meeting where the building's budget for the coming year is under discussion.

When teachers know how library allocations have been spent, how they will be spent, and the benefit to them and their students, they are much more likely to be supportive. Only when teachers feel disenfranchised or underserved by the library program will they question supporting library resources. Librarians must take the initiative to reach out to teachers, to encourage use of the library and its resources, and to make the resources as accessible as possible. Often teachers want their own classroom libraries because they consider the library too remote or inaccessible. The benefits of centralizing resources need to be well publicized, including the following:

- Circulation and inventory control systems already exist so that it will not be necessary for teachers to create a record-keeping system.
- Cataloging reduces duplicate purchases so that more resources can be available.
- Pooling dollars for a central collection rather than dividing them among classrooms makes it possible to buy expensive items when the need arises.
- Access to all materials is improved for both teachers and students, assuming borrowing policies that maximize access are in place.

FIGURE 4.1

Budget Proposal: Elementary School Library Media Center

Item	Comment	Spent
Books	Reading themes, grades 5–6	$1,369
	Reading themes, grades 3–4	$1,211
	Children's Choice Award books	$235
	Books to support author residency	$116
	Books to support social studies, 5–6	$118
	Books to support social studies, 3–4	$165
	Books to support social studies, 1–2	$50
	MC/NS collection building	$178
	Professional books	$55
	Reference books (almanac, author biography)	$125
	Award winners, student interest	$191
	Pattern books (kindergarten)	$425
	Total Books	**$4,238**
Supplies	Printer cartridges, computer paper	$574
	Total Supplies	**$574**
	Grand Total	**$4,812**

Note that there was very little purchasing for books for student self-selection; most purchases were curriculum related.

PROPOSAL FOR NEXT YEAR

Item	Comment	Estimated Cost
Books	Books for reading themes, grades 3–6	$1,600
	Books for reading themes, grades K–2 (includes some science and social studies literature)	$2,000
	Science trade books	$1,300
	Social studies trade books	$600
	Books for student self-selection	$500
	Total Books Request	**$6,000**
Computer Networked Resources	Tumble Books subscription for read-alongs plus BookFlix	$1,500
	Virus protection	$500
	Total Software Request	**$2,000**
Supplies	Computer paper, printer cartridges	$650
	Total Supplies Request	**$650**
	Grand Total Request	**$8,650**

District-Level Funding

Budgets for capital investments are typically centralized. These are larger, long-term expenditures, and concern for equity among schools is perhaps one justification for retaining these decisions at the central office. These expenditures affect the school library program because they typically include equipment such as projectors, computers, furniture, and peripherals. Centralized decisions typically include which computer platform to use, how many computers should be purchased, what capacity is really needed at each level, what peripherals schools need, and how frequently projectors and electronic whiteboards need to be replaced. Yet, they all impact the school library program at the building level.

To influence capital expenditures, either the district library coordinator or, if there is not one, a school librarian must develop and nurture a working relationship with the district's financial officer responsible for capital purchases. Finance officers want to spend money wisely, and so do librarians. With expertise on equipment specifications and reasonable replacement cycles, librarians can improve the value the district gets for its money. It is important to remember that the role of finance officers is to conserve financial resources, to spread funding over the many demands from groups throughout the district, and to sort out unreasonable demands that may be detrimental. This situation calls for the school librarian to accept and work within the spending parameters to acquire the best equipment possible. The advantage of quantity purchase is substantial, so working to amass orders is worthwhile. The finance officer will appreciate this one simple strategy, and the librarian can quickly be seen as a valuable colleague at the district level. Finance officers are also concerned about equity; because they are accountable to a governing board, fairness across the district is important to them. By maintaining awareness of the interests at work at the district level, the school librarian can increase library program resources.

Online resources such as e-book collections, databases, and other electronic subscriptions also are often centrally funded. In many situations, regional education agencies or state libraries support these resources. For resources not funded regionally, district-level purchasing or multischool cooperative purchasing becomes important for leveraging the best pricing. Again, this opportunity can demonstrate awareness of the importance of efficiency and economy-sensitive purchasing, which is likely to pay off in good will at the central administration offices.

Even in tight financial times, it is important to maintain optimism and commitment to the belief that library programs really make a difference in student learning. It can be discouraging to read of district-wide and statewide cuts in library funding. Yet, regardless of the situation, districts have money, and the question that remains is, what are the best programs in which to invest? The library program needs to be seen as such an essential program, and that can happen only when school librarians work closely with administrators at both the building and district levels. In exemplary districts, superintendents and librarians are working together in tight financial times. These examples need to be showcased. The American Association of School Librarians (AASL) identifies exemplary administrators with its School Administrator of the Year Award. Librarians can share the stories of these individuals with their own districts to show what can be done. A recent recipient, Donna Haye, hails from Atlantic City, New Jersey. She is recognized for taking several important steps as assistant superintendent to support the school library program at the district level. Haye made hiring a certified school librarian for every school a priority. She also instituted schedule changes that allowed for flexible scheduling, enabling school librarians and teachers to collaborate on projects. To update the libraries' collections and technology, she spoke before community and school boards requesting that funds be put on the ballot. Local voters agreed, and $566,172 was approved for school library use, including funding for expanding collections to include multicultural titles reflecting the student population (AASL, 2011). This example of support for school libraries demonstrates the importance of seeing that central-office administrators know and understand the potential value of a school library.

A wise school librarian maintains a wish list so that when unplanned funding becomes available, administrators know that this is where funds can be spent that will impact all students. School librarians should be ready to allocate funding of several hundred to several thousand dollars upon invitation.

Personnel

Of the four major district-level functions, the librarian may have the least involvement in personnel matters. However, some areas of district-level personnel practice affect the library program. Two particularly significant ones are staffing allocations for library professional and support staff and district policies on personnel evaluation. In highly centralized districts, staffing allocations for teachers are determined for each building at the district level. This practice is reasonable since staffing accounts for a large percentage of the district's budget—often exceeding 80 percent. Such a large investment demands close governance and accountability to the governing board. It seems that generally central office administration affords principals limited autonomy: "Stated differently, effective district leaders understand the importance of distributing tangible assets equitably. . . . At the same time, they recognize the importance of providing principals with enough latitude to be able to innovate and create a culture of high expectations within their schools" (Eck and Goodwin, 2010).

However, the building principal may or may not ask staff to participate and is often the only one who determines exactly how staff is allocated. For example, he or she may have autonomy to determine how many teachers will be assigned to each grade level, or how many paraprofessionals there will be and where those paraprofessionals will work. Specialized staff positions, such as guidance counselors, principals, and librarians, often continue to be determined at the district level. The district value for equity across schools accounts for this practice, at least in part. District-level policy thus directly affects the library program in setting its staffing levels. Often districts assign one certified librarian per school regardless of size, or they determine staffing by ranges of student enrollment, so that schools with an enrollment of up to 900 may have one librarian, schools from 900 to 1,800 may have 1.5, schools, over 1,800 may have two, and so on. Such quotas are usually advantageous for library programs in the district because they protect these positions from whims and changes as building-level administrators come and go. When staffing allocations depend on district policy, the library program needs to be readily seen as essential to teaching and learning so that district policy supports (or increases) those allocations. Without such visibility, the line item for library personnel in the district budget can be vulnerable whenever administrators need to respond with dollars to a new demand.

Performance appraisal is a process typically managed at the district level and implemented at the building level. Many school districts fail to provide a specialized performance appraisal form or process for school librarians and instead use a generic form designed for classroom teachers. Clearly, this practice creates significant problems in a comprehensive performance assessment because of the unique characteristics of the library media position. It is therefore important to advocate for performance appraisal practices that address all dimensions of the library media professional's position. A first step may be to refer to the district's position description for school librarians. Aligning the performance appraisal with the position description creates internal integrity regarding expectations.

A tailored appraisal tool and process not only afford the opportunity for review of the complete school librarian position but also provide a communication tool for school administrators to understand the work of the school librarian. Each district typically develops its own appraisal format. The tools used to evaluate the library professional need to be consistent with the district format. Some appraisal forms are somewhat open-ended, providing opportunities for the professional to set goals or targets and then submit documentation to describe how these goals have been met. Others are more prescriptive. In situations where a prescriptive model is in place, the librarian will want to ensure that all aspects of the position are represented in the criteria: management, teaching, curriculum involvement with teachers, collection development and maintenance, technology leadership, and support. The Topeka Public Schools (2012) provides one example of performance appraisal criteria for school librarians that acknowledges the unique character of the position. The appraisal instrument focuses on five domains:

Planning and preparation: developing long- and short-term goals for the school library program; demonstrating knowledge of state and national standards, current best practices, and the areas of information literacy and educational technology

The library environment: creating an environment of respect and rapport for students; establishing a culture of investigation and love of literature; utilizing space effectively to support the library program

Delivery of services and instruction: collaborating with teaching staff in design of instruction; engaging students in inquiry and enjoyment of literature; assisting teachers and students in use of technology; teaching ethical use of information

Professional responsibilities: emphasizing professional development; participating in the professional community; advocating for the library program; demonstrating professionalism

Library program management: establishing and maintaining library policies; demonstrating knowledge of resources; devising and implementing a plan for program evaluation; maintaining and developing print and digital collections of resources; managing a budget

A district-level performance appraisal process geared specifically to teacher librarians is ideal because it establishes equitable expectations for school librarians throughout the district. As performance evaluation becomes increasingly tied to student achievement, it will be necessary to establish criteria for assessing the teacher librarian's contribution to student learning. This trend could be disadvantageous to school librarians unless they can identify measures of student growth related to learning in the library. And measuring growth calls for specific outcomes for the library curriculum and an assessment and reporting system that indicates student learning. Or, it may be necessary to incorporate the assessment of information literacy competencies with the assessments of student work in the disciplines, and then report on those particular elements of student achievement. In short, if the library curriculum is an authentic component of student learning, it will be important to determine how to document its success. Later in this text, the discussion of the library curriculum will focus further on questions of student achievement.

Curriculum

Consistency, stability, innovation, and equity are values that drive district-level curriculum decisions, both vertically (across grades) and horizontally (across disciplines). Consistency calls for curriculum articulation, so that the sequence of learning experiences is appropriate and aligned district-wide. Likewise, stability is a value; although change is a common topic among schools, long-term and effective change in schools tends to be evolutionary. Innovations, which sometimes are initiated by teachers or principals, tend to concern the district bureaucracy because changes often require coordination and resources for implementation. Equity is the fourth value that district-level curriculum specialists strive to maintain. It is important to recognize the difference between equal and equitable. *Equal* suggests that each entity has the same resources, whereas *equity* connotes fairness, taking all factors into account. Sometimes, schools in lower socioeconomic neighborhoods need more resources or different kinds of support to accommodate disadvantages. Often, district-level curriculum directors become the arbiters of fairness. School librarians typically base decisions on the same values within the school context. Acknowledging the similarities between the perspective of the district-level curriculum specialist and the school librarian improves the likelihood that these two professionals can work together toward common ends.

Curriculum decisions at the district level influence the library program. If new science units are being developed and promoted, new foreign languages are being taught, or new courses are being added to the social studies program, library resources need to change to support these new developments. Likewise, if new strategies or technologies are being considered, then library programs need to provide appropriate materials and develop requisite skills.

While a traditional curriculum development model may be a top-down design, in fact, research suggests that truly effective school systems simultaneously provide opportunities for top-down and bottom-up influence (Cuban, 1984). Still, in larger districts, leadership in curriculum often comes from district curriculum generalists and specialists. They maintain awareness of new trends and directions in their specialties, following the literature and attending conferences and workshops to keep up to date. Often these central-office leaders provide staff development to share new ideas with teachers.

The standards movement in curriculum has intensified the centralization of curriculum development. State and district testing programs now call for a common curriculum across districts, and in some cases across states. This trend begs for proactive school librarians who will advocate for curriculum design that incorporates learning to learn, learning to use technology effectively, critical thinking, and literature. Implementing district-level curriculum development and change typically begins through committees led by district-level curriculum specialists. Committees tend to be a primary vehicle for increasing the ownership of new ideas and for disseminating ideas throughout a district. District-level curriculum directors and specialists are initiators and facilitators, and committees are useful for both roles. Curriculum cycles usually focus on a different content area each year. However it is organized, most districts have a schedule for curriculum review, and participation in such reviews is crucial for librarians. These committees offer opportunities to learn what and how teachers will be teaching. The school librarian can be the information specialist for a curriculum review committee (e.g., searching professional literature about the topics under discussion, locating relevant instructional resources, and searching for new trade books or electronic resources to support curriculum innovations). By actively participating when curriculum change is being planned, the librarian can help teachers anticipate topics or strategies for which there will be a wealth of materials or for which materials will be scarce. This level of participation is clearly preferable to waiting until all curriculum decisions have been made and then responding by saying, "It will take three months to get what you need," or "What you are asking for doesn't seem to exist!" Simply put, proactive is better than reactive. In some settings, being appointed to such curriculum committees will require initiative on the part of the librarian. If central-office curriculum specialists are unfamiliar with curriculum-involved school library programs, they may not even think of including a librarian on such a committee. So, initiating contact and articulating why librarians should participate in curriculum at the district level are often necessary.

Central-office instruction or curriculum supervisors perceive their positions as invisible (Pajak, 1989). They see their role as working to make those in more visible positions—superintendent, principals, and teachers—look good. Invisibility may be something that librarians share with curriculum specialists. Both roles involve facilitating the work of others, working behind the scenes. Having this role characteristic in common can bring the librarian and curriculum supervisor together, since both focus on supporting the work of the front line. This shared role can also generate competition as each seeks to be a helper. Making the distinction between the content specialist and the resource and instruction specialist is important to foster working relationships.

Many district vision and/or mission statements include the phrase *lifelong learners*. Clearly, the library curriculum aligns with this overarching goal to educate students who will be lifelong learners. School librarians should tune in to each opportunity to make this connection between the library curriculum and the goals of the district so that district-level leaders understand that relationship.

Technology

Technical support from the district level is an essential ingredient in school districts of all sizes. Networking increases the technical knowledge needed to maintain and upgrade equipment, telecommunication systems, and software. For student production in multimedia, technical knowledge is needed to help building-level librarians buy appropriate equipment and learn to use it effectively. Districts employ network specialists and technicians to assist in these specialized needs. Often, technicians are naive about teaching and learning but highly skilled in the technology itself. Librarians can be important intermediaries to help technical staff understand how various technologies will be used, so that they can select and deploy equipment in ways that will work most effectively for educational applications. For district-level planning to be implemented, there must be effective links between the district and building. On many matters, the principal provides that link, particularly in areas of staffing, facilities, personnel management, grade reporting practices, and other managerial topics. The librarian can also act as liaison between district and school by serving on district committees for policy, curriculum, professional development, or planning issues. Technology planning is one topic that particularly warrants involving the librarian as a liaison.

A Word about Small Districts

This chapter has focused on the impact of the district on the school library program and the influence that the library program can have at the district level. While many very small school districts have skeletal central offices, there also is an organizational unit known as the school district. That entity, however small, has its own mission and goals, its own beliefs about teaching and learning, and its own relationship to its community. Where districts are very small, perhaps a regional agency provides leadership, particularly in areas such as curriculum or technical support or staff development. Regardless of district size, each librarian has an overarching organization where visibility and advocacy for the library program constitute an important responsibility.

Board-Approved Policies

Policy guides decision making. For school libraries, policies that support access to information, intellectual freedom, and ethical use of information are central to the mission of the program. To ensure adherence to these principles, the district is wise to have board-approved policies that address selection of library resources (including a reconsideration of materials process), confidentiality of library records, and ethical use of information, including acceptable use of information resources. In Chapter 8, the selection of library resources policy is detailed. In short, this policy delineates criteria for selection of resources and a process for stakeholders to raise objections to resources held in the library.

Confidentiality of library records ensures users that they can borrow resources from the library without concern that others will know what they have borrowed. Such a policy creates a climate of freedom of access. Many states have passed legislation stating that library records are confidential records; however, in most instances there is *no* explicit statement that this legislation applies to school libraries. Confidentiality of library records can be seen to conflict with FERPA (Family Educational Rights and Privacy Act), which guarantees that parents have access to students' educational records until the age of 18. FERPA also includes a provision wherein information in student records can be disclosed to other school officials, such as a guidance counselor or a teacher, when there is a "legitimate educational interest." At issue is whether school library circulation records are educational records. If they are, then parents—and perhaps other educational officials—have access to students' library records. Because of this potential conflict, a policy that defines confidentiality of library records for the district is wise. On the one hand, it is useful for parents to have access to library records for young children so that they can help them be accountable for the items they borrow. On the other hand, access by any other person may have a chilling effect on the borrowing behavior of youth who may seek information on sensitive subjects.

Ethical use of information encompasses issues of copyright and acceptable use of information. A detailed explanation of acceptable use policies occurs in Chapter 11. The policy related to copyright is essentially a commitment of adherence to copyright law and to the provisions of the fair use doctrine.

Still, a district does well to state explicitly its commitment to comply fully with copyright law and guidelines and its expectation that employees and students take responsibility for compliance. Protective provisions may include indicating that the district will not extend legal or insurance protection to employees who violate copyright law. Another provision that might be considered is for the district to provide periodic instruction to employees and students on copyright law and fair use provisions. Additionally, district policy may call for copyright notices to be placed on all equipment capable of reproduction. The conventional statement for posting on or near equipment is, "The copyright law of the United States (Title 17, US Code) governs the making of photocopies or other reproductions of copyrighted material. The person using this equipment is responsible for any infringement."

School librarians can provide leadership for district administration on the development of policies and explanation of the implications of policy provisions. To create an environment of intellectual freedom and open access to information, such policies need to be in place and need the authority of board approval. As the district's information professional, the school librarian's leadership will bring perspective to these issues that support the principles of freedom of access.

Advocacy

While it may seem intuitively obvious to those in the library profession that school librarians belong on district committees, can play key roles in implementing district programs, and have contributions to make to district-level work in finance, curriculum, personnel, or technology, these roles are rarely obvious to decision makers at the district level. Thus, the importance of taking initiative cannot be overemphasized. School librarians must make the case for what their specialization can offer, and then must act on their promises. When we say we can provide information, we must provide it in a timely fashion. When we say we can contribute to the conversation about curriculum articulation, we must produce. When we say we have ideas about using technology, we must articulate them. When we suggest that we can save the district money, we must come up with purchasing recommendations that accomplish that. The "say-do ratio" must be high.

Working within the System

More than 50 years ago, Robert Presthus (1962) published an interesting analysis of how people work within organizations. His theory is particularly relevant for the school librarian working within the school district context. Presthus described three types of relationships with one's organization: the upward mobile, the organizational indifferent, and the organizational ambivalent. An upward mobile employee is optimistic about the organization and plays roles within the organization to advance. Such individuals identify so closely with the organization that they consider the success of the organization to be their success. An upward mobile employee is able to overlook inconsistencies in the system. Accepting the organization's goals commits the upward mobile to conform to whatever the powerful influences in the organization want. The organizational indifferent is a disenfranchised person who does not identify with the organization. An indifferent focuses on his or her own job and remains aloof from the larger system. An idealist, the organizational ambivalent speculates what the organization ought to be rather than what it is. This type is ambivalent toward his or her status in the organization, in contrast to the upward mobile. The ambivalent wants success but does not want to pay the organizational price because that price is often a compromise. The ambivalent may be characterized as something of an outsider who lacks the political will to work within the system. Each of these is a pure type, but rarely do individuals fit into only one category. Indeed, organizational behavior is often situational. Deciding how to respond to organizational demands requires reflection about stakes and potential consequences. For example, let's assume that a district-wide decision has been made that no R-rated movies are to be shown in schools. This decision will eliminate showing several films that have been used in high school classes for several years—films such as *The Killing Fields* in a social studies elective course on war. How the high school librarian accommodates this decision can be classified by Presthus's theory. The upward mobile will support the decision unquestioningly. Or, this type might diplomatically point out, using a carefully developed and annotated list, those videos for which exceptions might be made. The organizational indifferent will have no opinion. The organizational ambivalent may question the decision based on principles of intellectual freedom, feeling that a class of materials ought not to be censored and that such a ruling violates teachers' and students' rights. An organizational ambivalent would probably openly express his or her concerns about the ruling and might contact the American Library Association Intellectual Freedom Office for an opinion.

Another example might be a district technology committee that is determining where to allocate computers and decides to place computers in kindergarten rooms for the first time. Parents of young children, early childhood teachers, and the school board have expressed their desire to increase young children's access to technology in school. The librarian on the committee believes that it would be more developmentally appropriate for computer use and instruction to begin at first grade, when children can begin to take advantage of the computer's capabilities for more sophisticated uses, seeing the computer as a tool rather than a reward. Furthermore, the librarian might be concerned that resources are limited and other grade levels really need computer access for conducting research and other advanced learning activities. The upward mobile will recognize that the influential forces in the organization want young children to access computers and will accept this allocation, despite needs in upper grades. The organizational indifferent will have no opinion and probably would not participate on the committee in the first place. The organizational ambivalent might oppose the idea and express concerns about developmental appropriateness or the needs at other grade levels and may appeal to literature from early childhood education to support his or her position.

Deciding how to respond to district-level issues challenges the school librarian. Each response must be weighed in terms of what is at stake, what the consequences are of agreeing or not agreeing with the district, and what will benefit students and teachers most in the long run. There will be times when performing as the upward mobile may seem to be the long-run best choice, and there will be times when, despite the consequences, the organizational ambivalent's posture is called for. When one begins to respond as an organizational indifferent, it may be time to reconsider career intentions. Assessing the situation each time causes the school librarian to repeatedly assess his or her position within the district context.

Conclusion

District-level decision making involves four areas in particular that have direct effects on the school library program—finance, personnel, curriculum, and technology. School librarians can influence district-level decisions, but they must be proactive because few educational administrators have a sophisticated understanding of a school librarian's competencies.

Leadership Strategies

Teacher

Work to ensure that administrators place you on district committees related to curriculum development and revision. Emphasize your knowledge of resources and technologies as a potential contribution to the district.

Information Specialist

Provide information on fair use provisions and Creative Commons options so that teachers can readily comply with district policy on copyright.

Program Administrator

Participate in district-level policy and planning when you have special expertise. Often the school librarian has more understanding about some policies than any other professional in the school. After all, such issues as freedom to read, copyright, and confidentiality are part of the professional ethic and training for school librarians. Examples include the following:

- Materials selection policy
- Copyright policy
- Acceptable use policy
- Privacy issues
- Networking for access to information

Develop a positive professional relationship with the district's chief financial officer. Demonstrate your insight into the budgeting process, the importance of differentiating between needs and wants, the necessity of compromise, and the importance of fiscal accountability.

Develop a network among educators across the district. Present yourself as a problem solver.

Be a friend to the district's physical plant personnel—it is easier to get electrical connections where they are needed, move furniture to accommodate new technologies, and make other physical plant improvements when workers know they are appreciated and respected.

Periodically provide the superintendent with "good news" to share with the board. Choose substantive items to share, but remember that such news as major increases in circulation, visiting authors, minigrants received by the library, or participation in library events by local "celebrities" might also be good items because they show increased use, community involvement, and initiative.

Scenarios for Discussion

Scenario 1

The school board is considering a referendum seeking support for bonding for renovation and expansion of the libraries in the three high schools in the district. As one of the high school librarians, Heather is very eager to see the referendum pass as these facilities are dated and undersized. At her bridge group, she hears that there is a small but vocal group of citizens raising questions about the wisdom of such a project. It seems that they are beginning to mobilize to mount an opposition campaign based on their perception that libraries represent an antiquated idea and are no longer important in schools. What should Heather do?

Scenario 2

George is a school librarian in a high school in Happy Hollow School District. Veronica is a tenth-grader in the school. Her stepfather arrives at the school library and asks to see a list of the books his stepdaughter has borrowed from the library. He is "concerned" about what she might be reading. How will George respond?

REFERENCES

AASL (American Association of School Librarians). 2011. "Past Recipients." *Distinguished School Administrators Award.* American Library Association. www.ala.org/ala/mgrps/divs/aasl/aaslawards/distinguishedsch/aasldistinguished.cfm.

Cuban, L. 1984. "Transforming the Frog into a Prince: Effective Schools Research, Policy and Practice at the District Level." *Harvard Educational Review* 54, no. 2: 129–151.

Eck, J., and B. Goodwin. 2010. "Autonomy for School Leaders." *School Administrator* 67, no. 1: 24–27.

Pajak, E. 1989. *The Central Office Supervisor of Curriculum and Instruction: Setting the Stage for Success.* Boston: Allyn and Bacon.

Presthus, R. 1962. *The Organizational Society: An Analysis and a Theory.* New York: Random House.

Topeka Public Schools. 2012. "Library Media Specialist Evaluation." The Topeka Public Schools USD 501, Topeka, Kansas. www.topekapublicschools.net/assets/Staff/forms/administrative/evaluations/certified/FORM-Admin-Eval-Certified-Library-Media-Specialist.pdf.

5

The Community

This chapter:

- describes the value of community involvement;
- discusses ways the library program can communicate and cooperate with community entities; and
- identifies leadership strategies for cooperative community activities.

A now familiar adage is "It takes a village to raise a child." While the school plays a central role in children's development, children benefit when there is interaction between the school and its community. Parent organizations, school boards, and parent-teacher conferences represent typical school-to-home connections, but these relationships are directed primarily toward parents of school-age children or to select community members. The greater community can also share in raising its youth. Businesses, social agencies, museums, and libraries have human, physical, and fiscal resources that can complement the school's resources.

The Value of Community Involvement

Community involvement in the school library program can serve several purposes (Gorton and Schneider, 1991). Through involvement, parents and other citizens learn how the library program contributes to student learning. Understanding the program helps people support it verbally and fiscally. Moreover, when parents are involved, they are able to help their children academically and socially. Community participation also provides the school library program with new ideas and expertise.

The importance of community participation is evidenced in the requirements for school librarians who seek to meet the National Board for Professional Teaching Standards (National Board, 2009). These standards set expectations for school librarians to participate in the greater community through such activities as:

- seeking frequent input from the larger community of families, volunteers, and other school partners;
- crafting library orientation for particular segments of the community, such as families of English language learners;
- seeking partnerships with other educational and cultural institutions in the community, such as museums, public and academic libraries, and other community agencies;
- participating in community events, speaking opportunities, and committees; and
- inviting members of the community to participate in school library programming or planning.

Through such outreach to the community, the library program enjoys greater visibility and the opportunities within the program are expanded.

Family Involvement

The family is the core of the school's community. Teachers and the school principal communicate directly with families through parent-teacher conferences, parent organizations, athletic organizations, phone trees, blogs, websites, and newsletters. The library program lacks the direct visibility of the classroom or the football field; hence, the school librarian must be intentional and strategic in promoting family participation in the program, events, and resources of the school library.

Presentations

Making presentations to parent and community groups is one way to share information about the library program and gain support from people who influence either the school or the district. School librarians should seek opportunities to give presentations for parent organizations or for back-to-school events. For example, a school librarian can make a presentation to parents about choosing materials for the library, as parents often are unaware of the materials selection process. That naiveté can lead to challenges or mis-understandings about materials in the school library, particularly at the ele-mentary school level. Worse can be a sentiment that spending money on more materials is unnecessary when the library shelves already are full. Topics cov-ered could be the selection policy, including criteria for selection; reviewing sources and selection tools; or procedures for parents, teachers, and students to suggest items for the collection. Parents may think that purchasing for a library is akin to a shopping spree, but a presentation like this can help them understand the complexity of collection building. Another topic that may inter-est parents is Internet use. Given public concern about inappropriate Internet activities, the school librarian can alleviate some worry with a session in which parents see the educational value of the web. During such a session the librarian could explain local policies for responsible Internet use, dem-onstrate the use of subscription databases to help parents see the value they offer in contrast to "free" information on the Internet, or provide a tour of the library's website and the resources accessible there to support learning. To leave these topics unaddressed opens the door for criticism from parents who have too little information from less reliable sources than the librarian. Such informative meetings are likely to increase knowledge, confidence, and communication.

A school librarian can also offer parents programs about homework and study skills, particularly at the middle school level. Other areas of presenta-tion include strategies for note taking, examples of web resources helpful for school assignments, and school library online resources available to help stu-dents with their homework.

Literacy programs are a natural family–school library connection. Such pro-grams can target special populations. For example, if a school has ESL stu-dents, then a program might include sharing books that will help children build their English vocabulary, such as picture dictionaries and pattern pic-ture books. The school librarian might demonstrate online audiobooks or read-alongs, or encourage parents to join their children during a designated after-school time to use these materials in the library.

Another target audience might be families with preschoolers. A research study by Gregory and Morrison (1998) revealed some very specific outcomes from parents reading to preschool children. Among those outcomes were higher cognitive levels of the questions they asked their parents, improved structure of their oral language, and increased general knowledge that prepared them for school. A report by Morisset (1993) cited research findings that an effective way to promote language skills and develop strong social interactions among young children is through storybook sharing. She reported that the frequency of listening to stories in the home was found to be directly related to literacy and teacher ratings of students' oral language skills at ages five to seven. Meta-analyses studies (Bus and van IJzendoorn, 1999 and Scarborough and Dobrich, 1994) have shown that frequency of reading to children at home is a good predictor of early reading achievement. More recently, Segal-Drori and colleagues (2010) investigated parent-child shared reading of both printed and electronic books and reported that reading e-books with parental intervention resulted in significant development of word reading in emergent readers. These studies underscore the value of reading in the home. The school librarian can share tips on reading aloud to young children, suggest books appropriate for the very young (e.g., books with repetition, pattern books, rhymes, and concept books), or share strategies for reading to and with children (such as paired reading, where parent and child take turns reading or chanting refrains together). Mol and colleagues (2008: 8) define a strategy called dialogic reading:

> . . . which was designed according to the following three principles: (a) the use of evocative techniques by the parent that encourage the child to talk about pictured materials; (b) informative feedback by incorporating expansions, corrective modeling, and other forms that highlight differences between what the child has said and what he might have said; and (c) an adaptive parent sensitive to the child's developing abilities. In sum, during typical shared reading the adult reads and the child listens, but in dialogic reading the child learns to become the storyteller.

It can be invaluable to help parents see that how they interact with their child as they read together may in fact strengthen their child's readiness to read. Perhaps a program offered cooperatively with the public library would raise awareness of materials and services available there.

While presentations can be a part of monthly parent meetings or school open houses, perhaps even more effective are presentations at meetings of local service groups. In these settings, the audience includes not only parents but also other community members. Program chairs of Lions Clubs, Kiwanis, Rotary, and other service groups are frequently looking for ideas. A school librarian may find an eager response to an offer for a presentation for such groups. Of course, this is the time to make a presentation entertaining, informative, and upbeat, as well as to showcase the skills and knowledge of the school librarian and the value to education afforded by the library program. Reading from children's literature as part of the program or providing a video clip showing young people at work in the library are examples of ways to make the program engaging.

Newsletters

The need for communication between the school library program and the family extends beyond special presentations. No school newsletter should go home without at least one meaningful item from the school library. Brief, readable articles might suggest good books to read as a family, describe student activities in the library, promote events in the community, or advise about computer applications for the home. Library program visibility is key, and the message must be that the library program is fundamental to learning. It is more important that communications contain substance rather than that they be clever or cute. The School Library Link (www.theschoollibrarylink. com) is a ready-made online newsletter that school librarians are free to acquire online and make accessible via their website or print and send home in monthly mailings. Each month offers a thematic, two-page newsletter in PDF format aimed at parents. Examples of themes include online technologies; curriculum; chatting, tweeting, and alternative media; standardized test scores; lifelong readers; and summer reading (McGarry, 2009). Key features of this publication are the focus on themes of interest to parents, brevity, and attractive formatting. Whether the school librarian uses this newsletter out of the box or to stimulate ideas for creating a local version, the School Library Link provides an excellent example for helping parents know what they can expect the school library to offer their children.

Advisory Committees

Another way to involve parents is through advisory committees; for example, if the school is developing its technology plan, the committee should include parent representation. Periodically, the library program needs to be evaluated.

Districts often have a review cycle, where each program or curricular area has a major evaluative review every five or seven years. Usually, the review process begins with naming a committee or team. When such a team includes parents, they gain important insights into the program and as a result often become advocates. Moreover, parents provide an important perspective on whether the program is really reaching students as intended.

A typical review process includes these steps:

- Reviewing the current literature to determine the state of the art
- Comparing the results of the literature review and an assessment of the library's current status
- Developing a vision statement, goals, and an action plan

Even without a formal review cycle, a school librarian might consider a parent advisory council or a library committee within the school's parent-teacher organization. Such a group might meet with the school librarian two or three times a year. If a school librarian has such a council, it is essential that the council have a purpose and that the librarian bring real topics for discussion. For example, if the school librarian is having difficulty with children failing to return books in an elementary school, the topic of strategies to address the issue could be a topic for the group to discuss. Such conversation might include the pros and cons of fines or withholding borrowing privileges. These conversations can help parents understand the complexity of ensuring that children have access to resources and accounting for the resources of the library. Or, the topic might have to do with high school students' need for access to the library after school and the challenges of limited staffing to provide such access. Again, parents can begin to understand the role the school librarian plays in helping students succeed academically.

Parent Library or Parent Links

In some settings, offering a parent library may be a way to reach out (Harvey, 2007). One parent group that may find this especially helpful is those who have children with special needs. A partnership with either the special education or the gifted program may result in some funding for the resources as well as recommendations of titles that would be helpful to parents. A virtual parent library is another option. Essentially, a parent portal provides links on the school library website to help parents support their children's learning. For secondary students, that parent portal might include information about colleges, opportunities for scholarships, and other resources of interest. A partnership with the guidance office may be appropriate for this kind of information. Still, the library's website as a good point of connection is evidence that libraries are information centers.

Business Involvement

Local businesses have a genuine interest in the quality of local education. First, their future employees may come from the local schools. And, good schools can be a selling point for chambers of commerce in attracting new businesses into the community. Community pride helps keep local businesses thriving, as they benefit from a sense of confidence within the community. All these factors mean that business cares about its schools. Every chamber of commerce has an education committee—an indicator of the importance business places on quality local education. When real estate brokers market homes to families, one common question is whether the schools in the neighborhood are considered "good" schools. Bankers in the home mortgage market want to be able to assure families that an investment in the community is a good one for them and their children, and good schools are central to that assurance. Business and education are obvious partners.

Businesses enter into partnerships with schools for two reasons: to contribute to the public good by improving the quality of the school and to increase their own standing in the marketplace. Likewise, schools seek business partnerships for two purposes: to increase their resources and to improve the community understanding and respect for their programs. There are two important principles to guide school–business partnerships: maintaining a focus on the partnership and maintaining the school's authority over the substance of the relationship. Focus allows any given business to have a niche for its marketplace advantage; for example, a business can become known as the science partner or the fine arts partner or the reading partner, and this association gives the business an identity in marketing. Focus also allows the school to connect special-interest staff members with specific partnerships to nurture the relationships; for example, the school librarian takes care of the reading partners or the networking partners, and the art and music teachers take care of the fine arts partners.

Perhaps even more important is controlling the substance of the project. Does the business bring its own special interests or biases to a partnership? The school should be in the position to decide the what of the partnership, and the business's participation should be focused on the how. Educators, after all, are responsible for what is taught in schools and should be protective of their right to determine content lest inappropriate bias influence instruction. School librarians must set standards for business participation in order to maintain the integrity of the school library program (Tinnish, 1996). In a case study of a Cincinnati school–business partnership, Abowitz (2000) emphasizes the importance of continuous monitoring to ensure that the power balance is governed so that the interests of business do not overtake the interests of educators.

Effective partnerships take time. A business partnership is a new relationship, and relationships can be demanding. School librarians considering such a partnership need to expect to give it time to develop. Like any relationship, it will not survive without nurturing. That nurturing involves regular contact with a representative of the business; reporting progress to the business, particularly the impact on students; and public acknowledgment so that the community is aware of the contribution by the business.

While business partnerships can add value and public awareness for library programs, school librarians must be cautious to not expect that business support will supplant public funding (Larson, 2002). Support from private funding can influence school boards to expect private fundraising instead of public funding. Setting boundaries for what kinds of business support are welcome and knowing what the business expects in return are important ground rules for the relationship.

An example of a business partnership that has been ongoing for more than 20 years and continues to be a successful venture community-wide is the Community Reading Project, supported by a local bank in Iowa City, Iowa (Donham van Deusen and Langhorne, 1997). The program involves public and school libraries in promoting reading among all sectors. Booktalk luncheons are held at public libraries where school and public librarians are featured, as well as students and community members. The series of luncheon programs are booktalks promoting good reading for adults one week, children the next, and young adults another time. The bank and local restaurateurs provide the lunches, and the libraries provide the content. The audiences include a variety of citizens—members of book discussion groups, grandparents, parents, and businesspeople—all interested in recommendations for their own personal reading or for gift-giving. Another component of the partnership is an author residency, each year featuring an author who visits elementary schools. The school library program creates a curriculum to educate students in advance about the visiting author's work, and the bank supports the visit with financial support. The strength of this program is the role that the bank plays—it provides fiscal support and promotion and seeks community recognition for doing a good deed for the schools. The school and public libraries control the content of the programming entirely.

Public Library Connections

Miller and Shontz (2003) found that half of the school librarians they surveyed maintain ongoing communication by e-mail, telephone, or fax with their local public librarians. Further, approximately 25 percent reported that they distribute and exchange newsletters with their public library counterparts, and 60 percent reported that they promote public library summer reading programs. All of these are examples of ways to bring together two important resources for students. The school librarian is pivotal in the relationship between the school and the public library. No other staff member in the school is as well positioned to make connections with this valuable extension of the school into the community.

Summer Reading

Reading loss during summer months is well documented in the reading research literature. Mraz and Rasinski (2007: 785) summarize their findings regarding summer reading loss, which indicate the particularly significant loss among children in lower socioeconomic situations:

> A review of 13 empirical studies representing approximately 40,000 students found that, on average, the reading proficiency levels of students from lower income families declined over the summer months, while the reading proficiency levels of students from middle-income families improved modestly. In a single academic year, this decline resulted in an estimated three-month achievement gap between more advantaged and less advantaged students. Between grades 1 and 6, the potential

cumulative impact of this achievement gap could compound to 1.5 years' worth of reading development lost in the summer months alone.

They go on to report on their own research findings delineating the stronger effect on lower-achieving students:

Our research with 116 first, second, and third graders in a school in a middle class neighborhood found that the decoding skills of nearly 45% of the participants and the fluency skills of 25% declined between May and September. Lower achieving students exhibited a sharper decline than higher achieving students.

Yet, school library collections sit on shelves inaccessible for ten or more weeks per year, and school library doors are locked. These findings suggest that school librarians could make research-supported arguments for the need to provide some form of outreach or summer programming to alleviate this serious problem. The solutions seem to lie in improving access to reading material and providing opportunities for children to sustain or enhance their reading comprehension skills. Elementary school librarians could provide experiences to support reading comprehension skills through techniques such as literature circles, book discussions, and storytelling programs, given the support to make such programming accessible. Creative ways of reaching out to neighborhood centers, public libraries, and other agencies may allow the community to expand the accessibility of the school library program. At a minimum, school librarians can provide parents with encouragement to use the public library, lists of developmentally appropriate books for sustaining reading fluency, or links to websites that offer ideas for supporting reading skills during the summer.

Even high school students need to continue to read during the summer. One high school library has responded by extending its collection to the local public library:

One high school library in Wamego, Kansas gives the public library the option of receiving 400–600 of the newest fiction and nonfiction books for use during the summer. According to librarian Joanie Doperalski and high school librarian Dr. Nancy McFarlin, once school is out of session and inventory is been completed, books are pulled from the shelves at the high school library. They are then placed on reserve for the public library with the material type label of "summer reading." Those downloadable records are then sent to the public library, along with the actual books. The library creates a reading list, posts it on the library Web site, and makes it available in print for public library patrons. Upon return of books in August, the reserve status is deleted from the record and books are re-shelved at the high school library. (Van Dusen, 2007: 25)

Another high school approach to summer reading in response to concern about summer reading loss is the Barnstable Summer Reading program (Gordon, 2008). The school librarian worked collaboratively with teachers to develop a summer reading list and summer reading activities offered to students through a website designed specifically for this program. Gordon (2010) extols the importance of summer reading having a social dimension that can be carried out through blogging or other social media. She emphasizes the perspective of school librarians to support reading for enjoyment, not just as an extension of curriculum. She contends that school library summer reading programs afford opportunities to encourage such free voluntary reading. By offering Web 2.0 tools that provide a social platform for sharing, the school librarian extends opportunities for reading to be a social endeavor.

Homework Help

Supporting students' assignments and supporting literacy are two functions common to school and public libraries. For the most part, communication is key to these partnerships. One possibility here is a monthly telephone call or visit. The school librarian can report to the public librarian topics coming up in the curriculum. In a perfect world, this report would be comprehensive, but in the real world the list will not be a complete summary of every student assignment. Still, a good-faith effort is a start. If the school library is successful in creating an assignments section on the school library website, then providing the public library with a link is an alternative way to encourage public librarians to assist students seeking help with homework or school projects. Or, if teachers tend to post their assignments on the web, helping public librarians know where to look on the school's website for that information is a way of enlisting their help and reaching out.

Public libraries often host library card drives, especially in the fall when school is just under way, and school librarians can help in promotion, perhaps hosting a representative from the public library to encourage card sign-ups among students and teachers. The public librarian can report to the school librarian on programming planned for the coming month. The school can then relay this information to teachers and families. While a monthly set time may seem artificial, it is a way to open communication and may lead to additional contacts as the relationship develops. Links to each other's web-sites provide an easy connection for clientele. If students get better service and families know more about programs to help children, then the efforts at cooperation have paid off.

Shared Resources

On a larger scale, school and public libraries can both benefit from considering the subscription databases each makes available and by looking for opportunities to mount the same resources in both environments; consistency will help students and teachers feel at home in each environment. Where the opportunity exists to consider matched catalog software, the opportunities for cooperation are even greater. Librarians can team up to design instruction programs for both the public and school environments. The potential for a stronger position in price negotiation for purchase of common products should not be overlooked. And, looking for ways to negotiate licensing for complementary products—some in the public library, some in the school—is another possibility.

In small communities, cooperation for library services has taken the form of shared use of facilities and resources. In rural areas, such a shared use of resources results in services that would not otherwise be available locally. While some libraries would raise objections to shared resources because of their distinct missions and collection needs, a reality in rural America is that very small communities may be unable to provide information resources and expertise to the community without such creative solutions as school-community libraries. Governance, hours, and collection must be negotiated between the constituencies. However, the alternative of no local public library services where the small scale makes them fiscally impossible justifies collaboration and compromise.

Outreach to the Community

Cooperative activity with museums and other local groups is another means of community involvement. Art museums, science museums, natural history museums, and local historical societies have programs, exhibits, and outreach staff available to connect to the school. School librarians serve well as contact persons for these organizations because they know the whole curriculum. Besides organizations, every community has individuals with special knowledge, skills, or talents. One possible way to track community resources is to develop a community talent bank. Such a resource directory could include these items for each entry:

- Contact person
- Address
- Telephone
- E-mail
- Topics
- Curriculum areas (e.g., science, art)
- Description (e.g., a speaker, an exhibit, a demonstration)
- Limitations (e.g., age groups or group size limitations)

Developing such a directory can begin with the chamber of commerce education committee or with parent organizations. A simple form can facilitate collecting information. Then, the school librarian can assemble it into a database and make it available to teachers. Teachers must use the resources, once collected; some marketing may be required until the database becomes a standard resource. Such community involvement generates support and understanding of the school's program. In many communities the majority of voters are not parents; only about 25 percent of the adults in the United States currently have children enrolled in public schools. The majorities in most communities are young people without children or older citizens whose children are grown. Yet, schools depend on the support of these people for taxes and bond referenda. They need to feel some ownership of the schools. School librarians spotlight their role as "information central" by managing and organizing a community resource directory. This is one way for the public to see the library program's role—something not intuitively obvious to those who remember their school library as a closet-sized room with a few books.

Some communities have community improvement foundations. These foundations can serve as a starting point for tapping into local resources. The Council on Foundations offers at its website (www.cof.org) a community foundation locator for finding local and area foundations. This database is searchable by state. When seeking support from organizations, it is essential to educate yourself about the foundation's giving programs. Each typically has priorities, and education is very often among them. Make a personal contact with the organization or write a letter of appeal. It is important to approach the foundation with a proposal tailored to its goals. To approach a local foundation for assistance, Hughes-Hassell and Wheelock (2001: 122) offer a suggested outline that includes seven components:

- A request: What is needed and how will it be used?
- The need: What local area need will be met?
- The fit of the proposal with the foundation's initiatives: How will the library program with these added resources help the foundation progress toward its goals?
- Comparative data: How does the status of the local school library center compare with other situations in the state or nation?
- A human face: Provide an anecdote that gives the proposal a human face.
- Proposal details: Provide a timeline and description of how improvements will be carried out if the request is granted.
- Conclusion: Invite further conversation.

Another important community resource is the local press. In small communities, contact local news media whenever events are occurring in the school library. In larger communities, send press releases to local media. Some school districts require that press releases funnel through a district office, so it is important to know local protocol. By making these releases professional, the likelihood of their getting attention is enhanced. Often, larger newspapers and area television media have invitations on their websites for story leads. In small to medium-sized districts, the local newspaper provides an excellent opportunity for a weekly or monthly newspaper column. Such columns can include recommended good reading for students of varying ages, information about research on the importance of good school library media programs for student achievement, information about using the web for schoolwork, and advice about study skills. The target audience here is parents, but the entire community will see what is going on in the school library program.

Volunteers from the Community

Volunteers can play a number of roles in the school library. The increasing number of retirees in most communities as the baby boom generation reaches their 60s signals a volunteer workforce worth pursuing. Volunteers are certainly helpful to shelve, work in circulation, shelf-read, and provide other assistance to operations. However, volunteers also can be valuable in working directly with students. At the elementary level, many school libraries have some variation of programs where senior citizens arrive on a regular (often weekly) basis to read one-to-one with children. Whether the senior is reading to the child or the child is reading to the senior, the experience enriches the child's experiences with text and supports the development of language and reading fluency. At middle school, these volunteers may be very capable of helping students engage in research (Rankin, 2006). Depending on the needs of students, this may involve tutoring them through the research process, guiding students to search for information online, helping students figure out search terms for the library catalog, or listening to students read aloud their written work so that they can self-monitor their own composition.

School districts typically have policies for volunteers in the school. It is important to know what those policies are from the onset of any volunteer program in the school library. If there is not a specific guide for volunteers in the school, the following provisions are worthy of consideration:

- Background check or provision of local references
- Wearing a name tag during time on duty
- Participating in training related to important policies (e.g., confidentiality, food and drink in the library, discipline, safety procedures)
- Reporting planned absence from duty
- Dress code

Local norms will guide establishment of formal volunteer policies. Urban settings may require formal background checks for volunteers, for example, whereas rural communities where virtually everyone knows everyone may find such a formal policy not only unwarranted but even offensive.

Conclusion

In public schools, taxpayers have a vested interest in what happens in their community's schools. In private schools, the stakeholders also take interest in how resources are used to improve the academic achievement of the students who attend. In all cases, parents want to know about the school their children attend. The school library may not be as readily visible to all of these interested parties, yet once they become aware of the many ways the program benefits students, they can readily become advocates and supporters. Connecting with the community requires initiative on the part of the school librarian.

Leadership Strategies

Teacher and Partner

Design resources to support reading during the summer.

Develop a volunteer readers program and provide training for readers so that they are comfortable engaging children in reading experiences.

Information Specialist

Provide access to school library resources for parents.

Initiate communication with the local public library to develop such collaborative programs as an after-school homework center, intergenerational reading, or Saturday dramatics.

Explore opportunities for consortial database purchasing with public libraries.

Program Administrator

Plan and present parent meetings. Topics can include booktalks on books for a specific age or topic, a film festival of videos about parenting borrowed from a local public library or other social agency, a "how to help your child study better" session, an introduction to computer applications used at the school, or a review of online databases that are accessible from home.

Include an article in each newsletter that goes home (e.g., book suggestions, websites of potential interest to students, and brief descriptions of activities in the library).

Encourage parent or community-member volunteers, giving options for weekly or monthly tasks as well as one-time projects. Seek volunteers from senior citizen ranks and from business employees who are not parents but who have talents or time to offer. Remember to acknowledge parent help in newsletters and to treat volunteers to special events periodically to convey appreciation.

Make personal contacts with local businesses and identify ways they can be supportive. Focus the request to a single business so that each has its own niche, if possible.

Look for community foundations that can offer fiscal support to the library program.

Seek connections with local media to provide news about the library program.

Scenarios for Discussion

Scenario 1
A middle school serves a neighborhood with a large proportion of children whose parents speak Spanish and do not understand English. Also, some Spanish-speaking parents are not literate in Spanish. How does the school librarian communicate with parents regarding the library program, their child's performance with respect to library instruction, and ways to provide literacy development at home? How does the library program support families of global backgrounds? What is the relationship between the ELL (English language learner) program and the library program? How is that relationship fostered?

Scenario 2
In September, Mrs. Dillon, wife of School Board President Matt Dillon, became a new volunteer in the library where Marjorie serves as the librarian.

Given several options of ways she could be of help, Mrs. Dillon indicated that she would really like to reshelve books because she loves children's books and this would give her a chance to handle them and see what is currently available. Marjorie's assistant Celia has taught Marjorie how to shelve. Six weeks or so into the school year, Marjorie is finding that books seem to be frequently out of order, especially in the nonfiction sections. Close analysis reveals that on many shelves books recently circulated are at the end of the shelf—regardless of their call number. For example, a 626.6 Hit book is sitting after a 626.6 Lac at the end of the shelf instead of where it belongs in the middle of the shelf. Many similar examples appear as Marjorie reads shelves throughout high-circulation nonfiction areas. She asks Celia who has been shelving and finds that Mrs. Dillon has been working at that task in that area of the library. A week later, a student whose mother is pregnant is looking for the book *Before You Were Born,* and Marjorie cannot locate it at all. Looking for an alternative, Marjorie then finds that *Where Do Babies Come From?* also seems to be missing—not checked out, but not on the shelf. Should she suspect Mrs. Dillon? Should she raise her concerns with her? Should she ignore both problems? Should she talk to someone else? What should Marjorie do?

REFERENCES

Abowitz, K. K. 2000. "Democratic Communities and Business Education 'Partnerships' in Secondary Education." *Urban Review* 32, no. 4: 313–341.

Bus, A. G., and M. H. van IJzendoorn. 1999. "Phonological Awareness and Early Reading: A Meta Analysis of Experimental Training Studies." *Journal of Educational Psychology* 91:403–414.

Donham van Deusen, J., and M. J. Langhorne. 1997. "Iowa City Reads!" *School Library Journal* 43 (May): 32–34.

Gordon, C. A. 2008. "A Never-Ending Story: Action Research Meets Summer Reading." *Knowledge Quest* 37, no. 2: 34–41.

———. 2010. "Meeting Readers Where They Are." *School Library Journal* 55, no. 11: 32–37.

Gorton, R. A., and G. T. Schneider. 1991. *School-Based Leadership: Challenges and Opportunities.* Dubuque, IA: Wm. C. Brown.

Gregory, L. P., and T. G. Morrison. 1998. "Lap Reading for Young At-Risk Children: Introducing Families to Books." *Early Childhood Education Journal* 26, no. 2: 67–77.

Harvey, C. 2007. "Connecting the Library Media Center and Parents." *School Library Media Activities Monthly* 23, no. 6: 25–27.

Hughes-Hassell, S., and A. Wheelock, eds. 2001. *The Information-Powered School.* Chicago: American Library Association.

Larson, K. 2002. "Commercialism in Schools." *Teacher Librarian* 30, no. 2: 27–29.

McGarry, M. 2009. "The School Library Is the Link to Connecting with Parents." *School Library Monthly* 26, no. 3: 45–47.

Miller, M., and M. Shontz. 2003. "The SLJ Spending Survey." *School Library Journal* 49, no. 10: 52–59.

Mol, S. E., A. G. Bus, M. T. De Jong, and D. J. Smeets. 2008. "Added Value of Dialogic Parent-Child Book Readings: A Meta-Analysis." *Early Education and Development* 19, no. 1: 7–26.

Morisset , C. E. 1993. *Language and Emotional Milestones on the Road to Readiness.* Baltimore, MD: Center on Families, Communities, Schools and Children's Learning, Johns Hopkins University.

Mraz, M., and T. Rasinski. 2007. "Summer Reading Loss." *The Reading Teacher* 60, no. 8: 784–789.

National Board (National Board for Professional Teaching Standards). 2009. "Library Media/Early Childhood through Young Adulthood." National Board for Professional Teaching Standards Certificate Areas. National Board for Professional Teaching Standards. www.nbpts.org/userfiles/File/ ECYA_LM_AssessAtaGlance.pdf.

Rankin, V. 2006. "Strength in Numbers." *School Library Journal* 52, no. 1: 37.

Scarborough, H. S., and W. Dobrich. 1994. "On the Efficacy of Reading to Preschoolers." *Developmental Review* 14:245–302.

Segal-Drori, Ora, Ofra Korat, Adina Shamir, and Pnina S. Klein. 2010. "Reading Electronic and Printed Books with and without Adult Instruction: Effects on Emergent Reading." *Reading and Writing* 23, no. 8: 913–930.

Tinnish, D. 1996. "Big Business in the School Library." *Emergency Librarian* 2, no. 5: 8–11.

Van Dusen, M. 2007. "Open Up with Community Outreach." *Library Media Connection* 25, no. 6: 24–26.

PART II

The
School Library
Program

6

Collaboration

This chapter:

- describes models of the collaborative process;
- examines the role of the school librarian as a member of the instructional team;
- discusses how collaboration benefits students, teachers, and school librarians; and
- identifies leadership strategies for collaboration.

The increased complexity of today's world calls for teamwork. Robert Reich (1987: 126) observes in *Tales of a New America*:

> Rarely do even Big Ideas emerge any longer from the solitary labors of genius. Modern science and technology is too complicated for one brain. It requires groups of astronomers, physicists, and computer programmers to discover new dimensions of the universe . . . With ever more frequency Nobel prizes are awarded to collections of people.

Increased complexity characterizes the teaching profession as well. Concern for differentiated instruction, greater accountability for student achievement, the explosion of information, and advances in instructional and information technologies are among the factors that contribute to the complexity in teaching.

In many settings, long-standing tradition has kept teachers isolated in their self-contained classrooms. Many teachers entered the profession expecting to work alone with their students, having autonomy over their own classroom and students. Today, consideration of more competitive performance-pay plans threatens incentives for team-based work. Yet, that competitive model is out of step with a culture that recognizes that teamwork can increase effectiveness and productivity and can improve the work environment. Likewise, Kimmel (2011) found through analyzing discourse of teachers and school librarians that established models of librarians run somewhat counter to the call for collaboration. She references the "prevailing meanings of a school librarian as a helper, a story lady whispering 'shhhh,' and a specialist providing release time for teachers" (Conclusion, para. 1).

The School Librarian as Collaborator

Participatory Culture

Hamilton (2011) describes the library as a site of "participatory culture." Indeed, this image is precisely the ambiance to be created for a school library. She cites Jenkins in identifying essential conditions for such a participatory school library:

> *Low barriers to expression and engagement.* The school librarian must take the initiative to determine what might be interfering with teacher-librarian collaboration and adjust accordingly. For example, if teaching schedules cause inadequate opportunity for face-to-face meetings, then the school librarian can identify collaborative technologies that can complement brief interchanges. Or, can a Google document or a Google calendar be used and shared to guide planning for an upcoming research project? Can chat via Gmail be used to coordinate details for planning? Can a LibGuide be created and shared to communicate resources to be considered?

> *Support for sharing.* For example, if a graphic organizer is being created to guide students in note taking, can the school librarian initiate sharing various models or designs and seek teacher input by e-mail?

> *Informal mentorship.* The school librarian can take the lead in advising new teachers as research project assignments are scheduled, guiding the novice on how to organize students to take advantage of the library and its resources.

> *Belief that all members' contributions matter.* The school librarian sits in an ideal position to acknowledge the work of each teacher participating in a collaborative endeavor.

Social connection among the collaborators. By including everyone in all communications, the school librarian can engender a sense of belonging for all.

Without collaboration, the collection, curriculum, and staff of the library program have little purpose; an effective library program cannot function in isolation. So, librarians must seek to work collaboratively with classroom teachers in order to improve students' learning experiences. Collaboration depends on effective communication and supportive relationships. Special education teachers share with school librarians a need to collaborate with classroom teachers in order to be effective in their own work. Speaking for special educators, Knackendoffel (2007) lists several dimensions of the collaborative effort:

Collaboration is voluntary. Only the individuals involved can decide if their interactions will be truly collaborative.

Collaboration requires parity among participants. Each person's contribution to an interaction is valued equally, and each person has equal power in decision making.

Collaboration is based on mutual goals. To collaborate, professionals must share one goal that is specific and important enough to maintain their shared attention.

Collaboration depends on shared responsibility for participation and decision making. Equal participation in the decision making is important, but shared participation in task completion does not mean that tasks must be divided equally. Participation in the activity often involves a convenient division of labor.

Individuals who collaborate share resources. Example resources include time and availability to carry out tasks and specialized knowledge.

Individuals who collaborate share accountability for outcomes.

These same dimensions of collaboration describe successful collaboration between librarians and classroom teachers.

Since working together takes more time than working alone, there must be motivation to collaborate. Sometimes that motivation is intrinsic—people trust that the result of collaboration will be better teaching and learning and that it is worth their time. Sometimes, the motivation must be external because people lack confidence that collaboration will be beneficial. In these cases, administrators might impose expectations for collaboration, setting team or department meeting times and attending those meetings whenever possible. Sometimes, principals build the expectation for collaboration into the performance appraisal. In cases where collaboration is an expectation held by the principal, it is particularly important that the benefits be quickly evident to participants. In many schools, teachers have formal planning teams based on grade level or academic discipline. Depending on the school culture, these teams may meet weekly, monthly, annually, or as needed. These teams plan big-picture curriculum, instructional units, individual lessons, and/or special activities together. Whatever the meeting pattern and agenda, school librarians need to participate in order to be true collaborators with classroom teachers. Too often, teachers approach the librarian after they finish their planning. As participants, librarians can help teachers understand what librarians can offer to the planning process.

It is important for the principal to support the librarian as an instructional partner who should be part of curriculum planning. When such understanding is lacking, the librarian may start a conversation like this:

> I can alert teachers to resources both at school and elsewhere if I know what they are teaching and expecting of their students. My goal is to help save teachers time, to help them locate the best resources for instructional needs, and to help teaching be as effective as it can be. I also want to teach students the skills necessary to locate and use information. If I participate in planning, then together we can decide on how best to develop these information skills in our students.

Teamwork requires trust in one another's contributions to the team's work, a no-risk environment for openly sharing ideas, and a shared commitment to the group's decisions. Establishing ground rules from the beginning that recognize these requirements will improve the potential for collaboration. Specific and explicit strategies are useful for helping teamwork proceed (Holcomb, 1996):

> *Pose questions using nonthreatening language.* To protect the no-risk atmosphere, phrasing questions so that they do not put others on the defensive is important. No one wants to speak in a situation where

ideas are at risk of being criticized or attacked; yet, open discussion demands that disagreement be voiced. Tact and sensitivity are important. Ask, "Might Steinbeck be too difficult for some kids to read?" rather than state, "Steinbeck is too difficult."

Ensure that all are heard. Some people tend to be cautious about speaking up even in small groups. Someone must take responsibility for seeing that all voices are heard. A simple query such as "Mark, we haven't heard from you; what do you think of this idea?" is sometimes all that is needed. A round-robin approach, asking each person for comments, also works well.

Clarify terms. Careful communication is important for collaboration, so think about assumptions and see that they are explicit. For example, a clarification such as "When we say consensus, do we mean agreement by the majority, or do we mean unanimous agreement?" may prevent a serious misunderstanding later on.

Keep the discussion focused. "We began with talking about how we would assess students' learning at the end of the Civil War unit, and now we are talking about websites. We seem to have gotten off the track."

Engage in active listening. Elements of active listening are the following: paraphrase what others say, ask probing questions, jot down important points, withhold advice until all information is shared, and listen to advice in full before reacting.

A collaborative meeting must be organized in order to be more than a chat session. The group needs a facilitator. Meetings should begin with a stated purpose or an agenda, with opportunities for additions from participants. Likewise, meetings should have some kind of outcome—written and distributed minutes or an oral summary of what was accomplished. These features help all participants know that their time was well spent. One way to increase the productivity of collaborative meetings is to have a planning format. Figure 6.1 offers a model for such a planning document. When the school librarian uses such a form, it conveys several messages: (1) This is such an important meeting that the school librarian will formally record its content. (2) The school librarian has an instructional agenda. (3) The school librarian is committed to acting on the content of the meeting.

FIGURE 6.1
Planning Guide for Teacher–Librarian Collaboration

COLLABORATIVE PLANNER	
Unit:	**Course/Grade:**
Teacher(s):	Student assignments/tasks:
Content area essential questions/standards:	Library essential questions/standards:
Content area learning activities:	Library learning activities:
Teacher Responsibilities	**Librarian Responsibilities**

CALENDAR/DATES OF UNIT

Monday	Tuesday	Wednesday	Thursday	Friday

Notes for Future Revision

Models of School Librarian–Teacher Collaboration

In an attempt to characterize the unique features of school librarians' collaboration with teachers, Monteil-Overall (2005) proposed a four-level model of collaboration. It features at the lowest level coordinator, progressing to cooperation, integrated instruction, and ultimately integrated curriculum. She defined each level as follows:

> *Coordination* is a collaborative effort that requires low levels of interaction between teacher and librarian. As a coordinator, the school librarian organizes or synchronizes events, activities, and resources. For example, a school librarian might organize a "reading extravaganza" event for the school that promotes reading across the school community. The librarian might take central responsibility for the event and involve teachers and/or volunteers to assist in carrying out the event. The librarian takes responsibility for activities, scheduling, organizing—coordinating the event.

> *Cooperation* involves more interaction between teacher and librarian. Teacher and librarian cooperate on lessons or units of study by dividing tasks. Goals and objectives are developed independently, although joint instruction may be involved. Cooperation calls for each party to know what the other is doing, and then their teaching can be complementary.

> *Integrated instruction* reflects a deeper level of involvement and commitment by the librarian and teacher and also a deeper level of trust. Integrated instruction requires planning together and integrating learning activities that bring together, respectively, the teacher's and the librarian's expertise in subject content and inquiry. Instruction is planned to engage students in learning experiences that connect classroom and library units of study through jointly planned, implemented, and evaluated lessons.

> *Integrated curriculum* is a systemic collaboration across the curriculum. Teachers meet regularly with the librarian to integrate information literacy and content through joint efforts that involve cothinking, coplanning, coimplementation, and coevaluation across the curriculum. Such systemic collaboration often involves the leadership of the principal in developing a collaborative culture school-wide. This comprehensive collaboration requires commitment of time and

professional development as well as a belief that such collaboration results in better learning opportunities for students. Through such systemic collaboration, subject areas and library curricula are integrated at every grade level.

In an alternate model, Marcoux (2007) proposed five degrees of collaboration:

Consumption. Students "consume" library resources; for example, printing, photocopying, or weekly reading quotas.

Connection. The school librarian is informed about upcoming instructional units but has no input into the design or timing of it.

Cooperation. The school librarian is informed about assignments. There is minimal consultation about types of resources to be used and timing of the project. The librarian works with the students on how to use the resources and/or how to do their research.

Coordination. The school librarian knows about lesson goals, expected outcomes, the timing, and assessment criteria. The school librarian has shown students how to use the resources and has worked with students on how to do their research and how to develop their projects.

Collaboration. The school librarian and the classroom teacher have jointly planned and implemented instruction. Teaching is shared on all aspects of the lesson, and student assessment/evaluation is done jointly. Evaluation criteria include both content mastery and information literacy process.

The classic work on defining degrees of collaboration is Loertscher's *Taxonomies of the School Library Media Program* (1988). Loertscher designed a more detailed model of collaboration that acknowledged, importantly, that sometimes no collaborative involvement is appropriate; school librarians cannot and do not need to collaborate with teachers on every unit taught. His acknowledgment of that fact sets his model apart. Further, his taxonomy offers a more detailed set of levels of collaboration to articulate the nuance of initiative (who initiates the collaboration) as well as the degree. This taxonomy classifies involvement from minimal participation to a central role.

Loertscher contends that one's placement along the taxonomy is situational, and that each level is appropriate at some time or other.

> *Level 1: No Interaction.* In some situations the school librarian is not involved at all.

> *Level 2: Self-Help Warehouse.* The "warehouse" represents the library's resources. Collection development is a collaborative process. Teachers give the librarian suggestions of topics, themes, or titles. The librarian negotiates with teachers to prioritize needs and determine what will be purchased. This collaborative process is an ongoing one in which information is continually being shared in both directions. School librarians are reviewing the existing collection and making decisions for weeding; these decisions too are shared with teachers to reduce the chances of withdrawing materials that have value. The warehouse extends beyond the physical collection to include resources available online and from other collections. And, the organization and access systems of the warehouse are communicated clearly to teachers so that they can use it independently.

> *Level 3: Individual Reference Assistance.* Here, the school librarian works with the teacher to find an answer to a specific question. Reference work is a collaboration between the information seeker and the librarian. Active listening and probing questions are key to effective individual reference. It requires careful communication to determine a precise need. The Reference and User Services Association (2004) of the American Library Association adopted a set of guidelines for successful reference transactions. Five qualitative measures are included in the guidelines: approachability, interest, listening/inquiring, searching, and follow-up. According to the approachability guideline, "the initial verbal and nonverbal responses of the librarian will influence the depth and level of the interaction between the librarian and the patron. The librarian's responsibility is to make the patron feel comfortable in a situation that may be perceived as intimidating, risky, confusing, and overwhelming." These guidelines are highly relevant to individualized reference assistance as a collaboration between librarian and teacher. These guidelines acknowledge that libraries (and sometimes librarians) can be intimidating not only for children but also

for adults. Examples of *approachability* behaviors are smiling, establishing eye contact, and extending a greeting. Under the guideline for *interest*, behaviors include using both verbal and nonverbal cues to signal that the librarian is listening and understanding the query. For *listening/inquiring*, the librarian allows the teacher to fully state his or her information need before hurrying off to respond, rephrases the question or request, and seeks assurance that the request is fully understood. For example, the librarian might simply ask, "Can you tell me a little more about . . . ?" As a follow-up, clarifying questions help determine how extensive the information search should be or whether specific formats will be more useful. Under the guideline for *searching*, the librarian not only engages in the search for information but also informs the teacher of the search process and explains how to use sources if the teacher shows interest. At this stage, the librarian works with the teacher to broaden or narrow the search if too little or too much information is identified. Finally, under the guideline for *follow-up*, the librarian asks the teacher if the question has been fully resolved and makes referrals to other sources if it has not. Careful, friendly, and thorough individual reference assistance may serve as a starting point for collaboration at higher levels of the taxonomy.

Level 4: Spontaneous Interaction and Gathering. At this level, teacher and librarian engage in minimal collaboration. The teacher suddenly discovers a need for something and sends a request, often by way of a student or e-mail, to the library: "I need a picture that shows the difference between a moth and a butterfly." Or, "I need that video about how to deal with strangers because of an incident reported this morning." As collaboration increases, however, teachers grow more confident that the librarian will respond to such requests.

Level 5: Cursory Planning. Here, collaboration in the true sense of planning with teachers begins—but informally. Brief informal conversations occur where teachers talk about what they are planning to teach, and the librarian may interject ideas or resources. Often, such conversations are essentially brainstorming; generally, they are brief and unstructured. Yet, there is communication between the librarian and teacher and often some activity occurs as a result—the librarian locates a resource, a lesson is taught in the library, a time is set for more in-depth conversation, or an activity is designed.

Level 6: Planned Gathering. As a result of communication between teachers and the librarian about upcoming instruction, the librarian gathers resources. Clear communication between teacher and librarian is vital. This interaction extends beyond a teacher stating a topic and a librarian gathering everything available about that topic. That is not collaboration. Collaboration means that the teacher helps the librarian know what kinds of resources will be really useful, and the librarian focuses the selection of recommended resources to match the need. Several questions need to be answered:

- "How long will you be working on this unit?" The answer to this question will guide the librarian regarding how much to collect.

- "How will you use the materials?" If the response is that the teacher will be using them as resources for himself or herself, then concern for reading level is not as crucial.

- "Is there a particular focus to the unit?" The response will help the school librarian know, for example, whether to collect materials related to causes of the Civil War or merely to collect information about the battles in the war itself, or both.

- "What kinds of activities do you anticipate?" If the response is reading and writing, the kinds of resources considered will be different from those collected if the response is hands-on activities and field trips.

Gathering materials becomes collaborative only when these questions are posed. If the school librarian simply pulls together as many physical and virtual resources about classical mythology or World War II as he or she can locate, the process is not collaborative. More important, it may not be particularly helpful, since providing teachers with more materials or the wrong materials may actually create unnecessary work for both teacher and librarian and ultimately be counterproductive to the most common purpose of collaboration—improving teaching and learning.

Level 7: Evangelistic Outreach. Marketing might be another appropriate metaphor for this level of involvement. Marketing requires clear understanding of the customers' needs and desires. By working closely with teachers, the school librarian learns what will "sell" in terms of resources and services. In the school setting, one of the most effective approaches is providing professional development. Collaboratively planned professional development or, even better, development of professional learning communities—when the school librarian and teachers discuss what is possible and what is appropriate for them and their school—may indeed be the most successful. The librarian can lead such endeavors by suggesting menus of possible topics, and together the group can discuss the local value of each suggestion.

Level 8: Scheduled Planning in the Support Role. Formal collaborative planning occurs when the librarian participates in planning sessions with teachers and provides assistance in identifying resources or designing learning activities. In schools where collaboration is a part of the local school culture, formal team, department, or grade-level meetings occur routinely. Acting in the support role, the librarian responds to teacher initiatives, taking away from such sessions a to-do list that usually involves fetching resources or designing activities based on the directions of the teachers.

Levels 9 and 10: Instructional Design. Here, formal collaboration moves beyond the support role so that the librarian takes part in designing the unit. This team relationship engages teachers and the school librarian equally in collaborative planning, including determining the goals for the unit, perhaps some team-teaching, selecting resources, designing student assessment, and evaluating the unit at its conclusion.

Level 11: Curriculum Development. School librarians have a legitimate place on curriculum development committees at the school and district levels. This is the systemic level where the larger organization embraces the role and expertise of the school librarian. School librarians are, after all, teachers. Beyond that, their special expertise about resources, technologies, teaching, and learning strategies makes them valuable participants.

FIGURE 6.2
Models of Collaboration

Loertscher	Marcoux	Monteil-Overall
No Interaction		
Self-Help Warehouse	Consumption	Coordination
Individual Reference Assistance	Consumption	Cooperation
Spontaneous Interaction and Gathering	Consumption	Cooperation
Cursory Planning	Connection	Cooperation
Planned Gathering	Cooperation	Cooperation
Evangelistic Outreach	Cooperation	Cooperation
Scheduled Planning—Support Role	Coordination	Cooperation
Instructional Design	Collaboration	Integrated Instruction
Curriculum Development		Integrated Curriculum

Figure 6.2 shows a comparison of these three models of collaboration. Each helps to create a mental model of what it means for a school librarian to collaborate with teachers.

Group Task Roles

The school librarian has a unique position in collaborating with teachers as both an insider and an outsider (Donham van Deusen, 1996). The school librarian is a regular member of the teaching staff and as such is an insider. However, as a librarian rather than a classroom teacher, he or she is an outsider who brings a different perspective to the planning process—a perspective that incorporates what is being taught throughout the school in different grades or in different departments, a perspective influenced by technology and by a broad variety of resources. This unique insider-outsider view creates an opportunity for raising questions that can be at once naive and challenging—questions such as "How does this new fifth-grade unit relate to the existing sixth-grade unit on space exploration?" or "What do you really want to accomplish in this unit?" This outsider can pose such questions as naive queries that cause the teachers to reflect on their planning, to refocus, or to alter their direction.

Drawn from the classic work of Benne and Sheats (1948), potential group roles can be summarized as follows:

The *clarifier* gives relevant examples, offers rationales, and restates problems. As clarifier, librarians can pose questions to teachers: "What do you want children to learn?" or "Immigration is a very broad topic; what might be the focus of this unit on immigration?" Such questions encourage teachers to reassess their planning and to focus on their goals.

The *initiator* suggests new or different ideas. As initiator, the school librarian can offer suggestions and alternatives to teachers. Benne and Sheats state that the initiator may suggest a new organizational structure to address a difficult issue. Perhaps a school librarian might suggest, and subsequently facilitate, a faculty technology study group to examine educational technology issues and to determine in what direction the school should proceed. Or a suggestion for a short course for students on "netiquette" might be in order.

The *opinion giver* states pertinent beliefs about discussion and others' suggestions. As opinion giver, the school librarian might bring in a different viewpoint or perspective based on the resources or on the professional literature. For example, the librarian might remind teachers that students are not as selective as they should be when finding sources of information.

The *summarizer* reviews discussion and pulls it together. As summarizer, the school librarian can share the results of listening to teachers. As the outsider, it is natural for the school librarian to begin the summary with, "I want to be sure I have not missed anything important in our discussion, so let me summarize our decision . . ."

The *tester* raises questions to test whether the group is ready for a decision. As tester, he or she can measure what teachers say or do against the mission and philosophy of the school. Such a role may begin with a question such as, "As we think about our plan, did we keep in mind that every unit we teach needs to have explicit accommodations for our English language learners? Where is that accommodation in this unit plan?"

The *compromiser* yields when necessary for progress. After a recommendation that students will need more class time to define their research questions for a research project fails to garner support among tenth-grade English teachers, a school librarian may suggest that students e-mail their research questions to him or her for feedback.

The following group roles are less content oriented and focus instead on the interpersonal concerns of group work; yet again as insider-outsider, the school librarian is well positioned to support the interactions within the group by asserting himself or herself in these ways:

- The *elaborator* builds on the suggestions of others.
- The *encourager* praises and supports others.
- The *gatekeeper* keeps communication open and encourages participation.
- The *harmonizer* mediates differences and reconciles points of view.
- The *tension reliever* uses humor or calls for breaks at appropriate times to draw off negative feelings.

All of these team task roles involve the school librarian's ability to step away from the group and become an outsider to offer a perspective that could help direct, redirect, or refocus the team's efforts. Such a perspective is uniquely valuable to the potential for the team to adhere to its mission and to maintain awareness of its larger context.

Formal and Informal Collaboration

Opportunities for collaboration are not limited to formal meetings. For example, a teacher stops into a library and shares an idea about an upcoming unit, and the librarian responds with a suggestion, question, or idea. Collaboration has begun. Where this informal interaction leads depends largely on the kind of response the library media specialist makes. In this situation, the image of Loertscher's Taxonomy or the hierarchies of either Monteil-Overall or Marcoux should appear in the mind's eye of the librarian, who then reflects: "How much involvement does this teacher want from me? How much involvement is appropriate for this instance? Do I offer a few resources to help the teacher out? Do I suggest that I will search for a variety of resources to support this unit? Do I suggest that we sit down and do a little brainstorming about possible activities to engage students for this unit?" These informal opportunities for collaboration can have an impact; indeed, in many schools where collaborative planning is not a part of the local school culture, this is the only kind of collaborative opportunity. School librarians need to be opportunistic and grab each opportunity as it arises to begin developing collaborative relationships with teachers.

Benefits of Collaboration

Because collaboration requires time and energy and is more complicated than working alone, its benefits need to be made explicit. In particular, three outcomes are likely benefits of collaboration that includes the school librarian: reflective thought, school-wide coordination, and improved teaching and learning.

Reflective Thought

A number of scholars and educators (e.g., Feiman, 1979; Tom, 1985; Zeichner and Liston, 1987) have written about reflection, based in large part on Dewey's (1910) concept of reflective thinking. Schön's (1983) work brought reflective thinking to the forefront. Reflective teachers consistently assess the origins, purposes, and consequences of their work (Nolan and Huber, 1989). Pugach and Johnson (1990) describe reflection as an art of mediated thinking. They propose that reflection among teachers can be mediated and enhanced by collegial dialogue. They suggest that to facilitate reflective thinking, one practices restraint and allows teachers to think aloud. Their proposal that a facilitator can promote reflective thinking is relevant to the role that a school librarian plays in helping teachers plan. The librarian can raise questions to generate reflective thought among teachers, whether it is a question of how they would define their thematic unit on friendship, why and when their students should learn keyboarding, or what they want their students to learn about war. Kottkamp (1990) distinguished between prescriptive and descriptive communication in his discussion of how to facilitate reflection. He emphasized the importance of avoiding prescriptive communication as a facilitator (i.e., messages in the form of "you should . . .") and instead using descriptive language that avoids judgment. The intent of the librarian is not to tell teachers what to do, but rather to encourage them to verbalize, to think aloud. Such thinking aloud can lead them to insights of their own and help them communicate with one another. Because of the outsider status, the school librarian can pose naive questions that encourage deliberation among teachers, thus func-tioning as a catalyst for reflective thought. Holt (1993) encourages a deliber-ate climate in schools where teachers consider and determine both what and how to teach. The collegial relationship he describes reflects the exchange of ideas generated in planning sessions; the school librarian can facilitate that exchange by being an insider (a member of the staff), yet a somewhat naive participant as an outsider. The school librarian acts as a clarifier. By probing for his or her own clarification, the librarian encourages the teachers to clarify their thinking and planning for themselves. Poole (1994) describes this phe-nomenon when she characterizes one teacher as learning not from suggestions of a coach but from the process of reflection that was necessary to articulate her ideas to the colleague. Because the school librarian is an outsider, teachers need to articulate quite clearly what they are thinking. As in Poole's case, this process forces clarifying their thinking as well.

School-Wide Coordination

The school librarian has the advantage of serving the entire school community—all grades, all subjects. By working in collaboration with teachers throughout the school, he or she can share knowledge of the total system with others and help teachers broaden their view of their students' total school experi-ence. Teachers design instruction based on curriculum goals, but the poten-tial is great for gaps and redundancy. Collaboration helps counteract both of those concerns. In his description of the basic school, Boyer (1995) asserted that teachers are leaders who work together. He advocates perceiving the school as a community of learners. The concept of community carries with it the connotation that people are working together in the learning process.

Improved Teaching and Learning

It seems intuitive that when more than one mind is put to a task, better ideas, better planning, and ultimately better teaching and learning will occur. And although each member of a team brings special talents, knowledge, experi-ence, and intelligence to the process, the group working together can produce better planning than individuals working alone. In a case study of collabora-tion in high schools in California, teachers maintained reflective logs dur-ing research units. They affirmed the value of collaboration with librarians, noting the benefit of two teachers available to work with individual students and the more systematic approach to research taken by students with guidance from the library media specialist (Lange, Montgomery, and Magee, 2003). Of key importance is the ability of a team's members to behave in ways that take advantage of the synergistic potential of teamwork.

Conclusion

The library program has little potential to contribute to the learning experiences of students if it is left isolated from the learning events of the classroom. However, the initiative for bringing the library together with the classroom most often rests with the school librarian. Helping teachers understand how the library program can advance learning requires that the school librarian articulate the potential. One way is to share with teachers a model of collaboration such as Loertscher's Taxonomy or the models of Marcoux or Monteil-Overall. Another strategy is to transform the library program into a learning commons philosophy as described in Chapter 1 and help teachers envision its meaning through that lens. In some instances, educating the principal will lead to progress toward a collaborative environment. Whatever method the school library chooses to begin the move toward collaboration, this implementation of collaboration between library program and classroom is essential for the library to be relevant to learners.

Leadership Strategies

Teacher and Partner

As a collaborative partner, whether working with an individual teacher or a whole team or department, leave each interaction with a to-do list and complete the tasks promptly so that teachers gain confidence in collaboration.

Avoid being only a gofer for a team; school librarians have more than resources to deliver. Ideas for teaching and learning strategies, offers to teach or team-teach and assess, particularly when information processes are a part of the learning, are ways to contribute substantively to the quality of learning. Emphasize that adding the school librarian to the teaching of a unit effectively halves the teacher-student ratio.

Be sensitive to the requests of teachers. When a teacher asks a question, it may actually present an opportunity for collaboration if you are poised to notice it. For example:

- When a teacher says, "Do we have a copy of *Little House in the Big Woods?*" perhaps he really is asking, "Can you suggest a good read-aloud for my class for our westward expansion unit?"
- When a teacher asks, "May I bring my class to the library on Friday?" what she might be saying is, "We are going to do some research and I don't think my students know where to begin to find the information they will need."
- When a teacher asks, "Do we have any books on Canada?" the real message could be, "I am about to begin a unit on Canada, and I have no resources beyond the textbook."

Of course, sometimes the simple question is merely seeking the simple direct answer; effectively tuning in and knowing which kind of response is needed is an important first step toward becoming a partner.

Information Specialist

Lead a study group in reading a book about teamwork. For example:

- *Effective Collaboration for Educating the Whole Child,* by C. Kochhar-Bryant and A. Heishman (Corwin Press, 2010).
- *TeamWork: Setting the Standard for Collaborative Teaching, Grades 5–9,* by M. Wild, A. Mayeaux, and K. Edmonds (Stenhouse, 2008).

Initiate professional learning communities organized around topics of interest to teachers and contribute resources and ideas to lead toward relationship building.

Program Administrator

If collaboration is not already a characteristic of the school culture, initiate conversations with individual teachers and include offers to brainstorm ideas or to search for materials. Deliver high-quality information or resources promptly so that the teacher can see the benefit of working together.

Share with the principal intentions to collaborate with others in the school and seek help for ways to become more involved in planning with teachers.

Work to promote a vision of a collaborative relationship with the library by promoting a learning commons philosophy.

Scenarios for Discussion

Scenario 1

At Washington Elementary School, the school librarian is new and in her first school library position. The school faculty consists of many seasoned teachers and a principal waiting to retire within the next three years. The previous librarian retired after more than 20 years at this school. The collection is top-notch, and the facility is modern and conducive to learning and teaching. The computer lab has recently been updated. Students come from homes that value education and support the school. It is November, and the teachers are still mourning the loss of their previous librarian. They are reluctant to accept a new person in the role, and the principal is not about to make waves with the staff. What steps should the new librarian take to create a climate that's conducive for collaboration in this school?

Scenario 2

Susan has been the school librarian at North Middle School for three years. Individual teachers readily come to her for recommendations of resources or requesting that she teach a special lesson for their students, such as searching for information for assignments that require resources beyond the textbook or doing a booktalk with their classes. However, Susan feels as if she is stuck at Level 5 on Loertscher's Taxonomy. Does it really matter whether collaboration is systemic? Why or why not? If it does matter, what can she do to move toward a more systemic model of collaboration?

REFERENCES

Benne, K. D., and P. Sheats. 1948. "Functional Roles of Group Members." *Journal of Social Issues* 4, no. 2: 42–47.

Boyer, E. 1995. *The Basic School: A Community for Learning.* Princeton, NJ: Carnegie Foundation for the Advancement of Teaching.

Dewey, J. 1910. *How We Think.* Boston: Heath.

Donham van Deusen, J. 1996. "The School Library Media Specialist as a Member of the Teaching Team—An 'Insider ' and an 'Outsider.'" *Journal of Curriculum and Supervision* 11, no. 3: 229–248.

Feiman, S. 1979. "Technique and Inquiry in Teacher Education: A Curricular Case Study." *Curriculum Inquiry* 9, no. 1: 63–79.

Hamilton, B. 2011. "The School Librarian as Teacher: What Kind of Teacher Are You?" *Knowledge Quest* 39, no. 5: 34–40.

Holcomb, E. 1996. *Asking the Right Question: Tools and Techniques for Teamwork.* Thousand Oaks, CA: Corwin.

Holt, M. 1993. "The High School Curriculum in the United States and the United Kingdom." *Journal of Curriculum and Supervision* 8, no. 2: 157–173.

Kimmel, S. C. 2011. "Consider with Whom You Are Working: Discourse Models of School Librarianship in Collaboration." *School Library Media Research* 14. http:www.ala.org/aasl/slmr.

Knackendoffel, E. A. 2007. "Collaborative Teaming in the Secondary School." *Focus on Exceptional Children* 40, no. 4: 1–20.

Kottkamp, R. B. 1990. "Means for Facilitating Reflection." *Education and Urban Society* 22, no. 2: 182–203.

Lange, B., S. Montgomery, and N. Magee. 2003. "Does Collaboration Boost Student Learning?" *School Library Journal* 49, no. 6: 4–5.

Loertscher, D. V. 1988. *Taxonomies of the School Library Media Program.* Littleton, CO: Libraries Unlimited.

Marcoux, Betty L. 2007. "Levels of Collaboration: Where Does Your Work Fit In?" *School Library Media Activities Monthly* 24, no. 4: 20–24.

Montiel-Overall, P. 2005. "A Theoretical Understanding of Teacher and Librarian Collaboration (TLC)." *School Libraries Worldwide* 11, no. 2: 24–48.

Nolan, J. F., and T. Huber. 1989. "Nurturing the Reflective Practitioner through Institutional Supervision: A Review of the Literature." *Journal of Curriculum and Supervision* 4, no. 2: 126–145.

Poole, W. 1994. "Removing the 'Super' from Supervision." *Journal of Curriculum and Supervision* 9, no. 3: 284–309.

Pugach, M., and L. J. Johnson. 1990. "Developing Reflective Practice through Structured Dialogue." In *Encouraging Reflective Practice in Education: An Analysis of Issues and Programs*, edited by R. T. Clift, 187–204. New York: Teachers College Press.

Reich, R. 1987. *Tales of a New America.* New York: Time Books.

Reference and User Services Association. 2004. *Guidelines for Behavioral Performance of Reference and Information Services Professionals.* American Library Association. www.ala.org/rusa/resources/guidelines/guidelinesbehavioral.

Schön, D. 1983. *The Reflective Practitioner.* New York: Basic Books.

Tom, A. R. 1985. "Inquiring into Inquiry-Oriented Teacher Education." *Journal of Teacher Education* 36, no. 5: 35–44.

Zeichner, K., and D. Liston. 1987. "Theory and Practice in the Evolution of an Inquiry-Oriented Student Teaching Program." *Harvard Educational Review* 57, no. 1: 34–48.

7

Access for Learning and Teaching

This chapter:

- introduces the principle of physical access to information resources;
- describes alternatives for scheduling instruction in the library;
- explores access to the library for individual students;
- examines the possibilities of access beyond the school day;
- discusses circulation policies in the context of maximum access; and
- identifies leadership strategies for access.

Maximizing access to information is a fundamental tenet of the library profession. Libraries have an interesting history in the United States. The story of the founding of the Boston Public Library, in particular, speaks to the long-standing value libraries have placed on access to information resources. McCrann (2005) summarized the forces at work leading to the 1848 founding of this library, considered to be the first *public* library in the United States. Prior to its founding, Boston, a city that prided itself as being highly educated, was home to many private libraries accessible by membership. The notion of a library openly accessible to the public represented a new direction. Tracing the development as reported in Whitehill's *Boston Public Library: A Centennial History*, McCrann (2005: 228) quotes a trustee report that states:

> [I]t would be a "great matter" if as many books as possible would be carried into "poor families" and "cheap boardinghouses; in short, wherever they will be most likely to affect life and raise personal character." In the same report Ticknor wrote, "It is of paramount importance that the means

of general information should be so diffused that the largest possible
number of persons should be induced to read and understand questions
of social order."

While early town libraries offered free service to their residents and were supported by public funding, they required their readers to come to the library to
read. The Boston Public Library went on to become a publicly funded library
open to all town residents that allowed the free circulation of its resources
to the public—a radical library idea for its time. In the context of this history, access to the school library and its resources requires consideration of
several factors. While the virtual library provides access to online library
resources and also some opportunities to benefit from the school librarian's
expertise through online research guides and/or virtual reference or chat
options, access to the physical library is the focus of this chapter. Indeed, the
physical facility and its human and informational resources offer important
support for students' academic and personal information needs. Factors that
influence such access include the library's hours of operation and students'
opportunities to access the physical library during the school day, circulation
policies as they affect access to resources, and access to instruction in the
library in a meaningful context.

Student Access

Hours

To begin, access to the library needs to accommodate students as much as
possible. Before school and after school, students should be able to go to the
library to the extent that activity schedules and bus schedules allow. Adams
(2011), in speaking to concerns for homeless children, makes a case for
extended library hours, particularly after school, as a way of providing a safe
and supportive environment for these children to do homework, read, and
explore intellectually. While this is certainly a population in need of such
a supportive environment, other latchkey students would benefit from such
accommodation as well. Consideration of extended hours depends on several local factors and should focus on the needs of the students in the school
(Despines, 2001). It may be that simply ensuring the library is staffed and
students are allowed access for 30 minutes before and after school will meet
local needs. However, extending availability of the library may be warranted

where access to public libraries is limited or difficult due to distance and/ or available transportation, where family situations afford little opportunity for online access in the home, or where little home support for academics is provided. In such instances, the school librarian will want to seek support for extending access. While staffing needs can sometimes be met by shifting hours, most often in an active program additional staff affords the best service beyond the school day. Perhaps a retired school librarian in the area can be employed on an hourly basis to staff extended hours, or a position can be shared with a local public library. Options will vary by locale, but staffing needs to be a top priority. Building security is another consideration; often buildings have evening custodial staff who can provide security for the building. Many schools have frequent events after school so that the facility is already open and in use. Disciplinary issues may need to be considered, again based on local school culture, so having a school administrator on call may be a solution to consider if hours extend beyond administrators' work hours. Determining appropriate hours for extended time is also a local question. In many situations, just providing hours up to 5 p.m. meets the needs of students. Student athletes may be best served by early-bird hours before school starts.

Aside from extended hours, throughout the school day the library should be open and accessible. Closing for lunch, for testing, for completing library managerial tasks such as inventory, or for other special events impedes student access and has detrimental effects on the library program and its ability to serve students. Not surprising were results of a study of closure of school libraries that documented the fact that increased closures during the school year were accompanied by reduced circulation of materials to students (Dickinson, Gavigan, and Pribesh, 2008). Similarly, closing the library because a class is meeting in the facility is problematic. Where support staff are available to meet the basic needs of students coming to the library for individual needs, the library should remain accessible even when the school librarian is teaching. If no support staff are available, this situation should be discussed with the school principal to arrive at a solution that will keep the library doors open throughout the school day. Classroom teachers must also recognize the value of open and flexible access throughout the school day. Discussion of the hours of operation of the school library with administrators and school staff and faculty will generate ideas about the perceived need for students and the potential support to meet the needs.

Flexible Access

Flexible access is complex, and its implementation must be systemic. It is not enough to simply say to everyone, "The library is open all day. Students may come whenever they wish." Classroom teachers must enable access from the classroom and into the library. Some teachers establish systems for allowing free-flow between the classroom and the library. For others, concern about student accountability demands more formalized systems. Systems as simple as creating passes for use in each classroom can govern how many students arrive at the library at once. Two to four passes per classroom, depending on school size and library capacity, may meet the needs. Or, using Twitter or text messages or other mobile messaging options can also facilitate access. One would hope that whenever a student has an information need, there is a way to seek the solution in a timely fashion.

Regularly scheduled book checkout/browsing time is another way to provide access. Daily checkout times for primary grade classes may be appropriate in many settings. This allows children to develop a sense of responsibility in a consistent pattern of borrowing and returning (Fox, 2001). Whatever the system, access for all students must be addressed.

Learning Commons

The very phrase *learning commons* conjures an image of a shared space where active learning occurs and where students and teachers feel welcome and comfortable. Advancing a vision of the school library that encompasses the idea of a learning commons is one way to support access—for access demands not only that the library is available but also that entering it is desirable for users. A library as learning commons affords spaces for a variety of activities: quiet spaces, group work spaces, creative spaces, social spaces, and instructional spaces. Technology—and the expertise to assist in its use— expands the reach of the learning commons. How these spaces are realized will vary between elementary and secondary schools, of course, but still a variety of opportunities should greet students and teachers entering any school library. The staff in the library as learning commons must also project its welcoming attitude and sense of shared ownership of the space. In some high schools, food and drink are becoming a part of the commons experience (Martin, Westmoreland, and Branyon, 2011), as school librarians follow the lead of public and academic libraries where coffee shops and vending machines are commonplace features to extend hospitality and welcome.

Important to the concept of access is that the learning commons creates an atmosphere that will attract students and teachers and encourage them to take advantage of the opportunities in the library.

A learning commons can extend the types of resources and assistance available to teachers and students as well. Schools where reading or writing support is provided for students may do well to integrate such resources into the commons area, just as academic libraries integrate writing centers, math and statistics support centers, technology support, and other learning resources to create a one-stop center for learning (Donham and Steele, 2007). The learning commons concept is evolving. It is not just a facility but also an attitude and a merger of various support systems for learning that result in teachers and students seeing value in accessing the school library. Valerie Diggs (Diggs and Loerstscher, 2009: 38), who was a trailblazer in bringing the idea of the learning commons to high schools, sums up its impact:

> The Learning Commons provides CHS students and staff members the opportunity to ask questions, think about answers, and create new meanings. We have become central to teaching and learning because our mission is tied to the mission and ideals of our school and district, and we are committed to offering our services and space to all of our constituents.

Circulation Policies

Librarians sit in a tenuous position between encouraging access to resources and acting as stewards of resources within their domain of responsibility. On the one hand, school librarians aim to conserve and protect public resources entrusted to the library and to develop in students a disposition of responsibility. On the other hand, school librarians aim to maximize access and encourage student and teacher use of those resources. The tension between these positions of protecting and promoting may too often result in more protecting than promoting. In *Empowering Learners* (AASL, 2009: 12) is the statement "All children deserve equitable access to books and reading." School librarians must carefully consider what the implications of this directive are for circulation policies. Krashen (2004) in *The Power of Reading* cites multiple studies that demonstrate access to books is crucial in developing strong readers. If school library programs truly aim for students to grow into lifelong learners and become literate citizens, then it is imperative to design policies that foster reading and information seeking and enable access. Limiting children to checking out one or two books, denying access when a student has an overdue book, and demanding that fines be paid before access privileges are restored are policies that inhibit access and create environments that limit the attraction of library use.

In an informal online poll in 2009, more than 65 percent of school librarians who responded indicated they limited circulation to fewer than four books per student ("One Question Survey," 2009); in fact, 30 percent limited circulation to fewer than three books across grade levels. Such limitations of access seem to run counter to the intent of the professional posture in favor of promoting access. Adams (2010) asserted that librarians should hold students accountable in some way for lost, damaged, or overdue books. However, she emphasized that there are many ways to teach the lesson of responsibility. Library policies should be sufficiently flexible to take into account students' personal and economic circumstances and to ensure that students have full access to library resources. Students can work off fines or fees, for example, or they can bring donations for food banks or other charitable collections as fines.

Ruefle (2011: 35) described her experience with moving away from limits on the number of books students may borrow and allowing them to check out as many as they wanted or needed. She stated in response to concerns about the stewardship of resources:

> None of my worries about excessive overdues or lost books came to fruition. We still have overdue books and lost books, certainly, but those numbers have never increased from when we had the two-books-at-a-time policy, though our circulation has gone through the roof. Students are more attentive to their books because they feel more connected to the library. It's not just about letting students have more books; it's about saying you trust them as readers and you trust them with the materials.

Circulation policies need to favor access if they are to support the principles and vision of the profession to promote literacy, support curiosity, and encourage learning for life. While responsible stewardship is important, school librarians do well to recall that some level of loss is the cost of doing business.

Scheduling for Instruction

Formal instruction in the school library is an important aspect of access. For young people to become effective and efficient users of the information resources a school library provides, an articulated instructional program needs to be in place. Scheduling students for instruction or research activities in the library poses different challenges at elementary and secondary levels. In many elementary schools, going to the library is no different from going to the art room or the music room. While it is good to consider the library a classroom because teaching and learning occur there, the library is more than a classroom. The library program has a curricular agenda of its own but is only relevant to students when integrated into the rest of the school curriculum. Secondary schools, on the other hand, have followed a more traditional library model, where classes visit when they have a need. Unlike at the elementary level, secondary school library programs have had to assert themselves as a teaching space.

Sending students to the library each week for a 30-minute class meets several needs: teachers need to have planning time, and all students need to have access to the library. The librarian needs to know the students in the school and to cover the library curriculum. However, inherent problems reside in counting on a weekly class schedule to achieve what should be a library program's goal—making students independently effective information consumers. The work students do in the library and the lessons they learn ought to have application to authentic information problems. Inquiry skills in the library curriculum are not analogous to music or art curricula where there is disciplinary content. In the library, students learn about the intellectual tools needed to accomplish work within content areas and develop important dispositions such as critical literacy and persistence. Regardless of the school level, learning theory supports flexible scheduling of library instruction at the point of need for the student. Learning to access, evaluate, and use information requires the opportunity to apply the learning to a problem or need. Such a context allows students to reflect on the specific skill and take action to use it, in keeping with constructivist theory of learning (Donham et al., 2001). Need-to-know will motivate students to gain skills and dispositions because the learning will be relevant to their needs.

Elementary School Scheduling Alternatives

Most commonly, the literature describes flexible scheduling and fixed scheduling as the two classic alternatives. *Fixed scheduling* means arranging classes to meet in the library on a regular basis, usually once a week or once a scheduling cycle. Classes meet for perhaps 30 minutes, and activities might include direct teaching by the librarian, storytimes, booktalks, book selection and checkout, or work on information-based projects. With fixed scheduling, librarians can create the year's schedule, showing when each class will come to the library. Space left in the schedule becomes time for specific library tasks such as cataloging and processing, preparation, meeting with teachers, and reference work, or it can be available for scheduling other library activities.

Alternatively, *flexible scheduling* is a plan whereby the school librarian teaches classes when students have a specific information-based assignment or project; these classes do not have library instructional time unless there is a need for it. For example, a class might come to the library every day for five days or for one day two weeks in a row for instruction or work on an assignment or project, and then may not receive instruction again until a class activity requires it.

BENEFITS OF FLEXIBLE SCHEDULING

Concern about retention of learning from one session to the next is one good reason to support flexible scheduling. When a librarian sets out to teach a complex process, it may take more than one class period to develop the skill or understanding. In weekly scheduled classes, seven days may intervene between the first and second lessons. How likely is it that students will retain learning from the first week in order to build on it the second week? Another factor is transfer of learning. Application to real needs is less likely in weekly scheduled classes where the activities may be unrelated to classroom work. What is the likelihood that students will automatically transfer what they learn about indexes to using the index in their American history textbook, unless there is teaching for transfer and the teaching in the library is integrated?

Weekly classes can prolong activities over several weeks, and such scheduling can decrease students' enthusiasm. If a librarian is teaching about keyword searching, for example, it may take several weekly lessons or more to complete the instruction. By the third or fourth installment, students' interest can easily decline. Although they have only spent 50 or 75 minutes on the topic, that time spread over several weeks makes it feel much longer.

One critical attribute of flexible scheduling is that classes may come to the library several days in a row in order to accomplish a task. The work that students do during the flexibly scheduled class time grows out of assignments from their classroom teacher so that library activity is timely—students have genuine concern about what they will learn because it has immediate relevance. In a flexibly scheduled library media program, no two weeks are alike. A disadvantage of flexible scheduling can arise if students have no flexible individual access to the library except when their classes come for instruction. While flexible scheduling tends to be the norm in high schools, fixed schedules tend to be the norm in elementary schools (Creighton, 2008).

For school librarians who have a fixed schedule, the time when they meet with students is typically the time when teachers are free to plan. They are therefore unable to participate, even briefly, with teachers during planning. Flexible scheduling should allow them to book themselves with teachers for collaborative planning. Flexible scheduling allows librarians to teach complex skills by having classes meet daily when needed in order to build understanding from one day to the next, rather than from one week to the next. Flexible scheduling is not intended to reduce the teaching in the library, nor is it intended to reduce contact with students. In fact, a study of time use among elementary school library media specialists found no significant difference in how much time was spent teaching between those with fixed schedules and those with flexible schedules (Donham van Deusen, 1996). If flexible scheduling does reduce teaching, then its implementation should be examined to determine if some prerequisite factors have not been met. While there may be no one exact formula, these six key conditions make it more likely to succeed:

Information/inquiry curriculum matched with content area curriculum. Teachers are more likely to embrace a proposal when they can understand the instructional aims. This requires that the school librarian develop and align a curriculum that intersects with content area expectations at each grade level. A concerted effort to map that alignment is a key to gaining teacher understanding and support.

Flexible access to the library. Because flexible scheduling may result in students no longer having weekly library visits, they must be assured of access to the library in other ways. Flexible access is one option; another is arranging specific times to browse and check out needed resources. Whatever approach is adopted, the librarian must ensure that a move to flexibly scheduled instruction does not constitute an end to student access to the library. Well-implemented flexible scheduling can have a favorable impact on library circulation. While limited by its population sample, a study by Gavigan, Pribesh, and Dickinson (2010) did find that elementary school libraries with flexible scheduling actually showed higher circulation counts per pupil than those with fixed schedules.

Collaborative planning between teachers and the school librarian. Research suggests that in schools where teachers plan as teams (by grade level or content area), flexible scheduling particularly enhances the consultation role of the school librarian (Donham van Deusen and Tallman, 1994). Although not determined to be causal, the relationship is clearly correlative. This finding suggests that the school librarian ought to provide some leadership toward teachers working together as teams if this structure is not already in place.

Principals' expectations for collaboration between teachers and the school librarian. Research has found that where some form of flexible scheduling was in place and principals had expectations for the librarian to participate in instructional planning with teachers, more such participation indeed occurred (Donham van Deusen, 1993). The importance of the principal perceiving that the library program is a collaborative partner in classroom instruction cannot be overlooked. The school librarian must help the principal see the relationship between the library program and the classroom and demonstrate that relationship in practice.

Commitment to resource-based learning (use of resources beyond a textbook). Textbooks tend to provide a single perspective. Dependence solely on a textbook negates the experience of integrating information from various sources—a lifelong learner skill. Further, textbooks afford little opportunity for differentiation in readability or learning style.

Support staff in the library. Research suggests that when library programs include support staff, professional librarians do significantly more consultation with teachers (Donham van Deusen, 1995). In that report, the operational definition of the consultation included five tasks: gathering materials for teachers, helping teachers identify instructional objectives, helping teachers plan learning activities, team-teaching, and evaluating the instruction. Three groups were analyzed: those with no paid support staff, those with up to 20 hours per week, and those with 20 hours or more per week. Those school librarians who had more than 20 hours of paid support staff in their libraries reported over 150 percent as many instances of four of the five consulting tasks (all except gathering materials) than those who had no support staff. With support staff available in the library, the library professional can meet with a teacher or a team, and students can still access the center and locate and use resources there. Of course, building size must be considered in determining an appropriate number of support staff. No significant differences were found between those with no support staff and those with fewer than 20 hours of assistance. These findings suggest that, at a minimum, it may take 20 hours per week of support staff to begin to make a difference in the librarian's collaborative work with teachers.

If these elements are lacking, it may be inappropriate to advocate for flexible scheduling. Without the requisite conditions, a move away from fixed scheduling can become a move toward no scheduling, which means students have little or no access to the library and little or no library instruction.

Perhaps the greatest challenge in a fixed schedule is making the transition toward a more flexible schedule. Since every school is different, there is no formula for making that happen, but there are some strategies to consider in light of the local situation. Shannon (1996) reported on two schools as they transitioned to flexible scheduling. She identified the following factors to be addressed in the transition:

Effective communication and public relations practices require careful attention. An advisory board was one strategy that was implemented in Shannon's case study. Creighton (2008) also supports a team approach to implementation to increase teacher buy-in.

School- and district-level support is essential. The principal's understanding and support are key and dependent on the school librarian's ability to articulate the vision.

Adequate resources are necessary for the library program to deliver on promises.

Professional development affords opportunities for teachers to gain insight into the content of the library curriculum, the vision for the program, and the expertise available in the teacher librarian.

MIXED SCHEDULING

Mixed scheduling offers a compromise between fixed and flexible scheduling, as it incorporates both kinds of scheduling. Totally flexible scheduling raises the concern that many students will never come to the library. Perhaps the teacher is reluctant to schedule the class into the library, perhaps the students' class or activity schedule limits the opportunities to visit the library, or perhaps the students have no motivation to go to the library. These students are missing out on opportunities to hone their ability to access, evaluate, and use information. They are also missing out on browsing—a particularly important activity for younger children who are less independent library users. Another concern is the teacher's release time. In many schools, teachers are dependent on the release time provided while the school librarian takes their classes, and they are understandably reluctant to give up that time. Often, this time is guaranteed in the teacher contract.

In response to these concerns for students and teachers, the library can schedule weekly or cyclical visits for classes and also offer flexible scheduling. In creating a mixed schedule, setting the times for the regularly scheduled classes is affected by several factors. Ideally, fixed schedules should be planned during times when other classes are having "specials" (e.g., art, music, physical education, or foreign language) or during mathematics when it might be less likely that those classes would need flexibly scheduled class time. Also, these classes can be short, say 15 or 20 minutes in length, because their purpose is scheduled access, not for teaching. It is likely that during this time the school librarian will not conduct formal instruction beyond a few brief booktalks or a short introduction to some new resource or perhaps share a storybook with young children. Alternatively, teachers and the school librarian can arrange daily open-visit times when children who want to exchange books or look for something in the library can visit in groups or individually for a short time—15 minutes, for example. Setting aside specific times each day when teachers can feel comfortable sending students on their own also increases access. These visits are single purpose: to ensure that all students have regular and frequent access to the library. The majority of the library schedule remains flexible so that when a class needs sustained instruction or guided information work, that need can be met. The flexibly scheduled time remains a high priority. If space and support staff are adequate, flexibly scheduled classes can be double-booked during weekly checkout visits, once regular visitors establish an appropriate level of independence or support staff can monitor them so that the school librarian can work with classes. Supervision of regularly scheduled checkout groups can even be delegated to a volunteer; the times are predictable, and the necessary skills can easily be taught to. Although many school librarians may feel that the mixed schedule is a stop-gap measure, research suggests that the option is indeed worthy of consideration. In a national study of scheduling, Donham van Deusen and Tallman (1994) found that compared to librarians with fixed scheduling, those with mixed schedules participated in significantly more consultation with teachers. In the same study, those school librarians with mixed schedules significantly outperformed those with both fixed and flexible scheduling in how frequently they incorporated instruction with classroom curriculum activities. These research results highlight the potential for combining fixed schedule classes and flexibly scheduled classes.

The example of a mixed schedule in Figure 7.1 requires some explanation. This schedule for a four-section K–5 school is intended to show that mixed scheduling is a feasible option. Each class has a weekly scheduled checkout time to ensure that all students have regular access to the library. The teacher may or may not accompany the group, depending on local priorities for teacher release time. Generally, these regular sessions are scheduled at times unlikely to be sought for flexible scheduling. Preparation time is set for the school librarian each day. This time could be considered flexible as well and exchanged for designated flexible time slots to accommodate classroom schedules. Also, a weekly meeting time with the principal is built into this schedule. A time slot is reserved for a grade-level meeting for each grade weekly. Again, depending on local culture, this time may be to meet with a grade-level team, or it may be collaboration time with a particular teacher.

FIGURE 7.1

Feasibility: Mixed Schedule K–5 Building with Four Sections per Grade

	Monday	Tuesday	Wednesday	Thursday	Friday
8:00–8:30	Team K	Team 1	Team 2	Prep	Prep
8:30–9:00	Fixed 1-A	Fixed 1-B	Fixed 2-A	Fixed K-A	Fixed K-B
9:00–9:30	Prep	Prep	Fixed 2-D	Team 4	Team 3
9:30–10:00	Fixed 1-D	Fixed K-D	Fixed 2-B	Principal	Fixed K-C
10:00–10:30					
10:30–11:00					
11:00–11:30	Fixed 1-C	Fixed 3-D	Fixed 2-C		
11:30–12:00	Lunch	Lunch	Lunch	Lunch	Lunch
12:00–12:30	Fixed 3-A	Fixed 3-B	Fixed 3-C	Prep	Fixed 5-D
12:30–1:00	Prep	Prep	Prep	Fixed 3-D	Prep
1:00–1:30					
1:30–2:00					
2:00–2:30	Fixed 4-A	Fixed 4-B	Fixed 4-C		
2:30–3:00	Fixed 5-A	Fixed 5-B	Fixed 5-C	Fixed 4-D	
3:00–3:30	Team 5	Prep	Prep	Prep	Prep

The point is that time is reserved in the school librarian's week for collaborative planning with teachers. Shaded time periods are available for flexibly scheduled sessions; these slots afford opportunities for longer learning sessions—ideal if possible so that extended work can be accomplished. Teachers do not have designated time slots for their flexibly scheduled classes. Instead, they schedule classes to fit their teaching needs; for activities in reading, a given class may come to the librarian during reading class, but that class may be scheduled to come in the afternoon during science class if a project requires library resources and instruction in science. The classroom schedule drives the library schedule.

The model shown would accommodate three extended projects per class per year, assuming a week of instruction for each project with each session lasting one hour. In fact, many projects could require less library instruction time than that. The takeaway is that a mixed schedule is feasible. If a school librarian were successful in creating three extended instructional units per

grade per year, the library program would be well along in implen
comprehensive inquiry-based curriculum while retaining the access
of weekly visits by all elementary school classes.

Scheduling Instruction in Secondary Schools

Since flexible scheduling is the norm in secondary schools, the responsibility
for advocating for the importance of instruction in the library is substantial
at this level. Secondary teachers tend to place a high value on the content
of their curriculum. Further, they tend to assume that students at their level
already know all they need to know about the inquiry process, information
technology, and the importance of researcher dispositions of critical stance
and persistence, as well as the responsibility for ethical use of information.
Where departmental meetings are part of the culture, school librarians can
seek opportunities there to demonstrate what learning opportunities exist
when teachers schedule classes into the library. Attending to content area
curricula, learning about assignments, and examining assessment data that
reveal student learning needs are approaches to gaining a foothold in order
to encourage scheduling for formal instruction in the library. Of particular
importance is what message goes out among teachers after an instructional
experience in the library. Word of mouth among teachers can be a key advocacy tool, so it behooves school librarians to plan instruction carefully and
design lessons that engage learners in applying lessons to relevant work.

Secondary school schedules vary based on the culture of the school. Some
schools retain the conventional comprehensive high school schedule of six
to eight class periods per day. Others have adopted a block schedule plan
where classes meet on alternate days for longer periods. With conventional
scheduling, instruction in the library needs to be efficient. Complementary technology aids on the library website aimed at particular assignments or courses
help streamline the use of instructional time in the library. Students need
opportunities for applying lessons learned to the requirements they bring from
the classroom. The advantage of a block schedule's longer periods for instruction in the library is readily apparent—teachers need to vary activities over
the longer period, and the library provides a readily available option. Further,
block scheduling offers secondary school librarians the opportunity to teach
inquiry skills and strategies in greater depth. More research occurs at this
level, and class periods are long enough to accommodate direct instruction
and hands-on engagement in the context of a real need (Richmond, 1999). An

informal survey of school librarians who have block scheduling indicated from 30 to 100 percent increases in class use of the library. They cite a change in teaching methods, including more student research activities (Gierke, 1999).

Conclusion

Physical access to the library encompasses setting hours and policies that encourage and support use of the library space and resources. Further, it is imperative that the library program adopt an environment and ambience that encourages access. The concept of a learning commons may assist in conveying to potential users the intention of the library to be not merely accessible but also hospitable to the variety of its potential users and their learning needs. Scheduling formal instruction in the library brings together physical access to the library's resources and intellectual access to use those resources intelligently and efficiently to solve information problems. Such scheduling should aim to provide opportunities to integrate the library instructional program with the classroom curriculum to afford opportunities for students to apply the lessons. Physical access is, of course, complemented by the 24/7 access to library resources made available via the virtual library.

Leadership Strategies

Teacher and Partner

Provide in-service for teachers about the library curriculum. Demonstrate with local examples how inquiry skills can be incorporated into what teachers are teaching. Show an example of a class that could come to the library every day for five days in a row to complete a project (compared to dragging a project out over weeks because it is done one period per week).

Engage teachers in discussion of free voluntary reading and identify ways to help keep students reading (e.g., by infusing trade books into curriculum and assignment expectations, finding times for booktalks and other "marketing" techniques, and identifying browsing times for students).

Design lessons to help students adopt a responsible disposition for the resources in the library.

Information Specialist

>   Consider mixed scheduling in elementary schools as an appropriate way to accommodate as many needs as possible.

>   In schools with block scheduling, offer booktalks during classes to encourage students to use the library for reading. These sessions can be 15-minute segments of the longer class periods. In some classes, booktalks might be thematic to fit classroom units; in other cases, booktalks may be aimed at recreational reading interests.

>   Consider providing Skype or Meebo chat hours where students can access assistance (Hornberger, 2011).

Program Administrator

>   Meet with the principal to discuss options for scheduling for instruction in the library.

>   Review and design circulation policies that promote access. Be ready with alternatives to limiting access as a consequence for overdue or missing materials.

Scenarios for Discussion

Scenario 1

Hughes High School has transitioned to block scheduling, which is now in its second year. The school librarian keeps a calendar on the circulation desk where teachers can reserve space in the library for classes. The calendar asks them to key in whether they want space (S), instruction (I), or guidance (G) while they are there. Now that classes are longer, two social studies teachers have begun to schedule their classes into the library routinely for "research time." Their typical practice is to meet with their class in the classroom for 20 minutes and then parade them to the library to do research. They mark "S" on the library calendar, indicating that they just want to use the space. Each class has arrived in the library at least twice a week for the past month. The librarian has asked the teachers whether she can provide specific guidance or instruction for the projects students are doing. Both teachers have said, however, that their seniors probably don't need any help—they just need to be in the library where they can get at resources they need. Meanwhile, the students from these classes are at workstations around the library surfing the web. What's next?

Scenario 2

Martin is a new elementary school librarian, and he has found in the policy manual created by his predecessor the circulation rules and policies for the library. Each class comes to the library once a week for "book exchange." Kindergarteners may borrow one book; first-graders may borrow one book. Second-graders may borrow two books; third-, fourth-, and fifth-graders may borrow three books. Books are due in one week and may be renewed once. No books may be borrowed by any student who has an overdue item. Martin wants to be cautious about making changes as the newcomer in the school, but he would like to move toward a more promotional set of circulation policies. What steps should he take? What policies should he attempt to establish?

REFERENCES

AASL (American Association of School Librarians). 2007. *Empowering Learners: Guidelines for School Library Programs*. Chicago: American Library Association.

Adams, H. R. 2010. "The 'Overdue' Blues: A Dilemma for School Librarians." *School Library Monthly* 26, no. 9: 48–49.

———. 2011. "Serving Homeless Children in the School Library—Part 2." *School Library Monthly* 27, no. 4: 52–53.

Creighton, P. M. 2008. "Flexible Scheduling: Making the Transition." *School Library Monthly* 24, no. 5: 24–27.

Despines, J. 2001. "Planning for Extended Hours: A Survey of Practice." *Knowledge Quest* 30, no. 2: 22–26.

Dickinson, G., K. Gavigan, and S. Pribesh. 2008. "Open and Accessible: The Relationship between Closures and Circulation in School Library Media Centers." *School Library Media Research* 11. www.ala.org/aasl/slmr.

Diggs, V., and D. V. Loertscher. 2009. "From Library to Learning Commons: A Metamorphosis." *Teacher Librarian* 36, no. 4: 32-38.

Donham, J., K. Bishop, C. C. Kuhlthau, and D. Oberg. 2001. *Inquiry Based Teaching: Lessons from Library Power*. Worthington, OH: Linworth.

Donham, J., and M. Steele, 2007. "Instructional Interventions across the Inquiry Process." *College and Undergraduate Libraries* 14, no. 4: 3–18.

Donham van Deusen, J. 1993. "Effects of Fixed versus Flexible Scheduling on Curriculum Involvement and Skills Integration in Elementary School Library Media Programs." *School Library Media Quarterly* 21, no. 3: 173–182.

———. 1995. "Prerequisites for Flexible Scheduling." *Emergency Librarian* 23, no. 1: 16–18.

———. 1996. "An Analysis of the Time-Use of Elementary School Library Media Specialists and Factors that Influence It." *School Library Media Quarterly* 24, no. 2: 85–92.

Donham van Deusen, J., and J. I. Tallman. 1994. "The Impact of Scheduling on Curriculum Consultation and Information Skills Instruction." *School Library Media Quarterly* 23, no. 1: 17–25.

Fox, C. J. 2001. "Designing a Flexible Schedule for an Elementary School Library Media Center." *Library Talk* 14, no. 1: 10–13.

Gavigan, K., S. Pribesh, and G. Dickinson. 2010. "Fixed or Flexible Schedule? Schedule Impacts and School Library Circulation." *Library and Information Science Research* 32, no. 2: 131–137.

Gierke, C. 1999. "What's Behind Block Scheduling?" *Book Report* 18, no. 2: 8–10.

Hornberger, K. 2011. "Your Library: An Educational Lifeline." *Learning Media* 39, no. 3: 11–12.

Krashen, S. 2004. *The Power of Reading: Insights from the Research.* 2nd ed. Westport, CT: Libraries Unlimited.

McCrann, G. 2005. "Contemporary Forces That Supported the Founding of the Boston Public Library." *Public Libraries* 44, no. 4: 223–228.

Martin, A. M., D. D. Westmoreland, and A. Branyon. 2011. "New Design Considerations That Transform the Library into an Indispensible Learning Environment." *Teacher Librarian* 38, no. 5: 15–20.

"One Question Survey." 2009. *Library Media Connection* 28, no. 2: 47.

Richmond, G. 1999. "Block Scheduling: From Principles to Practice." *Book Report* 18, no. 2: 12–14.

Ruefle, A. E. 2011. "Rules or Reading?" *Library Media Connection* 29, no. 6: 34–35.

Shannon, D. M. 1996. "Tracking the Transition to a Flexible Access Library Program in Two Library Power Elementary Schools." *School Library Media Quarterly* 24, no. 3: 155–163.

8

Collection

This chapter:

- defines *collection* as a multidimensional set of resources;
- discusses selection criteria and policies;
- considers the demands of special populations for resources;
- discusses collection maintenance and evaluation;
- describes the process for reconsideration of challenged materials; and
- identifies leadership strategies related to collection.

In contrast to times past, today the definition of a library collection is dynamic and complex. Perhaps one way to conceptualize this collection is to limit it to those resources intentionally made available through the library—physical and virtual. This would include purchased resources in the library such as books, DVDs, and print magazines as well as the virtual resources purchased and owned by the library—namely, collections of e-books. Secondly, the collection also would include those virtual resources available through subscription, such as online databases, some online audiobook collections, and some online reference resources. A third dimension of the collection might be those virtual resources that the library program intentionally makes accessible, such as applications like Prezi, Moodle, Animoto, or Diigo as well as links to specific content pages such as Goodreads, the American Memory, Exploratorium, or Digital Vaults. A collection defined as these three types of resources calls for consideration of each category both separately and collectively—factors related to selection criteria for each resource and overall factors related to the content of the collection and its responsiveness to curriculum and user needs.

Purchased-to-Own Resources

Naively, administrators sometimes assume that electronic access to information will justify reducing the budget for materials. For several reasons, this is simply not true. For example, the elementary school's reading program demands print resources for children to read, and the mathematics program demands manipulative materials such as items to count and sort or items with which to measure. Students in science classes will continue to use models to understand scientific principles. Students seeking a quick answer to a fact question may find it most efficient to look in an almanac or another fact book. Voluntary "reading" will continue to occur between covers as well as on screens or through earbuds. A collection that includes both electronic and print resources is likely to continue to characterize school libraries.

High-use patterns should be documented to show that teaching and learning are dependent on the library's physical collection as well as its access to online information. The constant rate of book publishing for children and youth promises no imminent demise in print materials, and the infusion of books into content-area learning signals a continued demand. That means budgets will need to keep pace with the market prices. According to the *2011 Library and Book Trade Almanac*, the average price of a children's hardcover book was $24.29. Renewed emphasis in the Common Core Curriculum on students reading complex text suggests a continued demand for physical textual resources along with online text. Budgets for physical collections continue to be needed for books as well as other formats to complement online access.

Selection Policy for Physical Resources

Each school district should have a formal, board-approved policy governing materials selection and reconsideration. In her seminal study, Hopkins (1991) found that in those schools where a formal policy exists, school librarians felt less pressure to be overly cautious in their selection practices. The board-approved selection policy should include the following features:

> *Statement of responsibility for selection.* This statement is often a delegation of authority to a particular staff member:
>> • The responsibility for the selection of library information and materials is delegated to the librarian(s) employed by the

district. Responsibility for selection of classroom instructional materials is delegated to ad hoc and/or standing textbook selection committees. While the responsibility for final selection and recommendation of resources rests with the licensed school library personnel for library materials and with designated committees with text materials, recommendations will be welcomed from principals, teachers, students, supervisors, and community members.

Criteria for selection. General criteria might include these qualities:

- Consistent with the general educational goals of the district and the objectives of specific courses
- High in quality of factual content and presentation
- Appropriate for the subject area and for the age, emotional level, ability level, and social development of the students for whom the materials are intended
- Of aesthetic, literary, or social value
- Authored by competent and qualified authors and producers
- Written to foster respect for women and minority and ethnic groups
- Selected for strengths rather than rejected for weaknesses
- Suitable in physical format and appearance for intended use
- Capable of providing ideological balance on controversial issues

Selection procedures. Procedures for selection should accomplish the following:

- Ensure quality by advocating use of reviewing media and professional selection tools.
- Provide for gathering input from the library program's constituencies.
- Establish gift criteria consistent with those applied to new purchases.
- Guide weeding and periodic replacement of both materials and hardware.

Reconsideration process. It is essential to have a written procedure for any community member to request formally that an item be reconsidered for inclusion in the collection. This process should include the following elements:

- Composition and operation of the reconsideration committee
- Description of the review process
- Statement of the next course of action in the event of a failure to resolve the concern

When a person raises an objection, it is essential to adhere to a written process. Key elements here are the makeup of the committee, the timeliness of action, and the expectation that the person raising the complaint has read the entire document being challenged and has completed a request for reconsideration form. Many experts recommend that the committee be closely balanced between citizens and educators. Some suggest that a balance slightly favor citizens to afford the opportunity for them to express their views, and yet also consider that the presence of educators provides professional expertise and perspective. Further, a balance slightly in favor of citizens may lend greater credence to the outcome. However, the makeup of the committee is a local decision. Possible representatives for the school would include librarians, teachers, administrators, and high school students. Citizen representatives may come from parent organizations, school advisory committees, or community leader groups. Timeliness of response is important lest the issue languish or gain momentum.

Request for Reconsideration

The procedure for objecting to resources held in a school library is outlined as follows:

1. The staff member receiving a complaint regarding library materials shall try to resolve the issue informally. The materials shall remain in use. The staff member initially receiving the complaint shall:

    a. explain to the complainant the school's selection policy, procedure, and criteria.

    b. explain the particular place the material occupies in the educational program and its intended educational use, or refer the complainant to someone who can identify and explain use of the material.

2. If the objection to material is not satisfied informally, the person will be given a Reconsideration Request Form.

3. The individual receiving the initial complaint shall advise the school principal of the initial contact no later than the end of the following school day, whether or not the complainant has apparently been satisfied by the initial contact. The principal shall maintain a written record of the contact. Each school will keep on hand and make available Reconsideration Request Forms. All formal objections to library materials shall be made on this form.

4. The Reconsideration Request Form shall be signed by the complainant and filed with the superintendent.

5. Within five (5) school days from receipt of the "Request for Reconsideration" in the superintendent's office, the Reconsideration Committee will be convened. The following will constitute this committee:

    a. Superintendent's designee

    b. One building administrator designated annually by the superintendent

    c. One teacher designated annually by local teachers association

    d. One school librarian designated annually by the superintendent

    e. One community representative designated annually from the Superintendent's Advisory Committee

    f. Two representatives designated annually by the District Parent Organization

    g. One high school student designated annually by a high school principal

6. The superintendent's designee will chair the committee and be a nonvoting member. A secretary will be appointed to keep minutes of record to be used in the development of the written decision.

7. The committee shall consider input from the complainant and professionally prepared reviews of the materials when available, and the committee may request input from others with special knowledge as needed.

8. Within twenty (20) school days from receipt of the Request for Reconsideration, the committee shall arrive at a decision by consensus and forward that written decision to the superintendent, to the complainant, and to the relevant attendance center. The committee's final decision will be:

   a. to not remove the challenged materials,

   b. to remove all or part of the challenged materials, or

   c. to limit the use of the challenged materials.

Committee members directly associated with the selection, use, or challenge of the materials shall be excused from the committee during the deliberation on such materials. The superintendent may appoint a temporary replacement for the excused committee member, but such replacement shall be of the same general qualifications of that person excused. If not satisfied with the decision, any person may request that the matter be placed on the agenda of the next regularly scheduled meeting of the board.

The committee shall first meet each year before the end of September. At the first meeting, the committee will be instructed on the selection policy and process and issues related to intellectual freedom. Subsequent meetings will be called as needed. The committee shall receive all Reconsideration Request Forms from the superintendent. The procedure for the first meeting following receipt of a Reconsideration Request Form is as follows:

1. Distribute copies of written request form.

2. Give the complainant an opportunity to talk about and expand on the request form.

3. Distribute reputable, professionally prepared reviews of the material when available.

4. Distribute copies of challenged material as available.

A standard form for filing an objection is important to the integrity of the process. Figure 8.1 provides a model of such a form.

Hopkins (1993: 29) found that "support for retention of challenged materials from persons/organizations within or outside the district was greater for written challenges" and that written rather than oral challenges predominate when there is a selection policy in place. One can usually expect the due process afforded by a written selection policy to more likely result in retaining challenged materials. These findings underscore the importance of insisting upon a written, board-approved policy in order to protect intellectual freedom.

Responses to materials challenges must strike a balance between the individual's right to protest the inclusion of a particular item in the collection, the librarian's responsibility to select materials based on objective criteria rather than on personal beliefs or biases, and the institution's right to remove material deemed inappropriate after reasonable due process. Due process is a critical factor in reconsideration cases, and the lack of due process has been the turning point for cases taken to the judicial system. The intent of due process is to avoid arbitrary decisions based on an individual's viewpoint or bias. Challenges represent freedom of expression and should not be labeled as inherently harmful. By providing a procedure for reconsideration of challenged materials, the institution is in effect stating that it will indeed reconsider a decision and give that reconsideration due attention and due process. This is a circumstance that brings the library program and its constituencies together, and mutual respect is the intended result. The intent of the principle of intellectual freedom is to ensure the right of any person to hold any belief and to express such beliefs or ideas. Censorship, on the other hand, is a denial of the right of freedom of expression; it is a negative act and a way of imposing one's beliefs on others. School librarians strive to provide their users a full range of information and ideas and to protect users' free access to information and various perspectives.

In schools, the issue of challenged materials is complicated by the definition of a public forum. A classroom is not a public forum; students are required to attend school, and the curriculum is under the purview of the school board. In *Minarcini v. Strongsville City School District* (1976), maintenance of a book on a library shelf and maintenance of material required for a course were considered two distinct issues. This case involved a class-action suit brought against a school board by five high school students when the board refused to adopt certain titles recommended by an English teacher for a course. The

FIGURE 8.1
Form for Reconsideration Request

Author: _____

Title: _____

Type of material:_____ Publisher/Producer:_____

Request initiated by:

Name:_____ Telephone:_____

E-mail: _____

Address: _____

School in which item is used: _____

Complainant represents:

_____ Himself/Herself

_____ Organization: _____

---

1. Did you review the entire item? If not, what section(s) did you review?

2. Please list your specific objection, citing exact passages or scenes, page numbers, etc.

3. Do you perceive any positive cultural, educational, or historical value in this item?

4. What effect do you think this material would have on your child/children?

6. For what level would this material be more appropriate?

7. In its place, what material would you recommend?

Signature of Complainant: _____ Date: _____

board also ordered removal of the books from the school library. At the appellate level, the issues of library access and classroom requirement were separated. The court found that the board had oversight responsibility for selecting materials to be required of students, but that the library would continue to provide access to the books. This is an important distinction when addressing reconsideration requests.

Often in schools, issues of age appropriateness are central to reconsideration discussions. Parents, in sincere efforts to protect their children, may raise concerns about materials that are available in school library collections. Often, such concerns can be alleviated by conversations with parents to indicate that what one parent finds too mature for a child, another parent finds ideal. The library collection must be responsive to a larger public; if a parent has concerns about his or her child's selections, that issue ought to be addressed within the family. One proactive approach to concerns about materials is for the librarian to offer a parent organization program about the process of materials selection. Parents can learn the criteria identified in the selection policy, the reviewing media on which the school librarian relies, and other sources of information and factors considered in purchasing decisions. Knowing the complexity of selection and the care taken in these decisions may be enough to alleviate many parents' anxiety.

Still, complaints will come. Sometimes the complaint will go directly to the principal. Proactively, the school librarian should periodically remind the principal of the selection and reconsideration policies to prepare him or her for such a complaint. Caught unaware, the principal may be inclined to immediately concede to the parent and agree to censor an item. Such a response becomes very difficult to reverse. Hence, keeping the principal alerted to the appropriate response is important. Sometimes the complaint will come directly to the school librarian, who then has six steps to take in response to a complaint about an item in the collection:

1. Listen sincerely to the position of the complainant.

2. Stress the need to respect diversity of the many people who use this collection.

3. Inform the complainant of how the material is used and how it was selected.

4. Explain the procedure for formal reconsideration.

5. Provide the appropriate form for a formal request for reconsideration.

6. Inform the principal, because no principal wants to be blindsided by a potential controversy.

Two important factors about challenged materials are worth remembering. First, the citizen has the right to complain. Second, if a committee elects to remove an item, removal does not represent a failure on the part of the librarian, nor does it represent censorship when there is appropriate due process.

Selection Tools for Purchased Resources

Educators outside the library profession often assume that building a collection is simply a matter of going shopping. However, building a true collection is more complex than that. Collection development requires considering the needs of users and examining the available resources to choose those that are the best fit. Various resources assist the librarian in determining what is available. A school librarian is responsible to spend public funds wisely. This responsibility calls for careful consideration in the selection process, and most especially a call for quality of resources. In nonfiction, we seek authoritative information as a mark of quality. In fiction, literary characteristics that make for a "good read" include well-rounded character development, engaging plot, themes of significance and interest, and appealing style. To assess potential purchases, school librarians make use of professional selection tools and reviewing media to help in identifying resources to purchase. A sobering thought is the fact that resources purchased today may still be in the collection up to ten or even more years from now, based on the view of shelves in most school libraries today. Hence, selection decisions need to be made with care. Librarians engage in two types of selection for a collection—ongoing general updating and focused collection development projects. When proposing a budget for a collection, both types of purchasing should be included as lines in the proposal. Each year should see at least one focused project where the librarian works collaboratively with other educators in the school to assess existing resources and make specific purchases. Such projects are typically curriculum-driven and can be identified by analyzing unmet or underserved needs. For example, when a collaborative unit on the American Civil War reveals gaps in information or an antiquated, unappealing collection, this topic can be placed on a list for a focused collection project. When budget proposals are submitted to the administration, the librarian can call on the educator whose students' needs went unmet to support allocation of dollars to resolve the weakness.

For ongoing collection updating, many school librarians rely on the monthly reviews from *Horn Book, School Library Journal, Booklist, Library Media Connection,* or the *Bulletin of the Center for Children's Books.* Each reviewing source has its own criteria and its own style. For example, *School Library Journal* often considers the pragmatic in suggesting where in a curriculum a particular text might fit. *Horn Book* may detail more fully literary or aesthetic aspects of a text. In addition, school librarians rely on award and notable lists—state children's choice awards, notable/outstanding lists from the National Science Teachers Association (www.nsta.org/publications/ostb) and the National Council for the Social Studies (www.socialstudies.org/resources/notable), and national awards from the Association for Library Service to Children (e.g., Newbery, Belpré, and Caldecott awards).

For focused collection development projects, school librarians are likely to consult bibliographies or resources specific to their project. The *Wilson Core Collections* for the appropriate level (elementary, middle, or high school) can be a useful resource against which to check one's collection in a particular subject area because it lists well-reviewed resources currently in print and can be searched by subject. More specifically, a school librarian who is expanding the collection of books for emergent readers, for example, may consult a Bowker publication, *Beyond Picture Books: Subject Access to Best Beginning Readers* by Barbara Barstow. Or, to enhance and update a collection's historical fiction might take a school librarian to a source like Melissa Rabey's (2011) *Historical Fiction for Teens: A Genre Guide.* Purchase of a selection guide to inform decisions should be an item added to the library budget proposal. Some librarians rely on jobber resources (e.g., Follett's *TitleWave*) for selection decisions. Through readers' editorial reviews, Amazon.com has become increasingly popular as an easily accessible resource for identifying what is available from a particular author or on a particular subject. While commercial vendor tools can be handy and helpful, it is important to recall that they represent those resources held in inventory by that jobber—not necessarily all that is available or perhaps not even the best that is available. Hence, using professional resources to supplement jobber databases increases the likelihood of a comprehensive and high-quality result.

Electronic Purchased Resources

Included in purchased resources are electronic resources that are actually purchased and become part of the library's collection. Such resources may include e-books and audiobooks, including purchased reference resources. These are distinguished from online subscriptions, which distinction is important when presenting a budget proposal to administrators because they are investments in materials rather than rental of information access (as occurs in subscription databases or other year-to-year pricing structures). Examples of vendors for such purchased resources include digital content distributors like Overdrive or NetLibrary (EBSCO owned). Business plans for digital content are in a state of flux as vendors work out profitable models, so school librarians will need to be diligent in investigating any fees or annual costs associated with these "purchased" collections.

Curriculum Priority

Owned resources in school library collections must exist within fiscal constraints. Such constraints increasingly call for assessing how much of the collection will be driven by curriculum connections and how much will be driven by user interests—especially interests of students.

Curriculum-driven collections tend to have depth in those topics that the curriculum emphasizes. For example, a middle school where American history is taught is likely to have substantial depth in that topic, while it may have very little, if any, specialized resources on Asian history if not represented in the curriculum.

Student Needs and Interests

Results from the National Assessment of Educational Progress show that significant gaps in reading performance continue to exist between racial/ethnic subgroups (NCES, 2009). These data signal the need for providing collections of reading materials that are accessible for students reading below level. Nonnative speakers present another subpopulation of users for the library collection. One of the most salient features of this population is its diversity—in native language, world experience, cultural values and norms, and socioeconomic status. Peregoy and Boyle (2000: 238) describe this population and its challenges in the context of reading:

> What differ between native and non-native English readers are the cognitive-linguistic and experiential resources they bring to the reading

task, especially in terms of those variables that relate directly to reading comprehension in English, i.e., (a) English language proficiency, (b) background knowledge related to the text, and (c) literacy abilities and experiences, if any, in the first language.

A striking example is the difference between the native speaker of Chinese, who must adjust from symbols representing whole words or concepts to phonemes. Similarly, Arabic-language speakers must overcome a very different set of conventions as they approach a new alphabet. For the school library to provide resources that are age-appropriate and yet also developmentally appropriate for this group of students requires a conscious effort at seeking advice from teachers who specialize in teaching English language learners (ELL). Some clearly identifiable conditions call for consideration in collection development. According to the Federal Interagency Forum on Child and Family Statistics (2012: 3):

> A growing number of children in the United States have a foreign-born parent. The percentage of children ages 0–17 living with at least one foreign-born parent rose from 15 percent in 1994 to 23 percent in 2011. Twenty-one percent of children were native-born children with at least one foreign-born parent, and 3 percent were foreign-born children with at least one foreign-born parent

Not surprisingly, the growth in immigrant populations in schools has been accompanied by a rise in the size of the limited-English-proficiency population in schools to an estimated 21 percent of the total student population (NCES, 2011). While political climates change and the current wave suggests interest in establishing the predominance of English as the language of the nation, schools nevertheless continue to have children arriving at their doors speaking Spanish, Chinese, Japanese, Vietnamese, Russian, and a score of other languages. A majority of these students are Hispanic (Camarota, 2007). Providing materials that help these children develop their skills in English is an important contribution of the library program. Also important is providing materials in formats and styles that facilitate ELL content across all curricular areas. Marketing the library to these students is a critical part of advocacy. Electronic resources that offer voice as well as text may be particularly helpful to their language development.

Materials also need to show sensitivity to students' lives. In 2010, approximately 34 percent of all US children lived with only one parent (Annie E.

Casey Foundation, 2011). Children from single-parent families often have added stresses related to family conflict and the disruption and deprivations associated with living with a single parent. Their special needs deserve consideration in selection of resources to meet student personal reading and learning interests.

Subscribed Resources

The school library collection typically includes not only purchased resources but also subscription-based resources. Periodical databases and electronic reference tools are examples of subscriptions for most school libraries. A survey of states (Krueger, 2011) indicated that most states have some statewide periodical databases, although the extent of those statewide contracts varies. In addition, many states have statewide subscriptions to e-reference resources. Beyond those statewide subscriptions, however, school libraries typically purchase annual subscriptions to both periodical databases and online reference resources. These resources deserve careful consideration in the overall picture of the library collection because they may meet a substantial information need, and they can extend access to the library beyond the school day. When librarians build physical collections owned by the school, a budget shortfall for a year is problematic, but the library still has the accumulated collection of previous years to provide information. The subscribed part of the collection has no equity value; it is analogous to renting. The dollars must be available every year or all of the information goes away. As libraries move to online reference resources and online research databases, the advantages can be tremendous, including simultaneous use by many students, the possibility of access from both classrooms and homes, and 24/7 availability of authoritative and very current information. Librarians will need to pay attention to usage reports provided through these subscriptions in order to gauge use and make annual decisions regarding this virtual collection.

Accessed Resources

Besides subscription resources, the web offers access to a vast array of information resources, but they vary widely in quality, reliability, and stability.

To ensure access to quality information the school librarian can create web-pages or to use a product such as LibGuides (www.springshare.com) to create online resource guides for specific courses or assignments. This tool is particularly useful when a class is researching a topic that is a staple in the curriculum and when many students will be seeking information on the topic. (See chapter 10 for further discussion of LibGuides.)

Collaboration

Whether it is the purchased, subscribed, or accessed collection, school librarians usually have the primary responsibility for selecting resources. Yet the importance of collaboration with teachers on collection decisions cannot be overlooked. In the past, school librarians read reviews and based their selections largely on what the reviewers said, with an eye to what they thought their clients wanted. In integrated library programs, the emphasis may shift in favor of what the clients request, and secondarily to what the reviewers say. When school librarians are working with teachers' planning teams, they are in very close communication with what is being taught. That information helps prioritize according to curricular demands. As instructional units are discussed and evaluated, librarians learn what units have been frustrating for teachers and students because of resource deficiencies, and they learn where the collection has worked well. Direct involvement with teachers in planning and evaluating instruction is key to ensuring good collection development decisions.

Mapping the Collection and the Curriculum

Curriculum mapping and collection mapping are two strategies useful for assessing how well the collection fits the curriculum. *Curriculum mapping* is a strategy for identifying the instructional content for each grade level or course, and summarizing it on a chart to show the spectrum (Jacobs, 2000). Charting the curriculum shows the articulation from grade to grade and course to course. If there are gaps, they become more obvious, and if there are inappropriate repetitions, they too are made manifest. Curriculum maps identify potential areas for interdisciplinary integration. For example, when *My Brother*

Sam Is Dead is being taught in a middle school language arts program, the curriculum map for the social studies program may reveal study of the American Revolution in the history curriculum, suggesting possibilities for curriculum integration. A curriculum map can help align curriculum with district or state standards. A curriculum map is a valuable tool for the school librarian—it facilitates anticipating topics so that appropriate resources can be selected to support instruction. The map should include three types of data: content (key concepts/essential questions), specific skills, and assessments. These data are charted according to grade level, teacher, discipline, or other data elements useful for articulation within a school or a school district. The curriculum map is a collaborative endeavor; the school librarian works with teachers by grade-level team (elementary) or by department (secondary) to create the map. The curriculum map becomes in essence a data source for needs assessment. By comparing that content to the collection, the school librarian can identify gaps.

Having the curriculum map provides essentially a guide to curriculum-driven needs to be met by the collection. A next step, then, is to map the collection in order to see how well it aligns with the curriculum and where gaps suggest a need for focused collection development. *Collection mapping* is a technique for identifying topics and determining the depth of holdings on those topics. For the cataloged and owned resources, Lowe (2001) recommends that school librarians print out their shelf list from the library automation system. Essential fields to include are the call number, the title, and the copyright date. The data in this report can be compared to the curriculum to determine where resources align with curriculum needs and where they do not. By examining the Dewey range relevant for a particular curricular area, the school librarian can assess both how extensive and how current the collection is to meet the demands of the curriculum. Most library automation systems provide a report option that includes call number, title, and copyright. Figure 8.2 shows an example of a report that maps a small section of a collection.

The report can be sorted by call number to match the collection with the curriculum, or by copyright to examine the need for updating within the selected call number range. A broader view of the collection and its relationship to curriculum can be seen in a report like the summary shown in Figure 8.3.

Next is the subscribed collection. For each Dewey range mapped, the librarian will note online databases and reference subscriptions that support information needs in that topic. In collaboration with teachers in each topic area, the librarian will want to discuss what format or formats the teachers

FIGURE 8.2

Collection Map: Dewey Range 570–583

Call Number	Title	Copyright
571.8	Plant life cycles	2005
571.8	Plant development and growth	2006
571.8	Pick pull snap	2003
571.8	Plant life cycles	2005
574.5	Look again	1992
574.526	The most beautiful roof in the world	1997
577.3	A walk in the woods	1990
577.3	If I ran the rain forest	2003
577.34	Into the forest	1996
577.4	A tallgrass prairie alphabet	2004
575.6	Flowers, fruits, and seeds	1999
578.75	A close look inside the garden	2005
580	What is a plant	2000
580	A parade of plants	2004
580	Plant	2005
580	Plants	2008
580	Plant secrets	2009
581.3	From seed to plant	1991
581.4	Seeds, stems, and stamens	2001
581.6	Plants bite back	1999
582	The reason for a flower	1992
582	All about seeds	1993
582.016	How a seed grows	1992
582.13	Freaky flowers	2002
583	Weird man-eating plants	2011

FIGURE 8.3

Collection Data for Curricular Emphases

Category	Average Copyright Date	Number of Volumes
Science 520s (Space Science)	2001	65
Science 550s (Earth Science)	1999	55
Science 580s (Plants)	2003	27
Science 590s (Animals)	2000	110
Technology 600s	2002	190
Social Studies 910s (Geography)	2003	130
Social Studies 970s (American History)	2001	310

prefer for their students. While this information may not be as quantifiable as the physical collection mapping, it is essential information. If, for example, the physical collection map shows a significant weakness in geography resources but the subscription collection is rich in this area with such resources as *Culture Grams* or *InfoTrac Junior Edition*, then the question becomes one of which format will be most useful to the students based on learning tasks in geography studies.

Finally, besides the subscribed resources, the school librarian needs to consider what web resources the library links to that provide consistent quality information in the subject area under review. In this instance, for example, such sites as the CIA World Fact Book or AllAfrica should be considered for the extent to which they meet information needs for this discipline. The conclusion may be that a relatively small book collection for geographic studies is appropriate, whereas other topics and teachers may require more book resources. Collection development is a complex balancing act and needs to be an informed process. Collection mapping and collaboration with teachers add up to informed decision making.

Identified gaps become targets of a purchase plan. Library selection tools (e.g., *Neal-Schuman Guide to Recommended Children's Books and Media for Use with Every Elementary Subject*) or specialized books (e.g., *A to Zoo: Subject Access to Children's Picture Books* or *Best Books for Young Teen Readers*) can then be used to identify quality resources to fill these gaps.

Focusing collection development on curriculum can create challenges. A focused collection will have gaps. When the collection does not respond to a query, the school librarian must use outside sources to provide assistance. Seeking information on the web is one avenue. Interlibrary loan with neighboring schools or public libraries is also a possible solution. Curriculum changes from time to time, and when it does, the changes will affect the collection. For example, when teachers who have taught a thematic literature unit on the Middle Ages for several years abandon it in favor of a thematic unit on heroes and heroines, few of the resources that have been collected for the former theme will apply to the new one, and many items about the Middle Ages will go largely unused, except for the rare independent request. Such a curriculum change calls for a supplement to the library media budget to accommodate the new in-depth demands on the collection.

Collection Maintenance

Materials

Maintaining a collection is as important as developing it. Collection maintenance involves two major processes: inventory and weeding. Inventory ensures that the materials included in the catalog are indeed in the collection. Automation has streamlined the process so that the collection can be efficiently inventoried with a bar code reader or scanner. High-use collections may deserve annual inventory. At a minimum, sections of the collection should be inventoried each year so that over a three-year period the entire collection is checked. During inventory, besides ensuring that materials are physically present, the librarian can check for condition and appearance to see whether items should be withdrawn or replaced.

A few years ago, a school librarian boxed up her entire collection over the summer so that the library could be repainted and carpeted. After the shelves were back in place, she began to unbox the collection. After two years in the school, she knew that the collection needed serious weeding and now felt she knew the curriculum and clientele well enough to proceed with that task. With the relevant *Core Collection* at hand to ensure that she did not remove a classic or a title that authorities suggest is the best available for its purpose, she began unboxing and considering each title. By the time she had finished, she had reduced the collection by more than one-third, ridding it of a 20-year accumulation of books now dusty, dirty, tattered, and dingy. At the opening of the school year, one student arrived in the library and remarked that he expected to see new carpet and paint but didn't know there would be so many new books too. In fact, the new books had not yet been unpacked; it was only that the existing collection looked so much better now that the newer books were visible and the worn-out ones were gone. This example highlights one benefit of collection maintenance: a collection needs to contain accurate and current information, and it is better to have no answer than to have an inaccurate or incorrect answer to a question. A second benefit is that weeding is important in making the collection attract users and in communicating that it is a recent and useful collection. Third, a collection needs to be attractive to its potential clientele, and eye appeal is particularly important to the young. A collection that goes unweeded will simply grow, use more space, and fail to serve the clientele. Given that the library collection includes not only the physical resources on its shelves but also the subscribed and accessible resources, it is inappropriate to keep an out-of-date item just to have "something" on a topic.

A schedule for weeding can coincide with the inventory schedule so that the collection is reviewed periodically for content as well. Age is a reasonable first criterion for considering materials for weeding. Longevity will vary by content area, so technical topics will age more quickly than life science, for example. Generally, materials between five (e.g., technical topics) and ten (e.g., religion or social sciences) years old can be pulled from the shelf and reviewed using other considerations, such as circulation data, physical condition, quality of the illustrative matter, and so on. In some topic areas, age may not be relevant at all, as would be the case with anatomy or general art books. See Figure 8.4 for a sample weeding schedule. Weeding can be approached in a relatively objective way:

> Establish a cutoff date for circulation (say, five years) and identify all titles that have not circulated within that period. This task should simply be a matter of generating a report from the circulation system.

> Pull from the shelves materials not circulated since the cutoff date.

> Ask teachers to examine materials in their areas and to flag those items to be retained.

FIGURE 8.4

Weeding Table

Class	Subject/Format	Age	Last Circ → Years Ago	Comments
000	General	5	NA	
	Computers	2–5	2	
030	Encyclopedia	5–10	NA	Not longer than ten years
100	Philos/Psych	15	3	
200	Religion	10	3	Retain basics; weed or do not accept propaganda/proselytizing
290	Mythology	15	5	Be conservative with classics
320	Poli Sci	5	3	
340	Law	10		
330	Economics	5	3	
350	Government	10	5	
360	Welfare	5	5	Discard career materials after five years
370	Education	10	3	
380	Commerce	10	5	
390	Etiquette	5	3	
	Customs/Folklore	15	5	Retain basics; classics
400	Language	10	3	Discard texts; retain basics, including dictionaries for languages studied
500	General Science	5	3	Retain classics
510	Math	10	3	
570	Biology/Nat History	10	3	
580	Botany	10	3	
600	General Technology	5	3	
610	Anatomy/Physiology	5		
	Other 610	10	3	
620	Applied Science	10	5	
630	Agriculture	10	5	
640	Homemaking	5	3	Retain cookbooks
650	Business	10	5	
660	Chemistry/Food	5–10	3–5	
690	Manufacturing	10	3–5	Retain material of historical interest
700	General			Retain basics, especially art history
745	Crafts		5	Retain well illustrated
770	Photography	5	3	Avoid dated techniques or equipment
800	Literature			Retain basics; check Wilson indexes before discarding
910	Travel/Geog	5–10	3–5	Retain expensive well illustrated
920	Biography	3–5		
F/E	Fiction/ Everybody		2–5	Retain high demand; literary merit; award-winning; well written; well illustrated. Check Wilson indexes

SOURCE: Adapted from Belinda Boon, *The Crew Method: Expanded Guidelines for Collection Evaluation and Weeding for Small and Medium-Sized Public Libraries* (Austin, TX: Texas State Library, 1995).

Evaluate the remaining items by checking to see whether the titles appear in the relevant *Core Collection*, as appropriate for the grade levels served. If a title appears in one of these resources, it is likely to be the best currently available title on the topic and probably should not be weeded. Review it for accuracy and currency.

Evaluate for physical condition.

Delete the bibliographic records for those items to be weeded.

Discard materials according to institutional policy. Generally, items weeded from the library media collection ought not to be distributed to teachers for their classroom. If they are not suitable for the library collection, they are most likely not suitable for classroom use either. In some districts, weeded titles are sent to a central facility for recycling or disposal. Cooperate with the custodial staff and principal to develop a method for disposal of weeded items.

Where weeding indicates an unfilled need, the librarian will want to add the topic to a consideration file to be addressed as a priority for future purchases.

Subscribed Resources

Because subscriptions tend to be annual, a natural cycle for assessment and decision making occurs. Renewal, cancellation, and new subscription decisions should be informed by advice from teachers and resources already owned or "accessed," as well as by usage data. Vendors of online subscriptions typically provide usage reports. Since these continue to lack industry standardization, the librarian needs to determine the meaning of data points reported, such as the meaning of a *search,* a *session,* a *hit,* or a *view* for each vendor. While these various definitions may make comparison across databases difficult, each will provide an indicator of use. Use of print subscriptions can be assessed through circulation data; however, in-house use is common for these resources, and unless these uses are counted, circulation data may be incomplete. Wear and tear may provide an estimate of use.

Input from teachers and/or students assists in determining both renewal and new subscription selections. Finally, it is important to stay attuned to new products in the marketplace through vendor exhibits at conferences and reading professional publications.

Accessed Resources
Because no costs are associated with online resources to which the library facilitates access, it is easy to overlook the need to maintain these links. However, the volatility of the virtual world demands that links be checked periodically for accuracy. Dead links send a message to users that a website cannot be trusted to be up to date, and the library can quickly lose the confidence of students and teachers. This task need not be a professional one, as volunteers can be assigned to check all links periodically.

Equipment

Equipment is an important part of the library collection. The Parchment (Michigan) School District (2012) technology plan offers a clear set of criteria for equipment purchase and maintenance. Included in the document is a rubric for equipment standards, including replacement cycle, brand and model selection, platform and operating system, application software, management of equipment and peripherals, surplus equipment, and security; thus it offers a framework for decision making. Four levels of equipment standards are described. The highest level includes the following criteria:

Replacement cycle. Three years is the accepted life cycle of equipment.

Brand selection. The district purchases one brand of equipment.

Model selection. Model selection is limited, with few exceptions.

Computer platform. A common platform is used throughout the district, with few exceptions.

Operating system. A consistent version of the OS is used across the district.

Application software. Acceptable software is listed.

Donated equipment. Equipment must meet district standards and be less than two years old.

Granted equipment. Equipment purchased through grants must meet district standards.

Peripherals. Brands and models are limited.

Surplus equipment. Equipment is taken out of service when it reaches replacement age.

Warranties. Equipment is warranted to cover its life expectancy.

Security. Guidelines and a firewall are in place.

While these guidelines may seem restrictive, it is clear that the aim is consistency across a school district to facilitate support of both hardware and software. This index provides an excellent and comprehensive approach to assessing the status of technology in a school district, and offers specific guidance to equipment management. Selecting equipment requires attention to detail. Comparison among brands and models is important because equipment is expensive, expected to last a long time, and gets hard use in schools. When one purchases a new stove or iron for home use, usually one or two people at most will be using it. The fact that school equipment will have many users makes the decision particularly weighty. Ease of use, reliability, durability, safety, and performance are all important factors. Creating a checklist for these five criteria and examining various makes and models side by side will more likely result in sound decisions. Another factor to consider carefully in equipment purchase is the reputation of the vendor. When negotiating for volume discounts, when equipment problems arise, when warranty work must be done, when it would be helpful to have a demonstration of a new piece of equipment, the vendor is the first contact. In most districts cost is the primary consideration and bids often go to the lowest bidder, but vendor service must still be considered as part of the purchase decision. It is possible to request that specific desired services be included in vendor bids. For volume purchases, it may be appropriate to include in the proposal a price and turnaround time for repairs or parts. Demonstrations or in-service training sessions could also be written into the proposal. The inclusion of some of these services may eliminate a few low-cost bidders, but the result may lead to better service in the long run.

Leasing is an increasingly common method of providing up-to-date technology in schools. Lease agreements can enable more frequent refreshing of equipment in a school. An important consideration here is that leased hardware expenses must be budgeted annually. Leases will require routine renewal or renegotiation of the lease, forcing districts to budget regularly for equipment acquisition.

Donated equipment can often be more of a liability than a real benefit. The selection policy should include a disclaimer granting the school the right to use or dispose of donated equipment and stating the maximum acceptable age for donated equipment. Consider the following factors when deciding whether to accept donated equipment (Reilly, 2003):

Opportunity costs. Will accepting the donations preclude the purchase of more current technologies?

Software licensing. Does licensing require that any accompanying software be transferred to the school?

Hardware. Does it work? What maintenance challenges does it present (e.g., cost, availability of parts)?

Training. Do staff members know how to use this equipment?

Networking. Is the hardware compatible with your network?

Location. Where in your school will this equipment meet a need?

Equipment budgets can be defined for new equipment and replacement equipment. Any time new equipment (not replacement) is acquired, the replacement budget at the end of its life expectancy should be set to accommodate its replacement. For example, an added computer's initial cost should be added to the replacement budget for six years postpurchase. A replacement strategy known as *tiering* involves identifying installations that require high-end computers and placing new machines there, perhaps every three years, and then passing older machines down to installations where power and speed can be lower yet still serviceable. While there often may be complaints of receiving hand-me-down equipment, this practice does maximize the use of available equipment efficiently.

Computer peripherals such as printers, scanners, and removable storage devices generally have a functional longevity of approximately five years. That is not to say that new and desirable models don't become available more frequently, but the functions for which the devices were purchased can typically be met for about five years. A replacement budget for peripheral equipment can be estimated by adding the purchase price to the replacement budget for five years hence.

A replacement cycle is a guide, not a rule. The school librarian must make decisions about whether equipment really needs to be upgraded or replaced; the cycle serves only to encourage equipment review in a proactive manner.

An equipment inventory is necessary for insurance coverage. Some librarians create catalog records for their equipment and bar code the equipment for circulation. Another approach is to set up an equipment database. For each item, the minimum fields of information are item name, make, model, purchase date, repair history, bulb/battery type, and cost. Generating reports from the inventory will provide information for making solid proposals for replacement funds and sound decisions regarding equipment replacement.

Conclusion

Developing and maintaining an effective collection of resources requires vigilance on the part of the school librarian. Balancing among purchased, subscribed/leased, and accessed resources yields a collection that meets user needs for content, format, convenience, preference, authority, and recency. The school librarian plays a leadership role regarding the gathering and organizing of the collection, but is wise to enlist input from teachers and students to ensure that he or she remains aware of the rich resources that are available and that suit the library's needs. Scheduling time for collection maintenance is essential; administrators are often unaware of the time commitment that good collection development and maintenance require. A school librarian does well to help develop understanding of the tasks and to explicitly build collection development and maintenance into weekly and annual schedules.

Leadership Strategies

Teacher and Partner

Route publications with materials reviews to teachers and encourage them to initial those items that they would like to see in the collection. This allows them to consider quality from the beginning.

At the end of instructional units—particularly those demanding student research or resources for the teacher—ask teachers how well the collection met their needs.

Information Specialist

Reserve a special amount from the budget, perhaps 10 percent, for student-initiated purchases.

Involve staff members in decisions about replacement of equipment (e.g., gather feedback on how the equipment is used and what features it should have).

For both purchasing and weeding decisions, take into account information accessible via the web. Consider whether a particular information need can be served online or whether it requires purchased or subscribed resources.

Offer parent information programs on the materials selection process to help parents understand the complexities of this process and to seek their respect for the need for diversity and level of difficulty within a collection.

Program Administrator

Identify times for cleaning and checking equipment—at least annually.

Provide information to teachers and the principal about the condition of the collection, such as collection mapping data, to inform allocation of the school's resources.

Use usage reports from the library's automation system and from vendor reports to inform decisions about weeding, needs for additional resources, and renewal of subscriptions.

Scenarios for Discussion

Scenario 1

Susan is the teacher librarian at Harrison Middle School. The school has a new principal this year. The principal is visiting the library and notices *Staying Safe: A Teen's Guide to Sexually Transmitted Diseases* on the circulation desk to be checked in. She picks up the book and takes it over to Susan and asks, "Do you think we should have this book in our school library? Might some parent find this objectionable? I would suggest that you consider removing it from the library or at the very least keeping it in your office." What will Susan say and/or do?

Scenario 2

Two teachers at Roosevelt Elementary School frequently bring the school librarian publishers catalogs of items they want the library to purchase. Sometimes they are teacher resources that have reproducible pages for student seatwork. Sometimes they are high-low texts—usually in sets—that they would like to have available in multiple copies for classroom use. Meanwhile, the school librarian has an extensive consideration file of recommended library resources she has collected from reviewing journals and recommendations from other teachers. How should she respond?

REFERENCES

Annie E. Casey Foundation. 2011. "Data Center: KIDS COUNT." The Annie E. Casey Foundation. Accessed November 23. datacenter.kidscount.org.

Camarota, S. 2007. *Immigrants in the United States, 2007: A Profile of America's Foreign-Born Population.* Center for Immigration Studies. www.cis.org/immigrants_profile_2007.

Federal Interagency Forum on Child and Family Statistics. 2012. *America's Children in Brief: Key National Indicators of Well-Being Indicators 2012.* Childstats.gov. www.childstats.gov/pdf/ac2012/ac_12.pdf.

Hopkins, D. M. 1991. "Challenges to Materials in Secondary School Library Media Centers: Results of a National Study." *Journal of Youth Services in Libraries* 4, no. 2: 131–140.

———. 1993. "Put It in Writing: What You Should Know About Challenges to School Library Materials." *School Library Journal* 39, no. 1: 26–30.

Jacobs, H. H. 2000. "Upgrading the K–12 Journey through Curriculum Mapping: A Technology Tool for Classroom Teachers, Media Specialists, and Administrators." *Knowledge Quest* 29, no. 2: 25–29.

Krueger, K. 2011. *The Status of Statewide Subscription Databases.* AASL Exploratorium, Minneapolis, MN. Accessed November 18. www.aasl11.org/virtual.

Lowe, K. 2001. "Resource Alignment: Providing Curriculum Support in the School Library Media Center." *Knowledge Quest* 30, no. 2: 27–32.

Minarcini v. Strongsville City School District, 541 F.2d 577 (6th Cir. 1976).

NCES (National Center for Education Statistics). 2009. *Achievement Gaps: How Black and White Students in Public Schools Perform in Mathematics and Reading on the National Assessment of Educational Progress.* NCES Publication 2009-455. http://nces.ed.gov/nationsreportcard/pdf/studies/2009455.pdf.

———. 2011. "Fast Facts." National Center for Education Statistics. Accessed November 25. http://nces.ed.gov/fastfacts.

Parchment School District. 2012. *Parchment School District Technology Plan: July 2009–June 2012.* Parchment School District, Parchment, Michigan. www.parchmentschools.org/docs/district/plans/final_tech_plan_v2.pdf.

Peregoy, S. F., and O. F. Boyle. 2000. "English Learners Reading English: What We Know, What We Need to Know." *Theory into Practice* 39, no. 4: 237–247.

Reilly, R. 2003. "Electronic Junk Dealer or Technology Wizard: Managing Donations." *MultiMedia Schools* 10, no. 6: 61–62.

9

Literacy

This chapter:

- explores three purposes of reading;
- reviews research that relates to nurturing readers;
- examines aspects of literacy instruction to be integrated into the library program curriculum;
- discusses reading incentive programs and their impact on aliteracy; and
- identifies leadership strategies for encouraging and supporting reading.

Literacy is the ability to gain information or vicarious experience from reading. When a reader can both decode the words in a body of text and also exhibit understanding by restating, summarizing, or questioning, then that reader can be considered literate. If we think of developing literacy as a continuum, then illiteracy represents a point on that continuum where the reader is not yet making meaning out of what is read. Where one sets the point on this continuum that divides the illiterate from the literate is debatable, but at some point the capability to make meaning from text becomes viable. Although the primary responsibility for addressing illiteracy lies with the classroom teacher, the school librarian can play an important role in supporting literacy development.

Another dimension of the literacy issue is aliteracy—when one can read but chooses not to do so. The mass media raise concerns regularly that Americans are reading less. However, data suggest that reading books is an increasingly common practice for the US public. The Association of American Publishers (2012) reported that from 2008 to 2010, net sales revenue for trade category publishers grew 5.8 percent; trade juvenile (children, teens, young adults) sales fared well, gaining 7.1 percent over the three years in net sales revenue and 12.1

percent increases in net unit sales. Furthermore, a 2011 Harris Poll found that 65 percent of those polled said they had visited a public library in the past year (ALA, 2012). Even *Newsweek* announced that young people in the United States (ages 12–18) "are reading novels in unprecedented numbers" (Reno, 2008: para. 3). These facts suggest that, at least for many, reading is alive and well. This is clearly good news, but it does not mean that all Americans are readers; moreover, it does not mean that all children and youth are readers or that schools have no need to nurture readers.

In fact, a large-scale national study of more than 18,000 US elementary school children found that both recreational and academic reading attitudes on average gradually but steadily declined throughout the elementary school years, beginning at a relatively positive outlook and ending in relative indifference (McKenna, Kear, and Ellsworth, 1995). This study continues to be seen as a seminal study of the downward trend in children's attitudes toward reading as they progress through elementary schools (Roberts and Wilson, 2006). Developing, extending, and sustaining enthusiasm for reading among children and youth presents a challenge. Both illiteracy and aliteracy are legitimate concerns for the library program.

The Purposes of Reading

Often the word *reading* brings to mind reading stories or fiction. However, reading serves three major purposes, and all three demand consideration in school library programs—reading for literary experience, reading for information, and reading to perform a task. Reading for literary experience occurs in free voluntary reading and in reading and literature classes through reading novels, short stories, poems, plays, and essays. The reader explores the human condition and the interaction among events, characters' emotions, and possibilities. Students gain insight into how a given author creates character and uses language. They experience vicariously. Reading for information includes reading articles in magazines or newspapers, textbooks, entries in encyclopedias and other sources (both print and electronic), and nonfiction books. It requires that the reader be aware of the features found in informative texts, such as charts, footnotes, diagrams, and tables. Readers usually acquire information to meet a specific information need and use such reading strategies as scanning and skimming, note taking, and paraphrasing to extract the needed information. Reading to perform a task involves reading practical documents, such as schedules, directions, forms, recipes, warranties, and memos. Students must recognize the purpose and structure of practical documents to gain necessary information from them. The pragmatic approach of looking for information to accomplish a task differs substantively from savoring the style or intent of a text or literary work.

Rosenblatt's (1978) work provides insight into how one engages in reading depending on purpose. She describes a continuum of purposes one establishes as a reader. The continuum spans from efferent to aesthetic. The efferent reader approaches the text to take away information; the purpose is pragmatic, and the artistry of the writing is secondary to its content. From the efferent stance, the focus is on what will remain as residue after the reading experience. In contrast, the aesthetic reader attends to the reading experience itself. The text stimulates sensing, feeling, imagining, and thinking, and these behaviors make the aesthetic experience. Rosenblatt further emphasizes that the reader control stance relies on what the reader does, not on what the text is. Many texts can be experienced from different points on the continuum. Historical fiction is an interesting case in point. Often, teachers in social studies ask children to read historical fiction as they study a historical period. In reading *Number the Stars*, for example, to what extent is the purpose to learn information about the Danish resistance and to what extent is it to feel the experience of a young Jewish girl living through the horrors of those times? In reading *A Family Apart*, to what extent is the purpose to learn about the Children's Aid Society of the late nineteenth century and the movement of children to the West, and to what extent is it to feel the experience of siblings being separated from one another and from their birth families? An awareness of the reading purpose from the beginning can influence the reading experience. Readers travel along the aesthetic–efferent continuum as their purpose shifts. Awareness of the reading stance continuum can increase the sensitivity in designing reading response activities. As students read fiction, they gain confidence in their knowledge because the narrative form complements students' understanding of the time and people portrayed in a historical novel. Asking students to glean information from historical fiction may not be an appropriate activity when the power of the novel is to generate a "feel" for the time—a substantively different experience from reading a textbook. The question to consider, then, is: where along that continuum should the reader be to accomplish the current purpose?

Reading's power lies in its potential to develop in the reader new perspectives on times, people, and places, and to engender empathy for others' experiences and feelings. As students read fiction, they gain confidence in their knowledge because the narrative form complements and humanizes the factual.

The Library Program and Reading Instruction

The school librarian has an important role to play as a partner with classroom teachers in developing a literate community in the school.

Leveling and Book Choice

With renewed commitment to standardized testing has come an interest in assessing the reading levels of library books and limiting students to reading "at level." Carter (2000) urges caution in basing children's reading selection on readability formulas. She suggests that the Lexile score is not always an accurate indicator of readability; illustrative material may allow less facile readers to understand a text, and conversely, unconventional text structures may make reading more difficult than the score indicates. Similarly, while students may have one reading ability score, the differences between reading fiction and reading nonfiction may not have been considered. She also expresses her worry that students will not automatically progress to increasingly complex texts if they are limited to a specific Lexile level. The school librarian needs to keep in mind that there is a difference in selecting books to be used for reading instruction in contrast to free voluntary reading. Dzaldov and Peterson (2005: 223) assert that we are experiencing "leveling mania" and cite Booth's observation:

> When a child chooses a book, she or he takes responsibility for learning. Children usually select a book because they are interested in the topic. Therefore, whether the book reflects their reading ability may be secondary, since interest can motivate a child to read a book that may be difficult.

Fry (2002) reminds us that many a ninth-grade student who has been identified as reading at the fourth-grade level has been successful at reading the driver's education manual required for acquiring a driving permit, even if it is scored at the eighth-grade level.

Allowing children to select books that are beyond their reading level may conflict with classroom teachers' insistence on children having books at level. Moreover, in some settings teachers are urging librarians to label

AASL Position Statement on Labeling Books with Reading Levels

Librarians use spine labels to organize and identify library resources by call number to help patrons locate general subject areas or specific fiction, nonfiction, reference, audiovisual, or other items. Viewpoint-neutral directional labeling in libraries increases students' access to information and supports their First Amendment right to read. Best practice in school libraries includes books and other resources being shelved using a standard classification system that also enables students to find resources in other libraries, such as a public library, from which they may borrow materials.

One of the realities some school librarians face in their jobs is pressure by administrators and classroom teachers to label and arrange library collections according to reading levels. Student browsing behaviors can be profoundly altered with the addition of external reading level labels. With reading level labels often closely tied to reward points, student browsing becomes mainly a search for books that must be read and tests completed for individual or classroom point goals and/or grades. School library collections are not merely extensions of classroom book collections or classroom teaching methods, but rather places where children can explore interests safely and without restrictions. A minor's right to access resources freely and without restriction has long been and continues to be the position of the American Library Association and the American Association of School Librarians.

Labeling and shelving a book with an assigned grade level on its spine allows other students to observe the reading level of peers, thus threatening the confidentiality of students' reading levels. Only a student, the child's parent or guardian, the teacher, and the school librarian as appropriate should have knowledge of a student's reading capability.

Nonstandard shelving practices make it difficult for library staff and patrons to locate specific titles. More important, students may have no understanding of how most school and public libraries arrange their materials, thus further affecting book selection in other libraries.

(cont.)

It is the responsibility of school librarians to promote free access for students and not to aid in restricting their library materials. School librarians should resist labeling and advocate for development of district policies regarding leveled reading programs that rely on library staff compliance with library book labeling and nonstandard shelving requirements. These policies should address the concerns of privacy, student First Amendment Rights, behavior modification in both browsing and motivational reading attitudes, and related issues.

SOURCE: www.ala.org/aasl/aaslissues/positionstatements/labeling.

or organize books according to Lexile scores or other readability measures. The American Association of School Librarians (AASL) has issued a position statement regarding this practice.

A solution to the potential conflict between insistence on selecting books at level and selecting books freely based on personal interest may be to create local, more general categories and encourage children to select books from each category. An example of one local set of categories for difficulty levels follows:

Vacation books—Easy books in which the reader knows all the words and easily understands the meaning; books read for fun and to develop reading fluency

Just-right books—Books in which the reader knows enough words to be able to figure out meanings; books read to practice reading strategies

Dream books—Interesting but challenging books that are difficult enough to affect comprehension; books best read with the assistance of another person; books browsed for captions and illustrations

School librarians can use such categories as they advise children in reading selection. Consistency between the classroom and the library will help children assess their reading choices.

Alternative formats may be another recommendation school librarians can make for supporting literacy. Audiobooks and e-books provide alternatives that can engage children and help them develop fluency. The variety of products available to school librarians is rapidly expanding. The following are some examples:

- Scholastic BookFlix pairs classic fictional video storybooks from Weston Woods with nonfiction e-books from Scholastic.
- OverDrive allows students to check out titles online, and read or listen offline on computers, smartphones, MP3 players, and e-book readers.
- FollettShelf provides access to e-books online from anywhere.

Providing access to electronic books that deliver text, audio, and/or video is another way the school librarian can support readers and offer choice not only in content but also in format.

Complex Text in the Common Core Curriculum

The *Common Core State Standards for English Language Arts* (Common Core State Standards Initiative, 2012) has been adopted by most states in the nation as educators seek to strengthen the reading skills and experiences of students. Common Core encourages attention to increasing the complexity of texts that students read. To that end, it offers a definition of text complexity and urges educators to engage young readers in increasingly complex text. Inherent in this definition is the notion that judging text is more complex than quantitative measures of readability have suggested. Instead, text complexity is perceived as having three dimensions:

Qualitative dimensions refer to factors such as levels of meaning (e.g., satire can be read on multiple levels) or purpose; structure; language conventionality and clarity (e.g. figurative language is more complex than literal language); and background knowledge demand.

Quantitative dimensions refer to those aspects of text complexity, such as word length or frequency, sentence length, and text cohesion—aspects of text often measured by computer software.

Reader and task dimensions refer to motivation, knowledge, and experiences and to particular reader tasks such as purpose of the task assigned and the questions posed to the reader or by the reader.

This more comprehensive definition for determining the complexity of a text calls into question the practice of relying on Lexile scores or readability definitions alone for matching text to reader. In particular, the consideration of the reader's background and motivation is particularly relevant for the school librarian in guiding children to texts of interest to satisfy curiosity in students seeking reading resources. The Common Core standards call for instruction to move generally toward decreasing scaffolding and increasing independence in readers at any given grade level. Clearly, this can be perceived as a call for providing more opportunities for students to read widely—a call for a rich array of resources in the school library.

Consultation with Teachers

Developing enthusiasm for reading and identifying texts that will capture the interest and enthusiasm of young readers depend on both wide knowledge of literature for children and youth and genuinely enjoying the experience of reading. That said, the findings about teachers and their own reading habits and knowledge of literature raise concern. In their study of teacher reading behaviors, McKool and Gespass (2009) revealed that while most teachers expressed a value for reading as a leisure time activity, only a little more than half of the teachers surveyed actually read for more than ten minutes a day in their free time. This finding has significance for best practices in the teaching of reading. In this study, those teachers who read the most for pleasure outside of school were more likely to hold guided reading lessons, use literature circles, hold oral comprehension discussions, let students participate in periods of sustained silent reading, share insights from their own personal reading, and recommend books to students. These teachers considered reading a socially constructed activity and provided opportunities for students to talk about the books that they are reading in a variety of ways (McKool and Gespass, 2009). Knowledge of children's literature would appear to be a valuable asset if teachers are to provide an environment designed to encourage students to read. Cunningham and Stanovich (2004) examined the knowledge of children's literature of 722 kindergarten through third-grade teachers. They found that only 10 percent of the teachers were familiar enough with the most popular children's books for kindergarten through third grade to recognize over half of the 35 titles examined. In a study of prospective teachers, over a three-year period 51.5 percent were classified as "unenthusiastic readers," defined as expressing no enthusiasm for reading and having done little or no reading during the summer preceding the survey (Applegate and Applegate, 2004). These findings raise a significant question about the role of the school librarian in developing teachers' knowledge of literature for young people, advising teachers on titles to be introduced in their classrooms, and recommending activities to support literacy in classrooms. If schools implement Common Core, it is essential for teachers to be able to identify texts appropriate to their respective grade levels. School librarians, as literature experts, have work to do to assist those teachers who are not readers themselves and who lack familiarity with the canon of literature for young people. Support for such practices as sustained silent reading (SSR), literature circles, choral reading, reader's theater, teacher read-alouds, and reader-response journals requires identifying texts best suited to these practices, and school librarians can step in to offer recommendations. Particularly in a time when the renewed emphasis on reading for information has raised the expectation that every teacher is a teacher of reading, support for the school librarian is likely to be welcome—if librarians extend the offer.

Reading in the Library Curriculum

"Reading is a window to the world." So begin the belief statements in *Standards for the 21st-Century Learner* (AASL, 2007). The school library can be a significant contributor to widening that window to the world for children and youth through resources, access policies, collaboration with teachers, and instruction. The school library curriculum, while certainly concerned about students learning to access, use, and evaluate information, also needs to consider helping young people become competent and engaged readers. Creating a library curriculum that introduces young people to the best of literature for their respective ages and promotes discussion of that literature with questions that challenge them to draw inferences and make predictions and judgments affords a significant opportunity for creating excitement about literature and the experiences it provides.

Comprehension Strategies

Too often, assumptions are made when passersby see a school librarian sharing a text with children. One unfortunate perception may be that this is just a way of filling time. However, school librarians can use their opportunities for meeting with students to engage them in deep learning by applying specific comprehension strategies such as the following:

Activating or building background knowledge. Before beginning a text, raise questions that bring forward knowledge that will support understanding.

Using senses. Suggest that students pay attention to the sounds or smells or other sensory experiences of a text as it is read.

Making predictions. Invite students to consider a story and predict what will come next.

Drawing inferences. Encourage students to respond to such questions as "Why do you think the character responded in that way?" or "What is the significance of that object?"

Intentionally designing such strategies into the library curriculum helps ensure that they are indeed applied. Further, the school library can then articulate to significant stakeholders, including classroom teachers, that literacy learning is occurring during literature lessons in the library.

Reading Nonfiction

While fiction can dominate the reading classroom landscape, Common Core has placed renewed emphasis on the importance of reading for information. Indeed, the literacy demands of adults are primarily aimed at obtaining information from nonfiction texts (Venezky, 2000). Moss and Hendershot (2002) conducted a two-year ethnographic study observing sixth-graders' motivation for selecting nonfiction books. They found that students chose their nonfiction based on "the need to know"—that is, students read to satisfy a personal curiosity about a topic. This internal motivation to get information provides the backdrop for developing critical reading skills in students, skills that will serve them well as lifelong learners. If reading is indeed a meaning-making process, then nonfiction provides an excellent opportunity to employ critical thinking and constructivism by engaging students in such thoughtful tasks as the following:

Judging the accuracy of the content of books. Ask students to verify factual information by searching for another authoritative source to confirm or refute.

Investigating the author's credentials. Have students examine publishers' webpages for leads toward such information.

Using concept mapping. Work with students to construct graphic organizers of the information they discover in a text to see the relationships
among ideas.

These critical reading skills are the foundation for developing the information literacy competencies necessary in a world that often offers too much
information or unjuried information. While fiction reading offers excellent
opportunities for developing such skills as drawing inferences, analyzing
motivation, and predicting outcome, reading nonfiction can develop complementary skills of questioning the accuracy or authority of the source, assessing
the importance of currency of information, comparing and reconciling differences among sources of information, and observing potential bias. Together,
fiction and nonfiction offer reading experiences that will make literacy
instruction comprehensive. The school librarian can play an important role
in selecting quality nonfiction, marketing nonfiction to students, discussing
nonfiction with students, engaging them in critical assessment of what they
read, and advocating for nonfiction in the reading curriculum. Further encouraging students to pay attention to text structure (e.g., sequence, cause-effect,
question-answer, descriptive, and comparison) and text features (e.g., maps,
illustrations, pullouts, and glossary) in nonfiction will help students be more
successful readers in print media and develop habits that are likely to transfer
to reading in online environments.

Reading Digitally

READING ON THE INTERNET

Research on reading online and how this experience differs from reading
static text is nascent, yet already many have observed and are beginning to
understand the unique tasks the online reader employs. For example, hyper-
text can lead readers to several distinct types of information; a hyperlink
may lead to a definition of a term, an activity, or another related page altogether. Readers need to make sophisticated decisions about where and when
to follow links and how to navigate back when appropriate. Electronic texts
can integrate symbols, multiple media formats, photographs, cartoons, and
advertisements. With the plethora of media online, students need to learn to
extract information from visual sources. Students need to learn to interpret
information presented in forums and other nonjuried media and to differentiate between authoritative information and opinion.

Coiro (2011) lists four behaviors of effective online readers:

1. Adopting a problem-solving mind-set that prompts them to set a purpose and generate a "plan of attack"

2. Navigating search engines and disparate web structures as they select relevant information, investigate author credentials, detect "agendas," and corroborate questionable claims

3. Monitoring comprehension by adjusting their speed or direction as they encounter information

4. Engaging in reciprocal acts of reading, writing, and reflecting as they negotiate information

These online reading behaviors represent the critical stance that school librarians encourage students to adopt, along with metacognitive behaviors of self-monitoring. However, young people are often impatient to "find the answer" and will need to be prodded to maintain the critical stance that this information landscape demands. For many young people, reading online consists largely of skimming, scanning, and grabbing information. It is important to build dispositions toward deeper, more investigative, and penetrating reading online that is analogous to expectations for reading for information in static media, particularly as online text becomes a mainstay for informational reading. Such reading readily fits the information curriculum of the library and is valued by content-area teachers as well.

E-BOOK READING

The meaning of e-books is fuzzy at best. Some people envision text files accessible online, or think of books that can be read online and have animation or sound or of stories read aloud online. (Who could resist listening to James Earl Jones on the Screen Actors Guild Foundation Storyline?) Alternatively, some think of the books available to be read on an e-reader or mobile device. Whatever the format, e-books are an important consideration in the landscape of literacy in schools. Reading from a digital screen is comfortable and familiar for most K–12 students, so perhaps the e-book lacks the sense of novelty that it may have for adults. In a study of third-graders reading from print and digital texts, participants were found showed no preference for reading in either format; of greater concern to these children was the content available to them as they expressed their preferences based on their interest (Jones and Brown, 2011). Over half of the participants in that study wanted to continue to read both print and e-books. Electronic reading resources offer some attractive opportunities that deserve careful consideration:

- Projection with interactive whiteboards for class discussion
- Immediate vocabulary and pronunciation support
- Read-along options
- Hyperlinking to literary allusions or additional information
- Font size options

The school library should have as a primary concern supporting literacy with its collection. That priority calls for providing books in both print and digital formats and encouraging students to choose the format and content that suits them and their needs. A few examples of various sources of e-books are shown in Figure 9.1.

Nurturing Readers

The following practices have been identified in research as those that nurture and enhance students' reading motivation and achievement (Gambrell, 2011):

- Access to a range of reading materials
- Opportunities for success with challenging texts
- Opportunities for students to choose what they read
- Adequate time for students to engage in sustained reading
- Opportunities for social interactions about text
- Opportunities to engage in reading tasks that have relevance
- Incentives that reflect the value of reading and learning

Children arrive at school eager to join the community of readers. The anticipation of learning to read is part of the joy children feel about going to school. How can we sustain that desire to be a reader? Nurturing readers is a responsibility shared by teachers, parents, children and youth, the greater community, and librarians. Often, though, the school librarian or the public librarian must initiate and guide the collaborative effort.

FIGURE 9.1

A Variety of E-book Sources

Title	Format/Content	Access
FREE		
Project Gutenberg	Primarily text; primarily out of copyright	http://www.gutenberg.org
StorylineOnline	Well-known picture books read aloud by famous members of the Screen Actors Guild	http://www.storylineonline.net
Children's International Digital Library	Picture books in various languages; page views with illustrations and text	http://en.childrenslibrary.org
Starfall	Animated books with audio/ controlled vocabulary texts for developing phonemic awareness	http://www.starfall.com
Bartleby.com: Great Books Online	Text/classics and literary reference	http://www.bartleby.com
SUBSCRIPTION		
TumbleBooks	Online collection of animated, talking picture books; read-alongs, e-books, graphic novels, audiobooks, and educational videos; and streaming audiobooks.	http://www.tumblebooks.com
Gale Virtual Reference Library	Text and illustrations as available in the print versions/references from Gale's catalog	http://www.gale.com/gvrl/
Greenwood Publishing Group, eBooks	Text and illustrations as available in the print versions/references from Greenwood's catalog	http://www.greenwood.com.proxy.lib.uni.edu/ebooks/
Follett Library Resource Company	Text including illustrations of trade books with a "robotic" read-aloud option for some titles and dictionary and search capabilities/trade books from Follett inventory	http://www.flr.follett.com
OverDrive	AudioBooks and e-text for download to mobile devices/trade books	http://www.overdrive.com

Access to Books

Gambrell (2011) suggests that children need to have ready access to a wide range of reading resources. This research-supported assertion suggests that flexible, frequent access to the school library and its resources is essential. Further, the collection in the library needs to be substantial enough to allow for classrooms to borrow arrays of books for ready access there as well. Recommendations cited by Gambrell range from three to seven books per child readily available. This speaks to circulation policies that limit children's borrowing and suggests that libraries where limits are imposed may need to rethink policies or consider supporting classroom collections to supplement books children borrow independently. In addition, Gambrell's suggestion of opportunities to succeed with challenging texts opens the door for the library to encourage young readers to select books that push them.

Choice

Choice of what to read is an important consideration for nurturing readers. Gambrell (2011) asserts that students who are allowed to choose their own reading materials are more motivated to read, expend more effort, and gain better understanding of the text. Johnson and Gaskins (1992) found that the element of choice was very important to the fourth-graders they studied. Even when the teacher limits the choices to a menu of titles, still the opportunity to control what one will spend time reading has a positive effect. Providing choice demands that teachers have available alternatives that will meet their goals; those alternatives may need to relate to the same theme or come from the same genre, but they must also offer some variety in tone, protagonist, and level of difficulty. The school librarian can be instrumental in helping the teacher arrive at such alternatives.

Time to Read

Providing time to read is one more way to nurture readers. In Krashen's (2003) review of research, he concludes the obvious—the more students read, the better readers they are. A study of middle school students found the following:

> Voluntary reading of at least one chapter in a book other than a textbook
> declined from 61% in sixth grade to 29% in eighth grade. In sixth grade,

32% of students reported reading for their own enjoyment almost every day; however, by eighth grade, only 20% reported doing so. (Ley, 1994: 31)

Although there should be little argument against advocacy for time during the school day for reading—time for students to just read—the pressures of increased testing can challenge the arguments for SSR as a legitimate part of the reading program. References to the research on the effects of free reading on reading achievement must be highlighted whenever finding the time for it is challenged. SSR can be even more powerful in the development of the reading community when it extends to the entire school. SSR programs seem to work more easily at elementary schools than at secondary schools. Yet, it is often at the middle school level that reading diminishes among students. Identifying some time during the middle school day for sustained reading seems one simple way to encourage adolescents to continue to be readers. The schedule of the school day may require that this be a special added period, perhaps shorter than the standard class sessions, where all students and all teachers read. If reading is valued, there is a way to incorporate it into every student's daily school experience.

Social Reading

A variety of approaches can bolster children's perception of the social aspects of reading. Some possibilities include special reading events to create a reading community, literature circles, and book discussion clubs.

SPECIAL EVENTS

Special events can engender a sense of community among readers. One community effort that has been sustained for more than 20 years is the Community Reading Project, a winner of the John Cotton Dana Award for Public Relations in 1995. This project, supported largely by a local bank in Iowa City, Iowa, has for many years worked to turn an entire small city into a "community of readers" to help young people see that being a member of the community requires being a reader (Donham van Deusen and Langhorne, 1997). There are no prizes and no incentives beyond the opportunity to explore and enjoy reading. The development of community spirit occurs in part because the event has wide sponsorship; besides the primary bank sponsor, participants include the area public libraries, local bookstores, other local businesses, the senior center, the local university, and the community schools. Activities scheduled during a month in the fall include the following:

Book talk lunches. Each week during the month, the public library hosts a booktalk luncheon for a special target audience (e.g., parents of young children, parents of adolescents, adults, or businesspeople). Local librarians and booksellers, as well as general community members, are among those presenting the booktalks.

Visiting authors. The participating bank supports a children's book author in residence for one week each year. In anticipation of the visit, teachers and school librarians develop a guide to the author's work and use the guide to prepare children for the visit.

Read-In Day. One day is identified each year as Read-In Day, when schools devote a 15-minute period to reading. Organizations such as the local senior center have hosted activities for Read-In Day.

Events are promoted in newspapers, through service clubs and the chamber of commerce, on radio stations, and in displays in businesses. Each year has its own special events as well, but the intent is to focus attention on reading, to reach a threshold where a majority of the community feels a part of the reading event, so that it is indeed a community of readers and belonging is its own reward.

A simple fact is that enthusiasm is contagious. The adults with whom young people interact most at school are their teachers. Enthusiasm for reading among teachers provides an important model for students. School librarians can engender enthusiasm among teachers in both formal and informal ways. A few good booktalks at the beginning of faculty, departmental, or team meetings can be a step toward creating a community of readers among teachers. Sharing reviews or recently acquired books with specific teachers based on their personal or professional interests often generates interest in reading among faculty members, and offering to do booktalks in classes is a way to reach out to teachers as well as students. Teacher book discussion groups may serve to engage teachers more in reading and staying up to date with literature for children and young adults. The school librarian can organize these as brown bag lunch sessions or early-morning chats—whatever suits the local teacher culture. In the end, creating a community of readers among the teaching staff can be a major contributor to creating a community of readers among students.

Other events can focus attention on reading and can become a ritualized part of the school culture. Examples include the Battle of the Books program, in which students read from a preselected list of books and engage in team competition to respond to questions about the books (Dix, 2010). Celebrating Teen Read Week (YALSA, 2011) or participating in state-level children's choice book programs are also examples of events to encourage reading. While any of these special events represents a way to keep reading in the forefront and generate enthusiasm, they are best accompanied by sustained reading activities to consistently encourage and support reading.

LITERATURE CIRCLES

The social aspect of reading is inherent in the literature circle, a classroom construct common in middle and elementary schools. This structure brings students together to talk about a book with their peers. Unlike many typical reading groups in classrooms, literature circles feature student leadership. A literature circle typically has four to six members, and roles rotate among the members. Roles might include discussion leader, vocabulary enricher, connector, passage picker, artist, and character captain (Bussell, 2010). Roles can be defined within an individual classroom to suit the needs of the students involved, and the reading selection may influence the roles appropriate for a given circle. Designated roles provide scaffolding for students so that they can prepare with confidence and come to the circle with something specific to share. Ideally, students choose the title they want to read and discuss, and the circles are formed accordingly. Often the teacher has preselected texts that focus on a theme or a genre. What is most important is that readers build conversational skills for talking about texts in personal and thoughtful ways (DeVault, 2009). The school librarian can serve as an important advisor to teachers setting up literature circles by identifying titles that will provoke deep reflection, questioning, and discussion and that represent the variety of reading competency found within a given classroom (Carpinelli, 2006). It may, in fact, be appropriate for the school librarian to present brief booktalks on the available selections to help students choose a text of interest. In addition, of course, is the opportunity to return to the circle to answer the students who ask, "What might I like to read next?"

BOOK GROUPS

Several studies, including Johnson and Gaskins (1992) and Manning and Manning (1984), cite meaningful book discussion as an important contributor to positive attitudes toward reading. Research shows that students' verbal exchanges about content improve their learning and increase their level of thinking (Marzano, 1991). Peer interaction is particularly powerful; small group and paired discussion about books that readers have chosen offer opportunities for meaningful interaction.

Book clubs and book discussion groups have enjoyed a resurgence in popularity among adults in recent years. Middle schools and high schools are experiencing considerable success with such groups also. Whittingham and Huffman (2009) found that students who began with a negative attitude toward reading developed more favorable dispositions toward reading after even limited participation in a book discussion club. Lunch-hour meetings, after-school gatherings, and summer discussion groups are all variations, but the essential element is young people, with the guidance of an adult, coming together in a social context to discuss books (Jaeger and Demetriadis, 2002). Among the advantages of the book club is the removal of grade pressure so often associated with reading. Moreover, the book club creates a more lifelike setting for readers. Young people enjoy social engagement, and book discussion groups give them the opportunity to have "civilized conversations" about literature (Frank, Dixon, and Brandts, 2001). Book clubs provide opportunities for young people to practice roles and relationships that differ from the classroom—there is no hand raising or turn taking. Instead, the conversation flows, and participants learn to listen actively and to formulate their comments and interject them in socially conscious ways.

More relevant to the concerns about literacy, book clubs engage students in discussion of books they choose to read and allow them to shape their responses around the books in ways that matter to them. Book discussion clubs can create a literacy culture within the school that brings attention to reading and gives readers opportunities for a sense of belonging that is so important to young people. Chandler (1997) describes her experience with a summer book discussion club she organized for high school students. In many locales, summer vacation means more social isolation for students than adults might realize; a summer book discussion club offers a meaningful way to get together socially and to sustain reading. Often, it is possible to find service organizations or local businesses that will support book discussion groups to purchase paperback copies for the participants. Book ownership can be an enticing enhancement to the book discussion group experience. In some locales, youth librarians at public libraries are eager to partner with schools to develop after-school or summer book discussion groups. School librarians can take the lead in facilitating these opportunities for young people.

READER RESPONSE

Encouraging students' personal response to literature improves their ability to construct meaning. With experience in reader response, over time, students develop increasingly complex responses to literature that help them become better at constructing meaning (Eeds and Wells, 1989). When children's responses to literature are valued, they develop a sense of ownership, pride, and respect for learning. Out of this shared value of learning comes a sense of community.

The reader-response approach intends for readers' experience with text to be at the center of the discussion. Langer (1994) laments that "literature is usually taught and tested in a non-literary manner, as if there is one right answer arrived at through point-of-reference reading or writing." She goes on to describe strategies for opening up the classroom conversation about literature:

> Overall, teachers conceived of the "lesson" (extending across one or many days) as including three major sections: inviting initial understandings, developing interpretations and taking a critical stance. These replaced traditional lesson segments such as vocabulary review or plot summary and provided overall structural options to include or overlook in any given lesson. (p. 208)

Inviting initial understandings simply involves asking students to describe what is presently on their minds about the piece. Developing interpretations calls for teachers to extend students' perspectives by posing questions to challenge their thinking. Finally, taking a critical stance is the analysis of students' own understanding of the text and their generalizing to life. Langer endorses a sophisticated conversation about reading where the focus is on meaning. Such conversations about literature—and life—increase the sophistication with which students approach literature, engage them in thought, and create memorable experiences from their reading. For teachers to interact with students about literature, they must have significant books. Moreover, opportunities for teachers to discuss those books with another reading enthusiast—perhaps a school library librarian—can be valuable as teachers consider what directions their conversations with students may take.

Relevance

Reading that is relevant can mean reading texts that appeal to a student's personal interests. The school librarian can lead students to an array of online and print resources to meet those interests and engage them actively in learning about topics of interest to them. In the context of the curriculum, when collaborating with teachers the school librarian can develop thematic or conceptual text sets. Teachers new to thematic approaches to literature often confuse topical and thematic approaches (Donham van Deusen and Brandt, 1997). Figure 9.2 shows examples of themes that develop from topics.

Text sets can be created around concepts from the social studies or science curriculum to enrich learning and provide points of discussion—whether the entire set is read in common or whether the set is jigsawed. Such concepts

FIGURE 9.2

Thematic Units

Topic	Theme	Titles
Mentors	While families have great influence on us, often a pivotal person outside our family can change our lives.	*Eleanor* by Barbara Cooney *Ben's Trumpet* by Rachel Isadora *Jip* by Katherine Paterson *The Bobbin Girl* by Emily Arnold McCully
Family	Family life includes enjoying special traditions.	*Just in Time for Christmas* by Louise Borden *Maria Molina and the Days of the Dead* by Kathleen Krull *Pablo's Tree* by Pat Mora
Generations	Family stories help bridge generations.	*When Jo Louis Won the Title* by Belinda Rochelle *Aunt Flossie's Hats (and Crab Cakes Later)* by Elizabeth Fitzgerald Howard *Pink and Say* by Patricia Polacco *Grandaddy's Place* by Helen Griffith

as power or leadership or community can be the focus of a text set to accompany a social studies unit and provide fodder for discussion to complement and enliven textbook information.

Reading Incentive Programs

Incentive programs that feature rewards or prizes for reading are common. They range from a simple sticker for reading a book to elaborate accumulations of points that are applied toward grander prizes. The fundamental questions are, "Do these incentive programs work for the long run?" and "Is there a better way to encourage reading?"

EXTRINSIC REWARD PROGRAMS

Kohn (1993) argues against the use of extrinsic rewards to encourage reading—or any other desirable behaviors. One of his major arguments is that rewards work as long as the rewards last, but when the rewards end, so does the behavior. He suggests that offering an extrinsic reward for a behavior immediately devalues the desired behavior; in short, if reading is so wonderful, why are prizes necessary to get people to do it? Kohn concedes that rewards may indeed work for the short term. Many reading incentive programs are judged successful by the number of books the participants read during the event when rewards were available. Rewards are effective at producing temporary compliance. However, the more important question is whether participants in reading incentive programs extend their behavior beyond the duration of the incentive or regress to their old behaviors—will those who were readers continue to read and those who were not discontinue reading? Some believe that extrinsically motivated exposure to the enjoyment of reading may jumpstart the internal desire to be a reader. However, Kohn cites a considerable body of research to say that "any contingent payment system tends to undermine intrinsic motivation" (p. 140). The focus on the reward effectively turns the activity into a means to an end. He suggests, in fact, that offering such extrinsic rewards can easily result in students doing less than they might have done without the reward system, perhaps choosing easier books, reading fewer pages, or doing just enough to get the reward. To nurture readers, is the purpose temporary compliance or is it a lifelong behavior?

Does this mean that all incentives for reading are ineffective? Regarding rewards for reading, Gambrell (2011: 11) asserts:

Research suggests that nontangible incentives, such as teacher praise and teacher feedback, can increase student motivation. When teachers give frequent, positive, and honest feedback about student reading performance, it supports students' belief that they can read well and increases their motivation to read. With respect to tangible incentives offered for reading, research suggests that the incentives should be a natural extension of the desired reading behavior, such as books and extra time for reading.

The term *token economy* describes a system for assigning value to specific tasks and "paying" students with tokens (prizes or privileges) for performing those tasks. One of the most extensive and expensive token economies intended to encourage reading is a system of computerized tests on trade books, with accumulated points to be applied toward purchase of a wide range of prizes. What are the messages that such programs send? We read books not to discuss them, not to enjoy them, not to appreciate them, not to see ourselves in others' lives, but to pass a literal comprehension quiz, to earn points, and to "buy" trinkets. Documentation of enormous increases in library circulation supports such programs (Chenowith, 2001). However, one must ask whether the long-term effect of such programs will be to instill a love of reading. Will students for whom reading the last page of a story means taking a quiz to collect points embrace reading as a pleasure unto itself? Perhaps not! Miller (1995: 22) puts it succinctly:

> Would you really enjoy reading or want to read many books if you had to boot up the computer and answer 20 questions before you were allowed to read another one? Further, how would you like it if someone else totally dictated what you could read?

Perhaps a most alarming aspect of such a program is expressed by Cregar (2011: 43):

> In a not uncommon situation I have overheard, several primary-age children are told the books they choose must be near their AR-tested reading levels. The teacher steps to the shelves and begins to make suggestions. I hear no titles. Instead a reading-level-focused bidding takes place: "1.5? No, that's too easy for you. Get a 1.9 book. A 2.2 is too hard for you. Choose a book with a lower number." It is difficult to witness what is intended to be an environment that encourages interest-based browsing and self-selection of materials become a teacher-controlled, reading-level-structured, restrictive extension of the classroom.

Smith and Westberg (2011) set out to see what students thought of the Accelerated Reader (AR) program. Their findings suggest that students alter their reading choices based on AR points. Students in their study also reported extensive cheating on the AR tests and were critical of the texts as seeking details that "were not important to the story" (p. 4). One student went on to say that the "thoughtful reader strategies" taught during reading class did not help on the AR tests. Students in their study indicated that they changed the way they read under AR. One wonders whether they moved toward the efferent end of the Rosenblatt continuum and passed up the opportunities for aesthetic experiences in their reading.

In a study of 1,500 seventh-graders in ten middle schools, Pavonetti, Brimmer, and Cipielewski (2002) found that although participating students had read more books with Accelerated Reader, once the program was over they read no more than before, and in fact the researchers found a negative effect in some schools. Everhart's 2005 study in Scotland and England revealed gender differences in students' enthusiasm for the AR program, reporting that boys were equally motivated by praise and recognition as well as prizes, and that girls were motivated more by discussing books and reading with others.

SUMMER READING

One type of reading program that merits consideration is summer reading. Malach and Rutter (2003) summarize a century of research on the "summer effect" by stating that student learning declines or remains the same and the magnitude of change varies with socioeconomic status. Sustaining students' reading during the summer can help them maintain their reading skills. Kim and White (2008) report that summer school programs to prevent summer reading decline among low-income children have had mixed results. Allington and colleagues (2010) undertook an experimental study in which low-income children received books to read over three successive summers. The children chose the books for themselves, and each child received 12 books. The researchers found that students who had received free books had significantly higher achievement than those who had not. Furthermore, the achievement gains were comparable to providing summer school programs and far less expensive. However, in a study by Kim (2007), no such growth was found; he suspected that inappropriate book choice contributed to the lack of success of this experimental program. In a related study, Kim and Guryan (2010) found that matching books to children's interests and reading level and providing direct instruction in comprehension strategies before summer began yielded spring-to-fall gains. In this instance, gains were achieved when parents provided assistance by listening to their child read and recording their child's fluency based on simple instruction from classroom teachers. School librarians can support summer reading programs through recommending summer reading titles that match reader interest and capacity, encouraging public library use to access books, and when feasible, offering library access during the summer.

Parental Influence

A recent study indicated significant associations between students' value of reading and the frequency of interaction with their parents in reading activities (Siah and Kwok, 2010). Parental activities included encouraging after-school reading, visiting libraries, purchasing leisure reading books, and talking about reading activities. In another study, children benefited when parents encouraged voluntary reading, read aloud, modeled reading themselves for recreational purposes, recommended good books, and discussed books at home that they and their children were reading. These same interviews indicated that students who were in schools where they were given opportunities to read self-selected materials and who were given access to materials that they were personally interested in reading were more likely to engage in voluntary reading than those in classrooms where these practices were not evident (McKool, 2007). The school librarian can help parents in this role.

Parents may need to become aware of their own importance in their child's potential as a reader. Perhaps they need to learn about good books or need help in reading aloud to their children, such as with strategies for reading aloud and guides to selecting books that are especially suited to reading aloud. Perhaps parents need ideas for how to support reading at home or need help in becoming readers themselves. Principals are often seeking topics for parent nights; "helping your child be a reader" may be a very attractive topic. Sending home or posting on the library website frequent suggestions of good books for family reads or reading suggestions for children can help parents. Designing reading events at school that involve parents can be another way of making them aware of their importance: a read-along-with-parents project might be an example of this. Neuman (1995) describes a community-supported parent tutoring program in Philadelphia where parents volunteered to work as a tutor/mentor with one or two children at a time. The heart of this program is the training that these parent volunteers receive—it undoubtedly also influences the way they will encourage their own children's reading at home. The school librarian can find allies among parents to help nurture readers. Clearly, outreach to children from less supportive families is an important concern. School librarians may need to take active interest in the reading activities of children who have little reading support at home. This can take the form of regular formal or informal reading conferences with identified children.

Conclusion

The school library can be a major player in fostering literacy in both print and online formats. Whether supporting readers individually through readers advisory sessions; working with groups of readers through booktalks or by facilitating literature circles; developing and maintaining collections to support readers; collaborating with teachers to enhance literacy experiences; or direct teaching in the library curriculum, the school librarian's expertise in reading resources—print and online—is key to a strong literacy program.

Leadership Strategies

Teacher and Partner

Meet with groups of students for book discussions in cooperation with reading or social studies units taught in the classroom.

Hold individual reading conferences to discuss books with target students who need support to become readers.

Develop a library curriculum that includes literacy skills, knowledge, and dispositions, including comprehension strategies, understanding of informational texts, and critical reading dispositions for both print and online text.

Information Specialist

Market books to students by doing booktalks. School librarians who teach weekly classes can make use of those weekly times to do booktalks. In addition, make relevant booktalks a standard part of the beginning of content area units. Consider the possibilities as history classes begin study of the Civil War, World War II, and the westward movement, or as area studies of the Middle East or women's studies begin.

Market books to teachers. Use five minutes of faculty or team meetings to promote some of the latest, best books for youth—or an occasional book for adults!

Provide research to colleagues on token economies and extrinsic reward systems as they relate to reading motivation; lead and encourage discussion.

Program Administrator

Bring authors to the school to speak to students. Seek support from local businesses to underwrite each event and then give it—and your sponsor—as much press as possible.

Support and encourage providing time during the school day for students to read.

Provide parent programs about reading to engender support for reading at home.

Encourage read-aloud programs. Some schools have all-school thematic read-aloud programs that create a community spirit centered on reading (Boothroy and Donham, 1981).

Collaborate with the public library year-round to design, implement, and publicize programs and events to support reading.

Start a book discussion club for faculty. Discussion can focus on books for the students—to help teachers learn about new books their students might enjoy. Alternatively, discussion might focus on reading materials for adults.

Use research to advocate an increase in reading resources in the library.

Develop access policies than ensure all students access to resources.

Scenarios for Discussion

Scenario 1

School librarian Joan is enthusiastic to see more use of e-books in her elementary school; however, teachers are a bit leery of the idea and show little interest or knowledge in how the school might make use of e-books. There is considerable concern about literacy and meeting state expectations for reading test scores, and teachers are focused entirely on reading strategies that they anticipate will directly improve students' scores. How can Joan interest the teaching staff in e-books? Should she?

Scenario 2

In a middle school that serves a largely low-income neighborhood, the faculty is discussing the school's dismal reading scores and lamenting the annual summer slide. The principal has applied for funding from the district to offer a summer school program for identified children to try to address the issue, but the proposal has been rejected because it was simply too expensive. He had proposed to offer half-day reading class sessions to serve 45 students by employing three teachers and providing transportation every day for six weeks. What alternatives might the school librarian advance?

REFERENCES

AASL (American Association of School Librarians). 2007. *Standards for the 21st-Century Learner.* American Library Association. www.*ala.org/aasl/ guidelinesandstandards/learningstandards/standards.*

———. 2011. "Position Statement on Labeling Books with Reading Levels." American Library Association. www.ala.org/aasl/aaslissues/ positionstatements/labeling.

ALA (American Library Association). 2012. *The State of America's Libraries.* American Library Association. www.ala.org/ala/newspresscenter/ mediapresscenter/americaslibraries/execsummary.cfm.

Allington, R. L. et al., 2010. "Addressing Summer Reading Setback among Economically Disadvantaged Elementary Students." *Reading Psychology* 31:411–427.

Applegate, A. J., and M. J. Applegate. 2004. "The Peter Effect: Reading Habits and Attitudes of Pre-service Teachers." *The Reading Teacher* 57, no. 6: 554–563.

Association of American Publishers. 2012. "BookStats Publishing Categories Highlights." The Association of American Publishers. www.publishers.org/bookstats/categories.

Boothroy, B., and J. Donham. 1981. "Listening to Literature: An All-School Program." *Reading Teacher* 34, no. 7: 772–774.

Bussell, Evelyn R. 2010. "Literature Circles in the Library." *The School Librarian's Workshop* 30, no. 6: 17–18.

Carpinelli, T. 2006. "Literature Circles: A Collaborative Success Story!" *Library Media Connection* 25, no. 3: 32–33.

Carter, B. 2000. "Formula for Failure." *School Library Journal* 46, no. 7: 34–37.

Chandler, K. 1997. "The Beach Book Club: Literacy in the 'Lazy Days of Summer.'" *Journal of Adolescent and Adult Literacy* 41, no. 2: 104–116.

Chenowith, K. 2001. "Keeping Score." *School Library Journal* 47, no. 9: 48–51.

Coiro, J. 2011. "Talking About Reading as Thinking: Modeling the Hidden Complexities of Online Reading Comprehension." *Theory into Practice* 50, no. 2: 107–115.

Common Core State Standards Initiative. 2012. *Common Core State Standards for English Language Arts and Literacy in History/Social Studies, Science, and Technical Subjects—Appendix A.* Common Core State Standards Initiative. www.corestandards.org/assets/Appendix_A.pdf.

Cregar, E. 2011. "Browsing by Numbers and Reading for Points." *Knowledge Quest* 39, no. 4: 40–45.

Cunningham, A. E., and K. E. Stanovich. (2004). "Disciplinary Knowledge of K–3 Teachers and Their Knowledge Calibration in the Domain of Early Literacy. *Annals of Dyslexia* 54, no. 1: 139–167.

DeVault, N. 2009. "Literature Circles in Library Class." *Library Media Connection* 28, no. 1: 24–25.

Dix, S. L. 2010. "Waging a Battle to Promote Reading." *Library Media Connection* 28, no. 5 (March): 20–22.

Donham van Deusen, J., and P. Brandt. 1997. "Designing Thematic Literature Units." *Emergency Librarian* 25, no. 1: 21–24.

Donham van Deusen, J., and M. J. Langhorne. 1997. "Iowa City Reads!" *School Library Journal* 43, no. 5: 32–34.

Dzaldov, B., and S. Peterson. 2005. "Book Leveling and Readers." *The Reading Teacher* 59, no. 3: 222–229.

Eeds, M., and D. Well. 1989. "Grand Conversations: An Exploration of Meaning Construction in Literature Study Groups." *Research in the Teaching of English* 23, no. 1: 4–29.

Everhart, N. 2005. "A Crosscultural Inquiry into the Levels of Implementation of Accelerated Reader and Its Effect on Motivation and Extent of Reading: Perspectives from Scotland and England." *School Library Media Research* 8. www.ala.org/aasl/slmr.

Frank, C. R., C. N. Dixon, and L. R. Brandts. 2001. "Bears, Trolls, and Page-masters: Learning About Learners in Book Clubs." *Reading Teacher* 54, no. 5: 448–463.

Fry, E. 2002. "Readability Versus Leveling." *The Reading Teacher* 56, no. 3: 286–291.

Gambrell, L. B. 2011."Motivation in the School Reading Curriculum." *Journal of Reading Education* 37, no. 1: 5–14.

Jaeger, L., and S. N. Demetriadis. 2002. "Book Club on a Budget." *School Library Journal* 48, no. 3: 47.

Johnson, C., and J. Gaskins. 1992. "Reading Attitude: Types of Materials and Specific Strategies." *Journal of Reading Improvement* 29, no. 2: 133–139.

Jones, T., and C. Brown. 2011. "Reading Engagement: A Comparison between EBooks and Traditional Print Books in an Elementary Classroom." *International Journal of Instruction* 4, no. 2: 5–22.

Kim, J. S. 2007. "The Effects of a Voluntary Summer Reading Intervention on Reading Activities and Reading Achievement." *Journal of Educational Psychology* 99, no. 3: 505–515.

Kim, J. S., and J. Guryan. 2010. "The Efficacy of a Voluntary Summer Book Reading Intervention for Low-Income Latino Children from Language Minority Families." *Journal of Educational Psychology* 102, no. 1: 20–31.

Kim, J. S., and T. G. White. 2008. "Scaffolding Voluntary Summer Reading for Children in Grades 3 to 5: An Experimental Study." *Scientific Studies of Reading* 12, no. 1: 1–23.

Kohn, A. 1993. *Punished by Rewards: The Trouble with Gold Stars, Incentive Plans, A's, Praise and Other Bribes.* Boston: Houghton Mifflin.

Krashen, S. D. 2003. "The (Lack of) Experimental Evidence Supporting the Use of Accelerated Reader." *Journal of Children's Literature* 29, no. 2: 9–30.

Langer, J. 1994. "A Response-Based Approach to Reading Literature." *Language Arts* 71, no. 3: 203–211.

Ley, T. C. 1994. "Longitudinal Study of the Reading Attitudes and Behaviors of Middle School Students." *Reading Psychology* 15, no. 1: 11–38.

Malach, D. A., and R. A. Rutter. 2003. "For Nine Months Kids Go to School, but in Summer This School Goes to Kids." *Reading Teacher* 57, no. 1: 50–54.

Manning, G., and M. Manning. 1984. "What Models of Recreational Reading Make a Difference?" *Reading World* 23, no. 4: 375–380.

Marzano, R. J. 1991. "Language, the Language Arts, and Thinking." In *Handbook of Research in the English Language Arts*, edited by J. Flood et al., 559–586. New York: Macmillan.

McKenna, M. C., D. J. Kear, and R. A. Ellsworth. 1995. "Children's Attitudes toward Reading: A National Survey." *Reading Research Quarterly* 30, no. 4: 934–956.

McKool, S. 2007. "Factors That Influence the Decision to Read: An Investigation of Fifth Grade Students' Out-of-School Reading Habits." *Reading Improvement* 44, no. 3: 111–131.

McKool, S., and S. Gespass. 2009. "Does Johnny's Reading Teacher Love to Read? How Teachers' Personal Reading Habits Affect Instructional Practices." *Literacy Research and Instruction* 48, no. 3: 264–276.

Miller, D. P. 1995. "Computerized Carrots—Are They Truly Reading Motivators?" *Technology Connection* 2, no. 7: 21–22.

Moss, B., and J. Hendershot. 2002. "Exploring Sixth Graders' Selection of Nonfiction Trade Books." *Reading Teacher* 56, no. 1: 6–18.

Neuman, S. 1995. "Reading Together: A Community-Supported Parent Tutoring Program." *Reading Teacher* 49, no. 2: 120–129.

Pavonetti, L. M., K. M. Brimmer, and J. F. Cipielewski. 2002. "Accelerated Reader: What Are the Lasting Effects on the Reading Habits of Middle School Students Exposed to Accelerated Reader in Elementary Grades?" *Journal of Adolescent and Adult Literacy* 46, no. 4: 300–311.

Reno, J. 2008. "Generation R (R is for Reader)." *Newsweek Web Exclusive*, May 34. www.newsweek.com/id/136961.

Roberts, M. S., and J. D. Wilson. 2006. "Reading Attitudes and Instructional Methodology: How Might Achievement Become Affected?" *Reading Improvement* 43, no. 2: 64–69.

Rosenblatt, L. 1978. *The Reader, the Text, the Poem: The Transactional Theory of the Literary Work.* Carbondale, IL: Southern Illinois Press.

Siah, P., and W. Kwok. 2010. "The Value of Reading and the Effectiveness of Sustained Silent Reading." *The Clearing House* 83, no. 5: 168–174.

Smith, A., and L. L. Westberg. 2011. "Student Attitudes toward Accelerated Reader: 'Thanks for Asking!'" *Current Issues in Education* 14, no. 2: 2–7.

Venezky, R. L. 2000. "The Origins of the Present Day Chasm between Adult Literacy Needs and School Literacy Instruction." *Scientific Studies of Reading* 4, no. 1: 19.

Whittingham, J. L., and S. Huffman. 2009. "The Effects of Book Clubs on the Reading Attitudes of Middle School Students." *Reading Improvement* 46, no. 3: 130–136.

YALSA (Young Adult Library Services Division). 2011. *Teen Read Week* (wiki). American Library Association. Accessed December 30. http://wikis.ala.org/yalsa/index.php/Teen_Read_Week.

10

The Virtual Library

This chapter:

- examines the virtual reach of the library;
- delineates the priorities for the school library website as an entrée to its resources;
- emphasizes the importance of selectivity in providing access to online tools and resources that add substantive value to learning;
- discusses the nature of students' interaction with online text;
- raises issues of responsibility for Internet safety in implementation of online social learning tools; and
- identifies leadership strategies for the library's virtual presence.

While physical access to the library is important, the 24/7 access to which constituents are accustomed today makes the virtual library content and design particularly important. It is crucial that the library present itself online as welcoming, highly functional, well organized, and up to date. The school librarian can work in the virtual environment to support learning as students interface with information resources that at once afford opportunities for deep learning and occasions for distraction. In addition, safety concerns arise in the virtual environment, and the school librarian's technical expertise is a valuable resource for parents, teachers, and school administrators for setting policy and designing curriculum regarding safe Internet practices. The school librarian understands the organization of information and has a professional commitment to ethical use of information. These professional skills and values make the school librarian the go-to person for providing a virtual information environment to serve the needs of teachers and students.

The Library Website: Content

Less can be more. No one argues that there is a plethora of information available online. Because of the expanse of online resources and tools, school library websites can quickly become overloaded. Like a physical library collection, the school library website's content ought to be focused on the needs of its users and provide resources and information matched to their needs. Otherwise, the user may find little benefit to the school library website and choose simply to use a generic search engine. A study of school library websites emphasizes the importance of school librarians making informed content decisions based on knowledge of their users needs (Jurkowski, 2004). Because each user group will have distinct purposes for entering the library through its website, the use of portals or links from the homepage for each group—students, teachers, and parents—is worthy of consideration. Figure 10.1 lists likely content to be included for each user group.

FIGURE 10.1

Website Content for User Groups

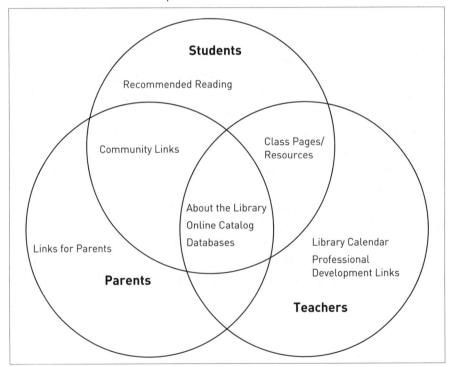

Content for All Users

All user groups share some common information needs from the school library. For example, access to the library's online catalog and subscription databases is valuable for all users. Hence, links to the catalog and databases should be consistently posted on all portals. Access to e-books for reference and for recreation also should be provided to all users. The way in which e-books are accessed will vary with the specific products. For purchased or subscribed e-books such as FollettShelf, access can be provided through the Follett OPAC Destiny or through a direct online link, or both. TumbleBooks for young children may be best accessed through a direct web link. In addition, links to free online e-book sites may suit the school community—for example, Project Gutenberg (www.gutenberg.org) at the high school level, or Starfall (www.starfall.com) for young children.

Under "About the Library" appear the mission of the school library; its hours, physical location, telephone numbers, and policies for circulation; selection and reconsideration of resources; volunteers; and ethical use of information (e.g., plagiarism, copyright, and acceptable use policy). Also posted there is information about the staff that ideally includes a brief bio of the teacher librarian with photo, support staff names and photos, and contact information for all staff. This information needs to be readily accessible for all user groups. *Library News* keeps the library website fresh and should be updated at least weekly, if not more frequently. Many school librarians choose to embed a blog in their website for providing news because it is easy to update and can take on a conversational and personal tone. News may include events in the library, the school, or the community or advertise new resources and suggest online websites that may pique the curiosity of students or align with school-wide activities or events. This section of the website provides an opportunity to show the vitality and dynamism of the library. Often, photos or videos are embedded to capture attention and convey the message that the library is a lively environment.

Content for Students and Teachers

Valenza (2006: 207) summarizes the value of the school library website when she states that virtual libraries "allow learners independence as they allow teacher librarians opportunities for intervention. As scalable strategies, virtual libraries allow librarians and educators to guide unlimited numbers of students, at home, or otherwise distant."

Student and teacher pages tend to emphasize resources for teaching and learning; for example, their portals might include "Class Pages," "Class Links," or "Curriculum Connections," or whatever title suits the local context. These pages connect students and teachers to resources selected specifically to match either courses or specific units or even specific assignments. Resources may be provided as pathfinders organized in a strategic sequence that guides students to begin with background building and move toward more specific resources as they focus their line of inquiry. Or, the resources may appear as a briefly annotated list of resources—print and/or online—to support classroom learning. Again, the motto "less is more" applies. These resources should be selected carefully to meet the developmental and curricular needs of local students. It is this selection and focusing of content that constitutes the added value of the school librarian's expertise. Too much information can simply overwhelm the users or cause them to take the convenient, albeit less vetted route to information via a generic search engine. Course pages facilitate working collaboratively with teachers to assess and meet the needs of students and teachers. A template for such pages may be a good approach so that students become familiar with a standard layout for their class resources. The commercial program LibGuides (www.springshare .com/libguides/school) is an excellent option for creating course pages; high school teacher librarians in particular will find this an attractive format for well-designed, easy-to-assemble pages that can be created, posted, saved and edited, and accessed ubiquitously. Students will appreciate the standardized format and convenient access. A sample guide is shown in Figure 10.2. The organizational tabs provide a step-through guide for the inquiry process. LibGuides allows for embedding video tutorials for how-to guidance, as well as links to subscription and open web resources. Librarians can embed videos, RSS feeds, podcasts, and other media into these pages to provide additional search assistance or information sources for students. In addition, these guides are mobile application–friendly. Examples of LibGuides from all types of libraries are accessible through the Springshare website at www .springshare.com.

An alternative is course management software like the open source Moodle (http://moodle.org), where teachers and librarians can create sites collaboratively to provide a range of course materials, including the librarian's selected information resources, research tools, and aids.

FIGURE 10.2

LibGuides for Student Research

SOURCE: Used with permission of Slaven Zivkovic at Springshare.

Figure 10.3 shows an example of a curricular page from an elementary school library website. This example offers links for specific topics from the fourth-grade curriculum. This is a highly selective list that does not overwhelm students and provides a carefully vetted set of links. By limiting the number of resources, the school librarian assists the users by not overwhelming them. A side benefit is the amount of time required for maintenance. Such a guide can be created as a wiki to make updating even more efficient.

The high school library page in Figure 10.4 provides resources with brief annotations aimed at a specific project. The use of logos from the databases helps students recognize where they are accessing their information. Be sure to secure permission for use of logos from the company for strict adherence to intellectual property considerations. It is ideal to request an electronic file of the image in order to provide best image definition and resolution rather than copying and pasting logos. By seeing these icons consistently on course pages, students develop associations with the available online resources. Annotations are brief and friendly to give students hints about what they can expect to find at each source. Databases are separated from websites as a way

FIGURE 10.3

Class Resources Page for Elementary School

What Makes Our Nation Great?

- Inflation Calculator
- Abraham Lincoln Boyhood Home
- Secrets of the Presidents
- Ben's Guide to Government
- The Democracy Project
- Interactive Map of Washington, D.C.

Monument Links:

- World Book Online - Searching using the NAME of your monument.
- Grolier Online - See Mr. Harvey for login/password
- National Parks in Washington D.C.
- U.S. Symbols
- DC for Kids
- Search Webpath Express in Destiny for other website (must be logged into Destiny to access)
- United States Capital Building
  - http://www.visitthecapital.gov
  - http://aoc.gov

President Links:

- Internet Public Library - POTUS Site
- The White House's Hall of Presidents
- Grolier's The American Presidency
- Biographical Information from The American President - PBS Special, 2000
- Portraits of the Presidents and First Ladies - Library of Congress Memory Collection
- Vincent Voice Library - American Presidents from B. Harrison to Present

SOURCE: Permission granted by Carl Harvey, School Librarian, North Elementary School, Noblesville, Indiana.

of creating an understanding of the difference between subscription and open sources of information.

Besides course-specific content, a set of generic how-tos can be a helpful addition to pages for students. Figure 10.5 shows an example of the kinds of guides that might be included.

Research guides like NoodleTools (www.noodletools.com) and KidsClick (www.kidsclick.org) provide guidance for various aspects of the research process. NoodleTools is a subscription tool that advises on selecting a search engine and provides a tool for notetaking and paraphrasing as well as citations in various standard styles. KidsClick, an open access tool owned and operated by the School of Library and Information Science at Kent State University, is essentially a search directory designed for elementary school age children. Topical searches lead to kid-safe content. Annotations indicate

FIGURE 10.4

High School Course Page

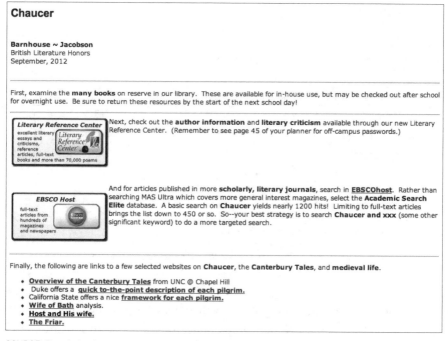

general reading level and illustrative material. Course or project pages allow the school librarian to extend the opportunities to learn specific strategies and techniques of the research process 24/7. A page designed for a specific course or project might include any of the following content:

- Instructions for the assignment
- An aid to focusing a topic or generating a research question
- Pathfinder to resources, from general background information to more specialized resources
- Link to a guide for the relevant citation style
- A note-taking guide or organizer
- A calendar for organizing work to complete the assignment
- E-mail link to the school librarian or online chat tool like GoogleTalk

FIGURE 10.5

How-To Guides

How-To Guides

Bibliography

For information on how to cite your sources, please see our **Bibliographic Citations** page.

Outline

How to Prepare an Outline Many word processing programs have built-in outlining functions, but many of us have found these to be more frustrating than helpful. We recommend that you use the following instructions for manually **formatting an outline**. These instructions work on most versions of MS Word (Mac or PC), as well as many other word processing programs. Also available here is a downloadable **Outline Template**.

Publication Templates

How to Create a Tri-Fold Brochure Use MS Word to create a simple tri-fold brochure. These instructions were written for Word XP, but should work for earlier versions as well.

Or download one of these sample brochures (created with MS Word) and use it as a template:

- **Tri-fold Brochure** Uses 8-1/2 by 11 (letter size) paper with landscape orientation. There are 6 "panels."
- **Tall Booklet Brochure** Uses 8-1/2 by 11 (letter size) paper with portrait orientation. There are 4 tall, narrow "panels."
- **Short Booklet Brochure** Uses 8-1/2 by 11 (letter size) paper with landscape orientation. There are 4 short, wide "panels."

Or download this sample newsletter (created with MS Word) and use it as a template:

- **Newsletter** Uses 8-1/2 by 11 (letter size) paper with portrait orientation.

SOURCE: Permission for use granted by Jill Hofmockel, West High School, Iowa City, Iowa.

Reading recommendations belong in the pages for teachers and students. For example, the school library may choose to subscribe to a reading recommender like EBSCO's NoveList or Gale's Books and Authors online reader's advisory tool. NoveList is focused on young readers and designed for a school setting with curricular connections and other resources well suited for the school librarians. The Gale product, including books for youth and adults, offers opportunities for reader community building that may be particularly attractive for developing a social reading network in a school or public library. Free sites like WhichBook (www.whichbook.net), Fantastic Fiction (www.fantasticfiction.com), or Goodreads (www.goodreads.com) are not designed specifically for young readers, but they may be alternatives to consider. WhichBook provides opportunities to characterize the type of book the reader is seeking according to various criteria along a sliding scale (e.g., happy–sad, easy–demanding, sex–no sex).

These tools assist students in choosing what they might enjoy reading next. A link to the local public library is appropriate here, especially if the library has pages devoted to reading recommendations for youth. Links to book award sites assist young readers in book selection, and many states have book award programs through state associations and offer lists of the year's readings. One example is the Illinois School Library Media Association book award program for K–3, promoted at www.islma.org/monarch.htm. A book blog or wiki is another way of promoting reading. The school librarian can post reading recommendations with minireviews, but more important, the site can be available for students and/or teachers to post book reviews as well (Church, 2006).

A calendar for the library is a useful resource to make available, particularly through the teacher portal or linked pages. An online calendar like Google Calendar allows for online access by teaching staff so that they can not only see what is happening in the library but also determine availability for scheduling their classes in the library. Providing such a tool again invites and encourages teachers to make use of the school library.

Content for Teachers

Through the teachers' portal, links to resources for professional development may be a useful subset of information. Links to online resources that relate to specific initiatives under way in the school can be particularly helpful. For example, if a school is committed to Positive Behavior Interventions and Supports (PBIS) or The Daily 5, then a cluster of links to resources related to the initiative can be useful. Also, links to state curriculum standards may be helpful for teachers and may encourage them to see the library website as their go-to place. Once again, the selection of resources relevant to the particular school and its teachers is the value of the teacher pages on the library website. The purpose is to select and organize resources for teachers, not to overwhelm them with so much that they find it exhausting. Another example of resources for the teacher page might be links to teacher tools. Examples of tools might be templates for creating web quests or graphic organizers. Many Web 2.0 tools might be considered here, but a well-honed list of tools that fit the teaching styles and technology skills and interests of the faculty is the goal. Kruger-Ross and Holcomb (2011: 2) assert:

> The Web 2.0 movement is predicated on the notion that online environments provide each user with the opportunity to interact with, change, adapt, and generate his or her own information, which can subsequently be interacted with, changed, and adapted (Hendron, 2008)—rather than simple posting and consuming of text and media. This creates value in

creating software and tools that are relatively inexpensive, if not free, with the understanding that users will help in the continued development of the software and will provide candid feedback to the software developers. Because many of these web-based tools are inexpensive (or free) and easy to access, their presence in K–12 classrooms has proliferated.

At issue then is the question of how a particular Web 2.0 tool will enhance learning and teaching. Advantages to evaluate include the tool's potential to assist in the following:

- Collaborative learning
- Organization and analysis of information or data
- Creation of new perspectives on information
- Generation of new knowledge or insights
- Interaction with distant human expertise

Tools that serve any of these purposes may be the ones to highlight for teachers on the library's website.

Content for Parents

Parent pages may provide recommendations for reading at home, information about online safety, links to community organizations serving families and children, and an invitation to volunteer in the school library. When these pages provide carefully selected links to resources and are marketed to parents through school–home communication media, the school library can be seen as an information resource for its entire community.

Mobile Apps

Mobile applications afford even greater access to information as cellphones become multipurpose information resources and other portable tablet devices such as iPads as well as iPods and their competitors gain popularity. In addition to the widely available consumer apps available at app stores for the respective platforms, vendors are eager to make their products accessible on mobile devices (Young, 2011). For example, Gale's AccessMyLibrary (AML) School Edition supplies students with free unlimited access to their school library's Gale online resources. Likewise, EBSCO Publishing offers EBSCOhost Mobile, a complete mobile platform for their databases. FollettShelf offers mobile access to the library's e-book collection. Individual publishers such as Dorling-Kindersley have app stores as well. While these developments again can extend the virtual reach of the school library, issues of equity arise and will deserve attention.

In summary, the content on the library's website needs to be selective and focused on the information needs of the users. Such a priority plays to the professional strengths and skills of the school librarian and adds value by providing an entrée to the web that assists users by increasing the efficiency of their access to information.

The Library Website: Design

Organization and navigation are key elements that contribute to a well-functioning website. Whether the site is designed on a website platform like GoogleSites, a blog platform, or a wiki platform, carefully organizing information is essential. To begin, routing users to pages or portals tailored to them avoids cluttering a general page with information not relevant to all users. Figure 10.6 shows a very simple example of a navigation frame that brings users to the resources most useful to them.

In the example, note that the navigation frame provides access to the library home page ("Welcome"), as well as the school and district home pages, so that these are always available to the user. Providing "bread crumbs" is another helpful navigational technique, as shown in Figure 10.7. School library websites are primarily aimed at providing access to information, and when that information can be located efficiently, users will be more likely to return.

Design elements are also important in considering the usability of the website. An overly cluttered or disorganized home page can discourage users quickly. In today's instant access world, web users are impatient and expect to quickly arrive at the information they need. This lack of patience calls for rational, intuitive organization and design. Williams (2004) suggests four basic design principles in both

FIGURE 10.6
Website Navigation Frame

Contents

▶ About the Library

▶ Class Projects

▶ Parent Information

▶ Special Events

▶ Student Links

▶ Teacher Links

SOURCE: Permission for use granted by Deb Dorzweiler, Penn Elementary School, North Liberty, Iowa.

FIGURE 10.7
Bread Crumbs

online and print publictions. Williams's rule of thumb is this: "Nothing should be placed on the page arbtrarily. Every item should have a visual connection with something else on the page" (Williams, 2004: 31). Her simple acronym—CRAP—can provide a solid foundation for thinking about design:

> *Contrast.* When considering contrast, the first design element is color. Choosing color for text and its background calls for seeking a high degree of contrast. Black text on a white background has the highest readability. Black and yellow is another combination that usually has a high readability, as do blue and white (Johansson, 2010). Some 8 percent of the population has some form of color blindness, and by choosing the wrong colors, a page can be virtually unreadable for them. Some colors present greater problems than others, especially red and green. Blues and yellows are somewhat less problematic. Strong contrast between text and background is important. Background contrast can help focus the reader's eye on a segment of the page; for example, if the background color in the navigation menu is different from the background color of the body of the page, the user's attention can be directed and focused. Beyond color, another contrast element is font. First, it is important to choose fonts that are readily available. Second, the concept of contrast suggests choosing one font for headings and a contrasting font for body text. In seeking contrast, headings might appear in a sans serif font such as Verdana, Arial, or Helvetica, while body text might appear in Times New Roman or Georgia. The serif fonts tend to be particularly readable, but the sans serif fonts are eye-catching, especially when they appear in contrast. Contrast can be a principle for creating the focal point on a webpage (Williams and Tollett, 2006). In other words, use the banner or logo or heading to provide contrast that catches the eye and helps establish focus on the page.

> *Repetition.* Repeating elements may simply be headings such as a consistent repetitive pattern of headings to guide the user's eye quickly down the page. Similarly, repetition can be applied by following a

consistent layout from page to page across the website. Repetition makes individual pages predictable and therefore more efficient for the user.

Alignment. The principle of alignment simply asks the designer to organize information in a way that helps the eye. If a heading is left justified, all headings in that set of information should be left justified, for example.

Proximity. Clustering similar information together is the concept of proximity. Categories help users quickly locate what they need; for example, bring together into a single list all databases or resources for a particular subject area or user group. Likewise, proximity urges the designer to pay attention to vertical space, as text line spacing that is too large forces the eye to travel farther and increases the need to scroll. On the other hand, some vertical space used to create divisions between clusters of information supports proximate groupings.

Accessibility is an important consideration in school library website design. Besides color choice sensitive to color blindness, looking to universal design principles that afford access across various disabilities is essential for providing equitable access to resources. Web resources provide specific information to assist in addressing accessibility questions; for example, the University of Washington's "World Wide Access: Accessible Web Design" at www.washington.edu/doit/Brochures/Technology/universal.design.html or the University of Wisconsin's "Designing More Usable Websites" at http://trace.wisc.edu/world/web.

Images on websites deserve careful attention to ensure that they load efficiently. The smaller the file size, the more quickly it loads (Williams and Tollett, 2006). Therefore, when adding jpeg files (typically photos or other images with extensive color gradation) to the website, there is payoff in taking time to save at medium- to low-quality levels to speed up loading. For gif files, 72 ppi is typically adequate resolution for the web.

Student Online Behaviors

Working online presents opportunities, challenges, and concerns for students. As schools make online access increasingly available with more deployment of laptops and other devices, it becomes essential that educators be aware of the unique characteristics of reading online versus reading offline, research about multitasking, social learning, and Internet safety.

Reading Online

Accessing and using online information imposes reader demands that differ from accessing information in printed texts. Reading researchers are beginning to explore the unique character of online reading. These lines of research are intersecting with research and theory in the library and information science (LIS) professions, and bringing together the expertise of reading specialists and the LIS perspective promises new insights into the online reading experience. One such insight is the idea that reading online is frequently a problem-solving process (Mokhtari, Kymes, and Edwards, 2008). Online reading of informational text tends to be in response to an information problem; as such, maintaining focus on a purpose in an environment of constant distraction is one key to success. Coiro (2011) suggests that four cognitive processes are involved in online reading comprehension:

> *Planning.* Skilled readers, she contends, generate a "plan of attack" in which they determine their purpose, anticipate potential challenges, and envision a plan as they enter the online reading environment. Such a planful approach is not innate in today's students, who are naturally inclined to dive into their quest and use their intuition as they proceed. A pitfall of this intuitive approach is the myriad distractions students will encounter as they read on the Internet. Online readers need coaching, modeling through such techniques as think-alouds, and scaffolding with such tools as graphic organizers to develop habits of purposefulness and focus. That said, there are times when rambling intuitive browsing to satisfy one's curiosity is appropriate, and there are times when focused investigation is important. Coiro's point is that purposefulness is a factor that supports comprehension.

> *Negotiating online text.* Coiro suggests that skilled online readers navigate a variety of text structures and a diverse range of perspectives. Strategies include making judgments about relevance, credibility, and bias as well as corroborating findings. While all reading is a transaction between reader and text, online reading is complicated by the potential for multiple texts through linking. Intentional judgments or

decisions about when to digress, what to believe, and when to verify—
required in the online reading experience—are not intuitive strategies
and must be coached, modeled, and taught. The natural inclination of
the novice online reader is acceptance of what is found.

Monitoring comprehension of and pathways through online texts. Coiro
describes skilled online readers as those who stop to revisit their purpose and monitor their understanding of content as well as the relevance of their reading path. Such metacognitive behavior requires
intermittent reflection. Self-monitoring is a behavior that can be supported through formative assessment techniques and intervention by
teachers and school librarians.

Responding to online texts. According to Coiro, skilled online readers are actively engaged in "reciprocal acts of reading, writing, and
reflecting." She describes this process as summing up key ideas, making connections across various online texts, probing, and integrating
one's own ideas. Raising students' awareness of these processes may
be the first step toward developing habits that contribute to deeper
comprehension during online reading.

Researchers investigating online reading have identified several specific strategies that constitute distinctions between effective online reading and offline
reading (Zawilinski et al., 2007). Examples of online reading comprehension
strategies include the following:

- Using the search engine results list to select sites most likely
  to be relevant and authoritative, in contrast to clicking on the first
  result and proceeding with a click-and-check approach through
  the list
- Using the design features (e.g., navigation, "About . . ." headings, and
  links) of websites to support comprehension and to increase efficiency
  in locating needed information
- "Text walking" (i.e., skimming the web page prior to close reading to
  assess its usefulness)
- Verifying factual information for accuracy with second sources
- Examining sources for bias
- Digital note taking

- Synthesizing information across both text-based and visual sources of information
- Using standard interface techniques (e.g., back button and find feature)

While many of these comprehension strategies have analogs in print reading, the online environment poses challenges and opportunities for teaching skills and strategies that will enhance learning from online information sources. The school librarian can provide support to teachers and students through direct instruction as well as development of online aids and organizers to support comprehension.

Of particular value is consideration of the ways in which online reading affords opportunities for deep learning. When students read a printed text and encounter a term, reference, or allusion that is foreign to them, their typical behavior is to skip over it and attempt to make meaning out of the text without that particular knowledge. A trip to a reference book or other source to learn the definition is not much of a temptation for most young readers. However, when reading online, finding out about the term or allusion is often a click away. This is one of the powers of the linked environment of the Internet. So, an allusion to *King Lear* in a text can be understood with a quick diversion to get a little background information. "Vooks" with their embedded online video promise enriched reading experiences. The downside of this linked environment is the temptation to continue with the diversion so that it becomes a distraction from the initial intended purpose of the reading. Modeling behaviors that discipline the reader to remain focused and supporting the notion of purpose-driven reading can contribute to maximizing the learning potential of online reading.

The e-book and e-reader product lines are emerging at a rapid pace. Print reference collections are quickly disappearing in favor of e-reference collections such as Gale's Virtual Reference Library, Credo Reference for college-preparatory high school students, and online encyclopedias from classic publishers such as Britannica. PlayAways (audio) and PlayAway Views (video) and Overdrive's e-books and audiobooks afford opportunities for reading in interactive formats. These reading formats will both pose challenges and offer opportunities as teachers and students apply comprehension and critical reading strategies to these reading environments.

Multitasking

The pervasive reach of technology—cellphones, iPods, tablets, netbooks, and laptops—raises interesting questions about multitasking. The educational technology literature, in fact, now encourages educators to take advantage of the presumed ability of this generation of students to multitask. Indeed, some tasks can be performed together effortlessly, but the greater the cognitive overlap, the greater the interference (Borst, Taatgen, and van Rijn, 2010). These researchers suggest, for example, that two behaviors that use language facilities such as writing and talking have considerable overlap and therefore interfere cognitively with each other:

> [A]lthough several tasks can be active at the same time, a particular resource can only be used by a single task at a time. For instance, if two tasks want to use the visual system at the same time, only one of them can proceed, and the other task will have to wait. In the case of the visual system, this is quite obvious: People can only look at one object at a time. However, the same mechanism is assumed to hold for more central resources like memory. For example, if two tasks want to retrieve a fact from memory at the same time, only one task can proceed; the other task will have to wait. On the other hand, no interference is predicted if one task wants to use the visual system and one task wants to retrieve a fact from memory. Thus, as long as the resource requirements of the different tasks do not overlap in time, threaded cognition predicts no interference, but as soon as a particular resource is concurrently needed by two or more tasks, that resource will act as a bottleneck and delay the execution of the combined process. This aligns with the intuition that if two tasks require the same cognitive constructs, the tasks will interfere. (p. 364)

Brain research evidence suggests that the brain does not multitask but rather engages in task switching, that is, shifting attention between or among tasks at hand (Rogers and Monsell, 1995). Further, while somewhat nascent, applied research suggests that attempts to do multiple tasks simultaneously can affect performance (Fried, 2008). In her study, Fried found that unstructured laptop use during class was negatively associated with student learning and posed distractions. Such findings call for educators to be vigilant in the ways in which they encourage task switching during learning episodes.

One conclusion from Fried's study of laptop use is that laptop use may be most effective when it is intentionally integrated into classroom activities. While the research base continues to develop, such a recommendation may indicate that well-constructed back channeling is one way to intensify student engagement and perhaps increase student learning. Jarrett and Devine (2010) offer recommendations for effective implementation of back channeling using a Web 2.0 resource called Today's Meet (www.todaysmeet.com). When the teacher poses questions through the back channel, all students can participate, and the teacher can review the discussion log to see who has and has not participated. Jarrett and Devine emphasize the importance of setting ground rules for the back channel so that students distinguish it from their social networking chatter. They also advise instructors to prepare questions in advance so that the back channel affords opportunities to deepen learning and to engage students in discourse that clarifies and extends their understandings.

Increasingly, 1:1 laptop deployment is affording opportunities to use technology to increase student engagement and to deepen learning. A responsibility of the educator is to ensure that it is improving and deepening learning, not distracting students from learning. Again, educators need to maintain awareness of research that suggests that task switching can affect attention and achievement and is influenced by the nature of the cognitive tasks in which students are engaged. Formative assessments to ensure that students are attending to the essential understandings of lessons may become even more important in the 1:1 environment and other settings where students have ready access to technologies that can either enhance or distract from intended learning.

Social Learning

The interactivity of online resources and tools creates an environment of social learning that allows students to interact with each other, with expertise, and with information in constructive and creative ways. Yet, that learning should be grounded in sound pedagogy and interconnected with the content and pedagogical intentions of the teacher. TPACK is a model for considering three important factors in the integration of technology—technology, content, and pedagogy (Mishra and Koehler, 2008). A strength of the model is that it intends for educators to consider the intersections of technology, content, and pedagogy by thinking about how each influences the other: How does the technology affect the content and/or how does the pedagogy affect the technology? For example, how does using a WebQuest affect student learning on the topic of the Civil Rights Movement? In what ways might the WebQuest afford opportunities for construction of meaning in ways that a textbook might not? Nelson, Christopher, and Mims (2009: 82) aptly suggest, "Teachers well versed in technology, pedagogy, and content no longer ask themselves, 'How do I use this technology?' Research recommends that teachers ask, 'Why do I want to use this technology?'" This important distinction has implications for teacher librarians who may advocate the use of Web 2.0 technology tools to teachers. The answer to the *why* question should incorporate what we know about the technology, the content, and the pedagogy, and warrants consideration when we make recommendations to teachers. When school librarians recommend social networking technologies, the question of why should we use this technology should be foremost, and the answer cannot be for fun, for motivation, or only for developing technology skills. The answer should relate to enhancing content learning. Examples of such criteria are as follows:

> *Constructive.* Does the tool engage students in constructing meaning? Examples of technologies with potential are wikis, blogs, and collaborative applications available in GoogleDocs. These encourage students to articulate what they are learning and/or to pose questions. It is essential to provide rubrics or clear standards and expectations for the content of students' entries so that what they compose is substantive, reflective, and insightful.

> *Integrative.* Does the tool encourage students to draw information from a variety of sources and organize or integrate it in meaningful ways? An example of a technology that is integrative is social bookmarking with a tool like Diigo. For example, tags can show relationships among various sites, and sticky notes can provide discussion questions that cause students to compare and contrast information or integrate ideas from various perspectives.

> *Creative.* Does the tool encourage the student to truly create and communicate in ways that evidence new insights or new understandings?

Digital storytelling with a tool like VoiceThread has the potential to meet such a criterion. However, this tool will reach its potential only when expectations call for students to meet standards for substantive original content and creative, articulate communication.

Complex. Does the tool encourage investigation into the complexity of the subject at hand? Use of tools that allow students to skim the surface of a subject—often the case with presentation tools, for example—does not meet the TPACK standard of considering not just technology but also how it interfaces with content and pedagogy. Complexity may involve looking at issues from multiple perspectives and bringing together information that requires analytical comparisons and evaluation or examination of biases.

In short, the school librarian can support a social learning environment by identifying those tools with the greatest potential for truly enhancing learning. Moreover, the school librarian can assist teachers in developing standards and rubrics for students that set criteria for work worth its time and effort. When technology serves only to decorate low-level learning, it is an irresponsible use of resources—a result that school librarians can work to avoid. In the wide array of options among the many Web 2.0 tools, the school librarian who adopts a critical stance and demands that technology tools meet a standard of supporting enhanced, deep learning may wonder:

To what extent does the brief message of a microblog such as Twitter support deep learning? How can we implement such a technology to en-sure reflective thought or critical analysis?

To what extent does presentation software such as Prezi, PowerPoint, KeyNote, Glogster, or Storybird engage students in deep learning rather than allow them to skim the surface of information? How can we create presentation expectations that preclude surface-only learning?

How can standards for blogging be set so that students provide evidence to support their assertions in postings or demonstrate logical reasoning or open-mindedness?

How do photo-sharing sites such as Flickr and Picasa or video-sharing sites such as GoogleVideo, OurMedia, or Animoto provide opportunities for learning that is not only creative but also calls for analysis, synthesis, and evaluation?

By posing and responding to such questions as these, the school librarian progresses from not merely caring about how to use Web 2.0 tools to thinking about why.

Internet Safety

The Broadband Data Improvement Act of 2008 requires schools receiving federal E-Rate discounts for telecommunications services to educate their students about appropriate online behavior, including interacting with other individuals on social networking sites and in chat rooms and cyberbullying awareness and response. The law requires the Federal Trade Commission to carry out a program to increase public awareness and provide educational strategies to promote the safe use of the Internet by children. A number of resources are available to support this effort and the school librarian can provide access to these via the school library website (Rivero, 2010). Each resource is appropriate for specific audiences and can be posted on the appropriate pages or via the portals created for the school library website. Examples of resources worthy of consideration are:

> *SafeKids.com (www.safekids.com)*—A site for parents and teachers to glean information about safety on the web for children and teens, including parenting and teaching strategies

> *iKeepSafe (http://ikeepsafe.org)*—A site with resources for parents, educators, and children regarding Internet safety

As with other library website resources, school librarians should be selective and not overwhelm users with too many options for education about Internet safety. Instead, the school librarian should review sites and select those that best suit the grade level, local policies on Internet use, and audience (parents, teachers, and students).

Another issue somewhat related to Internet safety is privacy of student information; for example, if student photos are used on the library website, the school library should acquire permission and avoid personal identification.

Conclusion

While the physical school library may have limited hours of access, the virtual school library through its website is accessible 24/7. The content on the library website and the intentional design for efficient access combine to raise the visibility of the library among all constituents. The expertise of school librarians has traditionally included selection of quality resources to match the needs of the users in the school community. The website provides a venue for that same expertise in selection of best resources and tools to meet local needs. The classic Ranganathan's fourth law of librarianship—"Save the time of the reader"—applies readily here. The web can be an overwhelming environment, but the school library website can serve as an intentionally vetted entrée that saves the time of its users. Just as librarians select physical resources based on standards for excellence, so quality criteria can be applied in selecting among the wide range of Web 2.0 tools to fit the pedagogy and content of the school and engage learners in deep learning.

Leadership Strategies

Teacher and Partner

Guide teachers in use of the TPACK model to design use of Web 2.0 technology applications so that student learning is deepened and enhanced, not merely decorated.

Raise awareness of research related to multitasking and task switching to prevent the Internet from distracting students from essential learning.

Use the library website as a teaching tool by providing course/assignment resources tailored to students' specific needs.

Offer direct instruction on Internet safety, including the value of privacy.

Information Specialist

Design the library website so that specific user groups can efficiently locate useful information.

Select information resources, including websites and e-books, to align with the curriculum and information needs of users.

Program Administrator

Apply design principles that make the library website readable and intuitive in its navigation.

Market the library website to all constituencies—students, teachers, and parents.

Scenarios for Discussion

Scenario 1

You have just signed your contract for your new position as school librarian, and you are taking a closer look at the school's website. You notice that there is no link to the library from the school's home page. How will you respond to this? Is it an issue you will bring up with the principal and/or the technology director? How might you advocate for getting a link to the library on the front page?

Scenario 2

A social studies teacher in the middle school where you work as school librarian brings his class to the library for a lesson you will teach to help them start a project that will involve investigating questions about the Civil War. The students arrive with their laptops and take their seats. The teacher settles in toward the back of the library classroom and reminds the students that they will be back channeling with him during your lesson. How do you respond today? How will you plan for the next time this teacher's class comes for instruction?

REFERENCES

Borst, J. P., N. A. Taatgen, and H. van Rijn. 2010. "The Problem State: A Cognitive Bottleneck in Multitasking." *Journal of Experimental Psychology: Learning, Memory, and Cognition* 36, no. 2: 363–382.

Church, A. 2006. "Your Library Goes Virtual: Promoting Reading and Supporting Research." *Library Media Connection* 25, no. 3: 10–13.

Coiro, J. 2011. "Talking about Reading as Thinking; Modeling the Hidden Complexities of Online Reading Comprehension." *Theory Into Practice* 50, no. 2: 107–115.

Fried, C. B. 2008. "In-class Laptop Use and Its Effect on Student Learning." *Computers and Education* 50, no. 3: 906–914.

Jarrett, K., and M. A. Devine. 2010. "How to Use Back Channeling in Your Classroom." *Education Digest* 76, no. 1: 41–44.

Johansson, D. 2010. "Color Contrast." Colors on the Web. www.colorsontheweb .com/colorcontrasts.asp.

Jurkowski, O. 2004. "School Library Website Components." *TechTrends: Linking Research and Practice to Improve Learning* 48, no. 6: 56–60.

Kruger-Ross, M., and L. B. Holcomb. 2011. "Toward a Set of Theoretical Best Practices for Web 2.0 and Web-based Technologies." *Meridian: A Kindergarten through High School Information and Communication Technologies Journal* 13, no. 2. www.ncsu.edu/meridian/winter2011/krugerross.

Mishra, P., and M. J. Koehler. 2008. "Technological Pedagogical Content Knowledge: A Framework for Teacher Knowledge." *Teachers College Record* 108, no. 6: 1017–1054.

Mokhtari, K., A. Kymes, and P. Edwards. 2008. "Assessing the New Literacies of Online Reading Comprehension: An Informative Interview with W. Ian O'Byrne, Lisa Zawilinski, J. Greg McVerry, and Donald J. Leu at the University of Connecticut." *The Reading Teacher* 62, no. 4: 345–357.

Nelson, J., A. Christopher, and C. Mims. 2009. "TPACK and Web 2.0: Transformation of Teaching and Learning." *TechTrends* 53, no. 5: 80–85.

Rivero, V. 2010. "Tools for Learning: Safety, Security and Access." *MultiMedia and Internet Schools* 17, no. 3: 24–27.

Rogers, R. D., and S. Monsell. 1995. "Costs of a Predictable Switch Between Simple Cognitive Tasks." *Journal of Experimental Psychology: General* 124:207–231.

Valenza, J. K. 2006. "It'd Be Really Dumb Not to Use It: Virtual Libraries and High School Students' Information Searching and Use—A Focus Group Investigation." In *Youth Information-Seeking Behavior II: Context, Theories, Models and Issues*, edited by M. K. Chelton and C. Cool, 208–256. New York: Scarecrow.

Williams, R. 2004. *The Non-Designer's Design Book.* 2nd ed. Berkeley, CA: Peachpit Press.

Williams, R., and J. Tollett. 2006. *The Non-Designer's Web Book.* 3rd ed. Berkeley, CA: Peachpit Press.

Young, T. E. 2011. "Smartphone and Library Apps: Where Are We, Where Are We Going." *Library Media Connection* 29, no. 6: 52–56.

Zawilinski, L., A. Carter, I. O'Byrne, G. McVerry, T. Nierlich, and D. Leu. 2007. "Toward a Taxonomy of Online Reading Comprehension Strategies." Paper presented at the annual meeting of the National Reading Conference, Austin, TX, November 30.

11

Technology Leadership

This chapter:

- explores the school librarian's roles as technology advocate, coordinator, manager, trainer, teacher, and policy maker;
- examines the process for educational technology planning;
- considers the role of the school in compensating for inequity of home access to online resources;
- discusses technology applications in the context of beliefs about teaching and learning; and
- identifies leadership strategies related to technology.

The values and principles of librarianship, such as commitment to equity, intellectual freedom, ethical use of information, and inquiry-based learning, cause the school librarian to bring unique perspectives to the technology leadership team in a school. While other team members may bring a high level of technical knowledge, these perspectives are important to sound decision making. While it may not be necessary for school librarians to be network or hardware technicians, it is essential that they be conversant enough in technology to contribute intelligently and productively to decision making. It is also important that the school librarian as an educator apply knowledge about teaching and learning to all discussions about instructional use of technology. The school librarian should be savvy about the technology planning process, technology applications in the context of teaching and learning, and technology access issues, as well as ethical policies and practices.

The School Librarian's Roles in Technology Leadership

For effectively integrating technology into a school's program, school librarians are well suited to play several roles: coordinator, manager, advocate, trainer, teacher, and policy maker. Too often, administrators have considered it necessary to add a separate position of instructional technology coordinator, and too often the qualifications for such a position call for a person who understands hardware and networking but not applications for technology in an educational environment. While the extensive deployment of technology in schools benefits from a technically trained staff to administer networks and support hardware and software, school librarians have several attributes that qualify them well for coordinating technology use in a school or a district. First, coordinating technology is akin to coordinating any other learning resource; this is already the work of the school librarian. What knowledge is required to provide such coordination? Clearly, a technology coordinator must be knowledgeable about what is possible to do with technology and what is worth doing. Maintaining current awareness of what is in the marketplace is a traditional part of the school librarian's work. More important, making judgments about quality based on explicit criteria is also a librarian's task. To coordinate technology requires knowing the curriculum, teachers' instructional styles, and students' learning needs; this knowledge of the instructional context is essential to all effective library programming.

Coordinator

Technology demands three kinds of support: the educational leadership that a library professional can offer, technical assistance for maintenance and repair, and networking expertise. A network specialist and technicians maintain and repair hardware, maintain file servers, attend to wiring and wireless installation, and install software and upgrades. These technical tasks are just that—technical—and do not require an educator's expertise. However, coordinating the application of technology for the overall school program does require an educator's expertise, and the most appropriate educator is the school librarian. What does the librarian as technology coordinator do? The school librarian in this case:

> maintains awareness of new technologies—hardware and software—and learns about relevance, fit, and practicality for the local setting; and

> shares awareness of new products and advises decision makers about advantages and disadvantages informed by such perspectives as teaching and learning, existing resources already in use, capacity, and professional development needs.

School librarians are accustomed to working across grade levels and departments. They are familiar with curriculum throughout the school as well as the entire teaching staff. This contextual knowledge complements their professional expertise in instructional and information technologies so that the case is easily made for their role in technology leadership.

Manager

The school librarian typically manages physical space, which is likely to include computer labs often located near or in the library. Librarians supervise a facility accessible to all departments or grades; when technology facilities or resources need to be scheduled and shared, the school library has systems in place for this operation. With access to the Internet, this supervision is particularly important for assisting students in their efficient and effective search for information and for monitoring Internet use. Another management task is inventory of equipment, a task easily accomplished using the library's automated circulation system. Each hardware item can be entered into the database and then checked out to its location in the building. Using this already existing system for equipment inventory means efficiency for the school. Managing software requires keeping track of licenses—an information management problem accomplished with a database program using such fields as title, version, publisher, vendor, purchase order number, date purchased, and license terms. Storage and organization of licensed software is a task familiar to the librarian.

A manager also is responsible for guiding policy. Here the school librarian's expertise is particularly valuable. Professional expertise regarding intellectual property, privacy, intellectual freedom, and Internet safety contributes substantively to school and district policy making on technology use. The school librarian needs to remain informed about current legislation and public policy on these issues, and share professional positions to inform policy development and implementation.

Technology Advocate

Building-level librarians serve as technology advocates. It is important, however, that their advocacy be spent on those applications that make a positive difference to teaching and learning. To advocate for just any use of technology or anything electronic is just as irresponsible as to spend library media dollars on poorly written books. Leadership is an important aspect of the technology advocate role, and sometimes leadership requires challenging technology uses that may not comport with the school's beliefs about learning or that may not play out as particularly sound ideas.

On a smaller scale, the school librarian can be an advocate for appropriate use of technology applications. For example, PowerPoint presentations have become pervasive in many schools, yet some would argue that this format has often been overused and inappropriately used. Whether Prezi (www.prezi.com) will suffer the same fate depends on how well lessons learned from PowerPoint are applied. School librarians may want to advise teachers of the worst habits of PowerPoint users (Cooper, 2009):

- Too many or too few words per slide
- Inappropriate backgrounds that distract from the content
- Too much animation and too many sound effects
- Too many slides for presentation length
- Overcomplicated graphics or charts
- Lack of presentation structure and content relationships

In a similar way, the school librarian may evaluate a Web 2.0 application like Glogster (http://edu.glogster.com). While this application provides opportunities for creativity and collaboration, when recommending such a venue for sharing work, the school librarian may become the devil's advocate to question whether the depth of inquiry of a project at hand is adequately represented in this medium. Sometimes the complexity of a topic calls for a formal written essay or a video presentation that affords opportunities for elaboration and development of ideas and issues. As advocate, the school librarian needs to urge not only technology use but also effective and appropriate technology use. Advocacy must be selective, and that requires analyzing the assumptions that underpin any technology use. The process of identifying appropriate technologies for the school is a collaborative process that involves both teachers and librarians and often includes infrastructure advice from network specialists.

Choosing applications needs to be based on explicit criteria. While this may seem particularly evident for purchased or subscribed applications, it is equally true for open source Web 2.0 tools and resources. All technologies have an opportunity cost—if librarians are spending teacher and student time on one application, they are not spending time on something else. School librarians need to apply the same quality demands regardless of the price. The set of evaluation criteria should be generated to match local beliefs about teaching and learning. Following are examples of criteria to consider when seeking applications of technology to be adopted:

- The application addresses skills and concepts central to teaching objectives.
- The application supports and enhances the curriculum.
- The application offers cross-curricular applications.
- The application is process-oriented.
- The program promotes active learning.
- The task could not be accomplished effectively with different media.
- The application appropriately provides otherwise unavailable firsthand experiences.
- The application promotes independent thinking, critical thinking, and investigative problem solving rather than rote thinking and out-of-context memorization.
- The application is developmentally appropriate for the target audience; that is, necessary reading levels do not vary greatly, and subject matter is appropriate to the intended age group.
- The application engages student interest and does not merely "decorate" low-level learning.
- Students feel a sense of accomplishment.
- Students with limited English-speaking abilities can use the program.
- The program offers options for students with special needs.
- Students can quickly begin to use the program with minimal prompting from an adult.
- Students' efforts are devoted to using the program, not learning how to use the program.

The criteria should show a direct relationship between the instructional beliefs of the institution and the decision making regarding what technologies to use in their schools. There is considerable expense in just purchasing a book, but add to that the costs of cataloging and processing the book even before the book is ready to be used. Implementation of technologies involves more than just the investment in software; it also requires decisions be made about the costs for using the technology. How many licenses are needed?

What staff development will be necessary for its implementation? Where will it be accessed? Are adequate bandwidth and hardware available? Such complexity calls for careful decision making because the cost in time and money goes well beyond the sticker price.

Students with special needs make unique demands on technology. A commitment to equity of opportunity draws the library media specialist into concern for the exceptional learner. First, the school librarian needs to be aware of the RtI (Response to Intervention) framework for supporting student learning. Batsche and colleagues (2005: 3) define RtI as "the practice of providing high quality instruction and intervention matched to student need, monitoring progress frequently to make decisions about changes in instruction, and applying child response data to important educational decisions."

The RtI framework is a structure of tiers. Tier 1 calls for research-based core practices focused on instruction. Tier 2 is supplemental intervention targeted at a small identified group. Tier 3 calls for more intensive, individualized intervention for students whose performance indicates a need for additional support (Basham et al., 2010). The National Center on Response to Intervention provides professional development assistance at its website (www.rti4success.org). When considering technologies for differentiating instruction and meeting the needs of special learners, the school librarian's awareness of these tiers can inform recommendations.

While there may be an assistive technology consultant available to the school, a wise school librarian maintains awareness of developments in this specialized application of technology in order to be conversant at the leadership table, and to advocate for those technological resources that will assist students with special needs and help teachers effectively differentiate instruction. One example of an accommodation is WordQ (www.wordq .com), an open source tool that features voice output to assist students with in-context word prediction, usage examples for confusing words, and predictions based on creative spelling of the user. It works with most word processing applications. Write:OutLoud (www.donJohnston.com/products/ write_outloud), a word processing application, features a high-quality text-to-speech component, an audio-based spell checker, a homonym checker, an easy-to-use bibliographer, and an easy-to-access tool and menu feature. Write:OutLoud also offers progress monitoring tools that collect data on word count, words used, number of words per sentence, number of sentences per paragraph, and similar information. Available for each student, data can also be examined across users as well as classes to provide the student progress data expected in the RtI initiative. While the specific tools available grow more numerous continuously, the point is that the school librarian should maintain awareness of current technology that supports special needs.

Trainer

Trainer is another role for librarians. Ertmer and Ottenbreit-Leftwitch (2010) assert that high levels of technology integration in schools is still lacking. While they cite high levels of teacher use of technology for communication as well as for instruction, close analysis indicates that instructional use tends to fall primarily into categories of presentation software like PowerPoint, web searching, or assigning students homework to be completed using specific software such as for word processing. Clearly, the school librarian has a crucial role to play in advocating for access as well as providing teacher development, so that students can take greatest advantage of whatever is available. Experienced teachers and novices alike need to learn about technology applications that can be helpful to them and their students. Cennamo, Ross, and Ertmer (2010) suggest that teachers need knowledge that enables them to select technologies that will support specific curricular goals and enable students to use technology for exploration, analysis, and production. Gradually, teachers entering the profession should bring increasingly sophisticated technology skills with them, but for a time some teachers will require training in these basic skills. Furthermore, technologies are continuously emerging and improving, so the school librarian will continue to help teachers select from what is available and assist them in learning to use it. The International Society for Technology in Education (ISTE) offers a set of teacher performance standards and indicators for implementation of technology in schools. These standards are accessible at the ISTE website (www.iste.org). They suggest that teachers can, for example, incorporate digital tools to promote student learning and creativity; demonstrate their own fluency in technology systems; use a variety of digital age media and formats; use current and emerging digital tools to locate, analyze, evaluate, and use information resources to support research and learning; and advocate, model, and teach safe, legal, and ethical use of digital information and technology. These are clearly professional skills and knowledge that school librarians possess; thus, they can serve as professional developers to help teachers expand their skills. School librarians can support, encourage, lead, and organize professional learning communities (PLCs). One hallmark of PLCs—collegiality—is also a hallmark of the school library profession. These professional development groups extend beyond the typical one-shot professional development event, as they are ongoing collegial groups focused on improving student learning. Because integration of technology can be complex, PLCs afford the ideal context for helping teachers build skills, knowledge, and confidence over time. The egalitarian culture of PLCs affords the school librarian opportunities to lead collegially, and it allows all members of the community to take turns leading as each is an equal member of the community and can share technology experience and expertise without reservation. School librarians may have more expertise than some members of the community and therefore may have more to share, but they also have the opportunity to be facilitators for active contributions from all members. Richard DuFour (2004), who is frequently associated with the concept of a PLC, outlines its core characteristics:

- The core mission is focused in the assumption that the purpose of formal education is not merely that students are taught, but rather that they learn.
- Teachers work in collaboration to analyze and improve their classroom practice.
- The work is results-driven, and the proof relies in information that documents improved student learning and not merely on raw data and inputs.

Most exciting and fruitful, PLCs engender a culture of collaboration, of sharing ideas. For professional development around the topic of technology, the PLC could be grade level or departmental, or organized around types of technology of interest (e.g., Web 2.0 tools, online information resources, or e-books). Crucial aspects are that the PLC is sustained over time, characterized by a collegial environment in which all participants feel free to share and to agree or disagree. Although technology may be inherently captivating, the focus remains on student learning. Administrative support to facilitate time for PLC work is, of course, essential.

True integration of technology is more than an add-on. Technology has been appropriately integrated in curriculum when an observer sees technology as a seamless part of the lesson; when the reason for using the technology is obvious; when students are focusing on learning rather than on technology;

when the teacher finds it difficult to accomplish his or her objectives without the technology; and when all students are benefiting from the technology (Roblyer and Doering, 2010). The school librarian will always need to be the "crow's nester"—the one who knows what is on the horizon and what is worth considering within the context of the school and its students.

As a trainer or professional developer for technology, the school librarian does well to understand the change process and possess the skills needed for helping teachers accept new ideas. For some teachers, integrating technologies into their curricula may require substantial changes in educational philosophy, classroom management, and curricular goals. After observing implementation of technology in public schools as a part of a longitudinal study in 14 states, Foa, Schwab, and Johnson (1996: 52) conclude:

> For technologies to be used effectively, teachers must be comfortable with a constructivist or project-based, problem-solving approach to learning; they must be willing to tolerate students progressing independently at widely varying paces; they must trust students to know more than they do about certain subjects and techniques, and in fact to take on the role of expert teacher at various times; they must be comfortable about not having complete control over what resources the student accesses or what the student learns and they must be flexible enough to change directions when technical glitches occur. For some teachers these practices are all second nature. . . .

More often, however, librarians are asking teachers to integrate dramatically new philosophies of education, curricular goals, classroom management techniques, and ideas about interdisciplinary and differentiated education into their daily practice. "No wonder the introduction of technologies is often perceived as threatening" (Foa, Schwab, and Johnson, 1996: 56). Sensitivity to teachers is nothing new to the school librarian, whose very curriculum is dependent on collaboration.

Hall and Hord (2001) describe the concerns-based adoption model (CBAM), a sequence of concerns that innovation raises. The sequence begins with *information concerns,* the need for introductory information about the innovation. As technology advocate, the school librarian makes teachers aware of a new use for technology—either hardware or software—that has potential to enhance or expand the current way of learning. In general, people tend to resist innovation when they perceive there is no need for it. A technology innovation must promise a substantial improvement in the learning experience before teachers, beyond the early adopters, will have enough interest to adopt it. In short, there must be some incentive to undertake the change, and ideally that incentive needs to be the intrinsic value of the technology. Before advocating for a technology implementation, the school librarian must have confidence that it is worth doing.

Next come *personal concerns,* where the novice wonders how an innovation will affect him or her: "What will I need to learn and how will I have to change to adopt this idea?" Fear of failure contributes to resistance to change. This anxiety typically calls for support and encouragement. Once personal concerns are alleviated, *management concerns* emerge: "How will I make this work in my classroom or schedule?" It is natural to want a sense of control, and teachers are accustomed to being in control of the content and flow of events in their classrooms. Therefore, innovations perceived as potentially eroding their control of instruction or their students are likely to bring resistance. Beyond management are *consequence concerns:* "What difference will this make for my students?" Sharing testimonies of successful adopters of a technology can help teachers see the potential benefits for their own students. Next, the CBAM model suggests that needs for *collaborating* and *refocusing* emerge. At this point, teachers need to work with someone else to fit the technology precisely to their situation—an opportunity for the school librarian and teacher to work together. If librarians are aware of these concerns when adopting an innovation, they can more easily appreciate the teacher's viewpoint.

Teacher

Besides working with teachers in developing technology competencies, librarians have a substantial role to play in teaching students about information technology. Specific skills to be taught are grounded in the ISTE NETS for Students (www.iste.org) and/or the *AASL Standards for the 21st-Century Learner* (www.ala.org/aasl/guidelinesandstandards/learningstandards/standards). It is important to keep this role in mind and to consider these questions: What are the skills and knowledge students need to be effective users of this technology? What implications does this technology have for teaching? How can these technology skills be integrated into the information skills curriculum? What ethical issues must students learn to address?

An example of a tool for integrated information literacy skills is the WebQuest. School librarians can work with teachers to create WebQuests as one effective way to engage students in making use of information online. A WebQuest is "an inquiry-oriented activity in which some or all of the information that learners interact with comes from resources on the Internet" (Dodge, 1995). WebQuests follow a general format of setting the stage, engaging the student in a task, providing links to a set of information sources that will help them complete the task, and guiding the process students will follow. The tasks are essentially problems that require students to select relevant information and apply it to solve a problem. QuestGarden (http://questgarden.com) is a searchable source for examples of WebQuests. A well-designed WebQuest asks students to apply the information they gather to a problem and create a product with which they transfer their learning to a defined audience. The expectations for a WebQuest are not unlike those for any good authentic assignment: it is designed so that students do more than merely report information findings and instead synthesize findings and integrate them into a response that represents application, synthesis, and evaluation of information. A common caveat about WebQuests is to ensure that expectations for students go beyond reporting findings, which can be accomplished simply through copy and paste. Done well, WebQuests can engage students in higher-order thinking as they take advantage of the expanded capabilities that technology offers.

Policy Maker

Policy making is another aspect of the technology role for school librarians. Librarians provide leadership in developing an array of policies that govern access to constitutionally protected material and that protect students, support appropriate use of technology, support provisions of copyright law, and offer equitable opportunities for use of technology.

ACCEPTABLE USE OF TECHNOLOGY RESOURCES

The Children's Internet Protection Act (CIPA) has created a challenging requirement for schools, in that the Supreme Court 2003 decision upheld the constitutionality of the use of Internet filters but ruled that libraries may override the filter if it blocks access to constitutionally protected material. Meanwhile, the use of filtering systems to limit access to websites is an expectation for schools receiving E-Rate discounts or Library Services and Technology Act (LSTA) funds. The Wisconsin Department of Public Instruction (Bocher, 2004) summarizes the requirements for school libraries:

1. A school or library must have some type of filter or blocking technology on all of its computers with Internet access. The filters must protect against access to certain visual depictions that are:

   Obscene: This is defined in section 1460 of title 18, US Code.

   Child pornography: This is defined in section 2256 of title 18, US Code.

   Harmful to minors: This is applicable only to Internet access by minors. It is defined in CIPA and means any picture, image, graphic image file, or other visual depiction that:
   a. taken as a whole, appeals to a prurient interest in nudity, sex, or excretion;
   b. depicts, describes, or represents, in a patently offensive way, an actual or simulated sexual act or sexual contact, actual or simulated normal or perverted sexual acts, or a lewd exhibition of the genitals; and
   c. taken as a whole, lacks serious literary, artistic, political, or scientific value.

2. A school or library must have an Internet safety policy and hold a public meeting to review the policy.

Traditionally, selection policies have provided guidelines for what schools buy. However, access to the web reduces the control educators have. This more open access to information has generated action to protect students and limit access. The best response is to inform students of what will constitute acceptable use of network resources in the school. Principles of intellectual freedom challenge the notion of schools censoring what will be accessible to students. Establishing that school-related information searching is the purpose for network resources seems an appropriate approach. Many schools have developed an acceptable use policy (AUP) to define parameters for using network resources. AUPs usually include the following components (Miller, 2004):

1. A description of the instructional philosophies and strategies to be supported by Internet access in schools. For example, an introductory statement might read, "Internet access is coordinated through a complex association of agencies, regional and state networks, and commercial organizations. To ensure smooth operation of the network, the following provisions regulate proper conduct and efficient, ethical, and legal usage."

2. A statement on the educational uses and advantages of the Internet in your school or division. A statement might include, "The use of your account must be in support of education or research."

3. A list of the responsibilities of educators, parents, and students for using the Internet. For example, parents should advise their children about privacy issues online.

4. A code of conduct governing behavior on the Internet. Here the AUP may include a statement indicating that cyberbullying will not be tolerated and describe the consequences for this behavior. In addition, a statement on vandalism may be appropriate: "Vandalism will result in cancellation of privileges. Vandalism is defined as any malicious attempt to harm or destroy hardware, software, or data of another user or any of the above listed agencies or other networks. This includes but is not limited to uploading or creating computer viruses or breaching security measures."

5. A description of the consequences of violating the AUP. The policy may simply state, "The use of the Internet is a privilege, not a right, and inappropriate use will result in a cancellation of that privilege."

6. A description of what constitutes acceptable and unacceptable use of the Internet. For example, a statement might include provisions such as, "Transmissions that violate any district, state, or U.S. regulations are prohibited. These transmissions include but are not limited to copyrighted material and threatening or obscene material. Use for commercial activities, product advertisement, or political lobbying is prohibited. You are expected to abide by the generally accepted rules of network etiquette. These might include but are not limited to the following:

Use appropriate language. Do not swear or use vulgarities or any other inappropriate language.

Do not reveal your personal address or phone number or those of students or colleagues.

Note that electronic mail is not guaranteed to be private. People who operate the system do have access to all mail. Messages relating to or in support of illegal activities may be reported to authorities.

Do not engage in illegal activities. These include but are not limited to threats, harassment, stalking, and fraud.

Do not use the network in such a way that you would disrupt the use of the network by other users.

Respect intellectual property of others by crediting sources and respecting all copyright laws.

Do not use another individual's account without written permission from that individual. Attempts to log on as a system operator will result in cancellation of user privileges. Any user identified as a security risk may be denied access to the district's computer resources."

7. A disclaimer absolving the school division, under specific circumstances, from responsibility

8. A statement that the AUP is in compliance with state and national telecommunication rules and regulations

9. A signature form for teachers, parents, and students indicating their intent to abide by the AUP, and that parents and teachers will accept responsibility for supervision of students

AUPs should include language about the use of social networking sites and blogs in order for schools to protect themselves against the possible violation of a student's First Amendment rights (Adams, 2008). For example, if a district states in its AUP that the use of social networking sites is prohibited during school hours, a student who posts something offensive on a social networking site while at school can be punished for violating the AUP, not because of the content of his or her speech. Prohibiting the use of social networking sites at school also helps to keep students safer from online predators. On the other hand, some districts see social networking sites and blogs as potential learning tools for their students. In these cases, the AUP should state that such sites and Web 2.0 tools would only be used at school under the permission of the supervising teacher. In addition to providing guidance on the use of technology resources, the AUP is also a means of ensuring student access to information and intellectual freedom. During the AUP review process, the school librarian should urge that the policy protect students' First Amendment right to receive information. The American Library Association's "Access to Digital Information, Services, and Networks" states:

> Information retrieved, utilized, or created digitally is constitutionally protected unless determined otherwise by a court of competent jurisdiction. These rights extend to minors as well as adults ("Free Access to Libraries for Minors"; "Access to Resources and Services in the School Library Media Program"; "Access for Children and Young Adults to Nonprint Materials"; and "Minors and Internet Interactivity"). . . . Libraries should use technology to enhance, not deny, access to information. (ALA, 2009)

The AUP should also make it clear that there are no guarantees of privacy to users of the network.

In order to ensure enforcement, it is crucial that the AUP be effectively communicated to all members of the school community. The first step in this process takes place when parents and students read and sign the policy. And to keep the issues prominent in each school, students and parents should sign the policies at the start of each school year (Dyrli, 2002: 29).

ETHICAL USE

Copyright of electronic resources is a complex issue. A primary purpose of copyright is to ensure ongoing creation. Those who create must have some means of protecting their creation and, ideally, gaining some compensation for it. This purpose must be balanced against dissemination of ideas necessary for continuing intellectual and creative progress. The fair use doctrine allows certain uses of copyrighted material (e.g., criticism, reporting, teaching, and scholarship) that would otherwise be copyright infringements. Four factors determine fair use:

Purpose or character of the use. Use in the regular course of one's educational activities usually satisfies the requirement that the use is for nonprofit educational purposes rather than for commercial purposes.

Nature of the copyrighted work. The fair use doctrine is more likely to apply to factual works or works intended for the educational market than to fictional or creative expression.

Amount and substantiality of the portion. Generally, the fair use doctrine requires the least possible use of an original work. The substantiality test means that the essence of the work (e.g., the theme of a musical score) is not used.

Effect upon the potential market. Fair use should not adversely affect the original author's economic opportunities.

Multimedia copyright guidelines were agreed to and released in 1997, the result of lengthy discussion between representatives of copyright holders and educators led by the Consortium of College and University Media Centers. Although these guidelines are not law, they represent an agreement on limits of use. The guidelines permit students to create multimedia works and retain them in portfolios for job interviews. Teachers may create and use copyrighted material in their multimedia productions in face-to-face instruction and may assign students to look at them independently. Teachers may also display their productions at conferences when using copyrighted material under the limits set by the guidelines. Quantitative limits set in the guidelines of how much can be used from a copyrighted work include the following:

Motion media (film/video)—up to 10 percent or three minutes, whichever is less, of an individual program

Text—up to 10 percent or 1,000 words, whichever is less; complete short poems; and three poems per poet or five poems per anthology

Music—up to 10 percent but not more than 30 seconds

Illustrations—no more than five images per artist; not more than 10 percent or 16 images from a single collective work

Another resource for guidance on intellectual property issues in a digital environment is the Center for Social Media (CSM; www.centerforsocialmedia .org). CSM offers guidelines for best practice in multimedia production. In contrast to the 1997 quantitative guidelines, CSM suggests a more open/qualitative approach to uses of creative works, but again, the principle of attribution is emphasized. CSM's best practice guidelines outline how to make use of digital works ethically in an educational environment. Two key questions guide the interpretation of fair use:

> Did the unlicensed use "transform" the material taken from the copyrighted work by using it for a purpose different than that of the original, or did it just repeat the work for the same intent and value as the original?
>
> Was the material taken appropriate in kind and amount, considering the nature of the copyrighted work and of the use?

Affirmative answers to these two questions suggest that the use is fair in an educational environment, according to CSM. The transformative criterion calls for true creation of a new work. These best practice guidelines emphasize the fact that guidelines such as the 1997 multimedia guidelines are not the law.

More recently, students' increased use of digital content has opened more doors for student projects. The Creative Commons (http://creativecommons .org) provides a way to share, create, and remix. Here, media creators have the opportunity to license their works. Creators of works may choose to license others to copy their work, make derivative works or adaptations of their work, distribute their work, and/or make money from their work. The creator governs the extent to which the work is shared. For student producers then, the Creative Commons provides a source for images, video, and other works that they can use according to the license provided by the creator. Consistent in the Creative Commons license is the expectation that users will attribute credit to the creator. This provision asserts the importance of respect for intellectual property. Searching via the Creative Commons search engine (http://search.creativecommons.org) yields results for which the user can see the license and know how freely the work may be used. The user can select to search for those works that are available to "modify, adapt, or build on." In essence, this option gives the user permission to use the resource in his or her own work—with attribution.

Librarians need to encourage students and teachers to be aware of copyright and its protective purposes. Students must learn that access to works on the web does not automatically mean that these materials can be reproduced and reused without permission or royalty payment; also, some copyrighted works may have been posted without authorization of the copyright holder. Attribution should be a concept that students apply in all their own creative work.

LIBRARY CIRCULATION SYSTEM POLICIES

Upholding professional ethics associated with intellectual freedom involves setting policies within the library circulation system and its use that encourage open access to the resources of the school library. Examples of settings include provisions to ensure confidentiality, such as setting the system preferences to eliminate the historical record of borrowing transactions once the item has been returned. This setting safeguards against attempts to review what topics or resources a student has been using. When students know that policies are in place to protect the confidentiality of their library records, they can feel greater freedom to pursue information of importance to them— even when it may be sensitive. Similarly, setting policies will ensure that anyone who has access to circulation records in the library understands the importance of confidentiality and does not divulge confidential information freely. Similarly, publication of overdue items needs to be managed in a way that is confidential as well; providing lists to teachers or posting lists publicly both violate the principle of confidentiality.

Physical Access to Technology

Because adequate and equitable access is a key professional value held by school librarians, it is important to be aware of technical issues that will facilitate access. In-school access to computers and the Internet has improved dramatically in recent years, especially since the introduction of the E-Rate, officially known as the Schools and Libraries Universal Service Program and created as part of the Telecommunications Act of 1996. This program applies fees from the telecommunications industry to fund discounts on local area networking, Internet service, and telecommunications services. Before the E-Rate, several studies had revealed significant differences in technology use based on the socioeconomic status of schools. While today nearly all schools report Internet access and deployment of technology, inequity continues across schools and school districts. A study by Hohlfeld and colleagues (2010) revealed apparent differences between high SES (socio-economic status) and low SES schools related to student use of software. They reported that students in the study in low SES elementary and middle schools appeared to use content delivery software significantly more often than their high SES counterparts. Conversely, students in high SES schools, at every level, appeared to be using production software significantly more frequently than those in low SES schools.

High-speed access is necessary for truly taking advantage of the potential of the Internet. According to a 2011 report from the US Department of Commerce, significant gaps exist in high-speed home Internet access among certain demographic and geographic groups around the country. Adults 25 and older with college degrees adopt broadband at almost triple the rate of those with some high school education (84 versus 30 percent). The rates for white (68 percent) and Asian non-Hispanics (69 percent) exceed those for black non-Hispanics (50 percent) and Hispanics (45 percent). Rural America lags behind urban areas by ten percentage points (60 versus 70 percent). These disparities underscore the importance of providing sufficient online access in schools as a step toward equity. Adequate school access requires not only adequate access points (computers, tablets, or other devices) but also adequate bandwidth to meet the speed requirements of today's online resources. In a report from the State Educational Technology Directors Association (SETDA, 2008), most schools in the country are at T1 (1.54 Mbps) connection speeds between school buildings, with some having additional capacity. With these bandwidth speeds, schools are trying to accommodate the technology needs of many concurrent users. Compared to the average household with broadband access of at least 5 Mbps with just a few users, bandwidth in many schools is significantly lower, considering many more concurrent users. Even in schools that are sufficiently connected with broadband, bandwidth demand is quickly exceeding capacity as they utilize advanced technology tools.

In a technology-rich learning environment looking forward to 2014, SETDA recommends the following:

- An external Internet connection to the Internet service provider of at least 10 Mbps per 1,000 students/staff
- Internal wide area network connections from the district to each school and between schools of at least 100 Mbps per 1,000 students/staff

In the five to seven years after 2014, SETDA recommends the following:

- An external Internet connection to the Internet service provider of at least 100 Mbps per 1,000 students/staff
- Internal wide area network connections from the district to each school and between schools of at least 1 Gbps per 1,000 students/staff

SETDA recommends that school districts consider the following questions when updating their broadband access:

- How many students use your network?
- How many teachers and administrators use your network?
- How many computers are connected to the Internet in your school district?
- Based on the number of students, teachers, administrators, and computers, how many concurrent users are on the network at any given time?
- What technology applications do you use?
- What technology applications are planned for the future?
- How much bandwidth is required for each technology application?
- How can you build scalability and flexibility into the network to ensure continuous improvement?

Districts can use these values to determine approximate bandwidth demand, and then use this information to scale the bandwidth required in the next three to five years. In a powerful technology environment supply also creates demand, and as educators see the benefits of technology applications, they will want to use even more technology tools and resources. Technology leaders can also access the School 2.0 Bandwidth Calculator to determine the amount of bandwidth needed to run current and/or future applications at http://etoolkit.org/etoolkit/bandwidth_calculator.

The past ten years have seen the emergence of 1:1 laptop initiatives (Holcomb, 2009). More recently, 1:1 netbook or tablet initiatives are underway as well. These initiatives hold promise for increasing adequacy and equity of access to online resources. Bandwidth is a particularly crucial consideration, however, when deploying devices to every student. Beyond improving access is how to integrate the use of technology so that it enhances learning.

Planning for Technology

Planning is "a set of formal and rational activities that seeks to anticipate conditions, directions, and challenges at some future point for the purposes of enhancing the readiness of personnel and the organization to perform more effectively and to attain relevant objectives by optimal means" (Knezevich, 1984: 88).

There are several key concepts in this definition. First, planning is formal and rational. The word *rational* emphasizes gathering information and making reasonable and informed decisions. Technology is an area where it may be easy to jump on the bandwagon of buying hardware or software for no reason except that others are doing so. A rational approach to planning calls for analyzing the school's goals and technology capabilities and then identifying the intersections where technology can substantively improve goal attainment.

Another key concept in this definition is the readiness of personnel and the organization in terms of staff involvement and careful consideration of the organizational context. A final key term is *optimal means*. Planning involves looking for the best ways to attain the organization's objectives. Quality is important whenever considering technological innovations; the marketplace is vast, and not everything in it represents optimal means. No school or district should be without a formal technology plan because of rapid change, high costs, the range of enthusiasm from zealous to resistant, the importance of broad-based ownership, and the complexity of integration into the instructional program. An effective external incentive for comprehensive technology planning is the E-Rate discount. Participation in the E-Rate Universal Service program requires a three-year plan. To qualify for a Universal Service discount, a technology plan (www.universalservice.org/sl/applicants/step02) must address these points:

- Establish clear goals and a realistic strategy for using telecommunications and information technology to improve education or library services.
- Include a professional development strategy to ensure that staff members know how to use technology to improve education or library services.

- Include an assessment of the telecommunication services, hardware, software, and other services that will be needed to improve education or library services.
- Implement an evaluation process that enables the school or library to monitor progress toward the specified goals and make midcourse corrections in response to new developments and opportunities as they arise.

For technology planning to be effective, some baseline work must occur. Establishing a mission for technology in teaching and learning is an important first step. Such a mission grows out of underlying assumptions about the nature of technology and learning. One such belief is that technology is a tool that allows people to extend their capabilities by working smarter or faster. Learning is the result of creating new meaning by relating new experiences and prior learning. Given these two beliefs, a mission for technology might call for students to use technological tools to access, manipulate, and communicate information. What is important is that the technology mission be closely tied to its larger context—the mission for the school.

A technology plan must be the product of broad-based teamwork. Key players include teachers, administrators, parents, local businesspeople, physical plant workers, and library professionals. Physical plant workers are likely to know secrets about buildings that can make critical differences in networking decisions. Local businesspeople and parents may be helpful in garnering support when they understand the program; they also bring a perspective that may generate valuable ideas or insights that are different from those of educators. Each stakeholder has something to bring to the discussions about technology, and each can serve as an advocate for ideas when implementation begins.

The technology planning process is never finished. While a long-term view is important for establishing mission and goals, short-term planning is ongoing because of the constant changes in available technologies. This is not a process to occur every five or even every three years; it is continuous. The long-term view must provide for budgeting. Technology is a capital expenditure, and without line items in the budget for technology, planning is futile. That budget must include consideration of several items:

> *Infrastructure.* Reliability, adequacy, bandwidth, and security are key attributes of infrastructure necessary to support the use of technology

district-wide (Johnson, 2003). Network administration is a crucial aspect of infrastructure.

New hardware. Today's iPad or netbook will be superseded by new devices that must be evaluated for their potential to enhance learning and teaching.

New applications

Annual licensing fees for software and databases

Hardware upgrades. Three years is about as long as a computer is likely to run effectively without being upgraded.

Replacement hardware. After about four years, a computer needs to be reviewed for its capacity to continue in its assigned purpose. Often by that time, processor speed, memory limitations, or storage capacity makes the machine less useful for a given application. Also, a machine may need to be reassigned to a less demanding task or retired completely. For each new computer installation, the budget four years ahead needs to include a replacement for it.

Staff development. Release time for teachers to participate in training, trainers' stipends, and the costs of facilities, equipment, software, supplies, and technology-related conference attendance are all necessary expenses.

Technical support. As more machines are acquired, maintenance and repair, either by in-house technical staff or by contractors, becomes essential. Existing employees cannot take on this additional work because it must be the highest priority of the individual. Besides, the workload will grow.

A sound technology plan should be results-driven, with a focus on how the technology will be used and what difference it will make (Jukes, 1996). The test questions are, What worthwhile activity can this technology allow that could not be done before? What worthwhile activity can this technology allow to be done substantially better? McKenzie (2002: 35) states, "We should only acquire new technologies that will improve student performance on learning tasks that match state curriculum standards or address important local learning goals." Such a standard needs to be considered during the planning process to ensure that resources are allocated where they will have impact, not simply to satisfy calls for fair and equal distribution or to keep up with neighboring districts.

Staff development needs to be ongoing and incremental and not a collection of one-shot events; it also cannot be a generic set of lessons or a one-size-fits-all approach. Instead, a sound staff development plan is directly relevant to what the participants will do. Staff development must also be thorough; a series of lessons with time for teachers to share ideas and to practice is more appropriate than covering many topics superficially. Before teachers can feel confident to add technology to their teaching repertoire, they must feel ownership; that can occur only when they have time to experiment, collaborate, and create for themselves. Ongoing PLCs around technology topics, supported by administrators with time and resources, increases the opportunities for the sustained attention on ways to integrate technology effectively. Teachers need to have adequate access to computers to build confidence and skill; providing access, either by lending computers for home use or providing computers to teachers for their classrooms, is essential. Teachers are far less likely to embrace technology when they must share computer lab space with students or when they must borrow a computer for limited times at school. Effective staff development calls for a readily available support system; when teachers forget a step in the use of a program or attempt something altogether new, they need a colleague to call, someone who is convenient, knowledgeable, and supportive. Such a person can certainly be the school librarian.

Just as staff development needs must be addressed, benchmarks indicating student competencies in using technology need to be clearly defined and assessed. The ISTE standards for students provide a framework for development of technology student learning outcomes. These standards address the following areas of technology skills and competencies:

- Demonstrate creative thinking, construct knowledge, and develop innovative products and processes using technology.
- Use digital media and environments to communicate and work collaboratively, including at a distance, to support individual learning and contribute to the learning of others.
- Use critical thinking skills to plan and conduct research, manage projects, solve problems, and make informed decisions using appropriate digital tools and resources.

- Understand human, cultural, and societal issues related to technology and practice legal and ethical behavior.
- Demonstrate a sound understanding of technology concepts, systems, and operations.

The school librarian can bring these student standards to the technology planning process to provide scaffolding for a technology curriculum as part of the overall technology plan.

An example of comprehensive technology planning is the three-year plan developed under the leadership of Mary Lynn Kovach, Technology Coordinator for the schools in Parchment, Michigan, accessible at www .parchmentschools.org/docs/district/plans/final_tech_plan_v2.pdf This plan integrates all aspects of technology planning: vision, goals and objectives, learning, parent communication, infrastructure, technical support, professional development, budget, and evaluation. Extensive appendices provide details and rubrics for implementation and monitoring.

Evaluation

Assessment of student performance is an important dimension of the evaluation process. Building curriculum based on the ISTE standards will include benchmarks against which assessments can be designed to ensure that students are developing appropriate technology skills. The Rhinelander (Wisconsin) School District has set grade-level benchmarks, keyed to the ISTE standards, to guide assessment (see www.rhinelander.k12.wi.us/ itlbenchmarks.cfm).

Conclusion

Technology planning is a complex process that must take into account the school and district fiscal capacity, perspectives on learning and teaching, and the needs of students. School librarians bring to the planning table a cross-age perspective that differs from teachers. They bring a technical perspective that differs from technologists because it is grounded in their understanding of learning. They bring awareness of emerging technologies and their potential to facilitate learning. They bring organizational systems that afford efficiency in managing technologies and organizing for online access to digital information. Further, school librarians offer important capabilities for faculty professional development as well as student instruction and bring understanding of ethical issues associated with technology use in schools. In short, they contribute to both planning and implementation of technology plans. School librarians must be ready to articulate what they offer to the technology program and then be ready to act.

Leadership Strategies

Teacher and Partner

Teach information technologies as part of the information skills curriculum.

Initiate and facilitate PLCs focused on integration of technology.

Information Specialist

Facilitate access to technology for teachers and students by reducing barriers:

- Consider home checkout.
- Purchase laptop or handheld devices such as e-book readers or iPads to expand access.
- Pursue special purchase plans for teachers' computers. Some school districts have worked with local vendors to make special purchase plans available with cooperation from local banks for low-interest loans and with the school district business office for payment by payroll deduction.
- Maintain awareness of the needs of exceptional learners and be on the lookout for technologies that can improve their access to information.

Program Administrator

Seek a position on school and/or district technology planning teams.

Be a leader/role model in the uses of technology for the entire school.

Maintain current awareness in the area of technology by

- using RSS feeds from such sources as AASL Hotlinks at www
  .ala.org/aasl/publications-journals/hotlinks;

- joining a Ning, such as the ISTE Ning at www.iste-community
  .org;

- following key leaders in technology on Twitter; for example,
  Joyce Valenza at http://twitter.com/#!/Joycevalenza;

- reading such journals as *Library Media Connection* or *Learning
  and Leading with Technology;*

- attending conferences sponsored by national organizations such
  as ISTE or Educause and/or their state affiliates;

- participating in webinars offered by professional associations
  like AASL or ISTE; and

- using Google Reader to organize your information feeds.

Establish criteria for technology applications and software selection to
promote a commitment to quality in the use of technology.

Use the automated circulation system to manage hardware inventory.

Remind teachers and administrators that technology must be used in the
context of the instructional program, not as an add-on.

Provide leadership in developing policies related to acceptable use of
resources, copyright, privacy, and intellectual freedom as these relate
to technology.

Collect data to document the uses of technology and its impact, and
include statistics on use of equipment, facilities, and software, as
well as sample documents and projects created by students, to demonstrate the qualitative impact technology has had.

Scenarios for Discussion

Scenario 1

Hitchcock Elementary School has a high percentage of students from lower
socioeconomic backgrounds. A strong before- and after-school program

(BASP) meets in the building. It benefits many students, and the new librarian wants to do her part to maintain a positive relationship between this program's staff and the school staff. It has been past practice for the BASP to use the computer lab in the library after school. School staff members have expressed concerns about problems with the lab use by this group in the past; for example, unsupervised Internet use, inappropriate downloading, changes to the desktop, and mistreatment of mice and keyboards. The librarian initiated a conversation with the BASP director about these concerns, but no changes have been observed. What next?

Scenario 2

Granger Middle School has recently gone to a 1:1 laptop model in grades 6, 7, and 8. Because there had been some community push-back on the initiative based on cost and concern about potential effectiveness, the principal is very eager to see maximum use of the laptops. She comes to visit with you in the school library and asks you to create a page on your library website where you link to as many different Web 2.0 resources and tools as you can. She hopes that by providing teachers with as many resources as possible, everyone will find something they would choose to use in their teaching. How will you respond? What might you recommend?

REFERENCES

Adams, H. R. 2008. "Dusting Off the Acceptable Use Policy (AUP)." *School Library Media Activities Monthly* 25, no. 4: 56.

ALA (American Library Association). 2009. "Access to Digital Information, Services, and Networks." American Library Association. www.ala.org/advocacy/intfreedom/librarybill/interpretations/accessdigital.

Basham, J. D., M. Israel, J. Graden, R. Poth., and M. Winston. 2010. "A Comprehensive Approach to RtI: Embedding Universal Design for Learning and Technology." *Learning Disability Quarterly* 33, no. 4: 243–255

Batsche, G., J. Elliot, J. L. Graden, J. Grimes, J. F. Kovaleski, D. Prasse, D. J. Reschly, J. Schräg, and W. D. Tilly. 2005. *Response to Intervention: Policy Considerations and Implementation.* Alexandria, VA: National Association of State Directors of Special Education.

Bocher, B. 2004. "FAQ on E-Rate Compliance with the Children's Internet Protection Act and the Neighborhood Children's Internet Protection Act." Wisconsin Department of Public Instruction, February 19. http://pld.dpi .wi.gov/files/pld/pdf/cipafaq.pdf .

CCUMC (Consortium of College and University Media Centers). 2012. "Copyright Matters." Consortium of College and University Media Centers. www .ccumc.org/index.php?option=com_content&view=article&id=44&Itemid=102.

Cennamo, K., J. Ross, and P. Ertmer. 2010. *Technology Integration for Meaningful Classroom Use: A Standards-Based Approach.* Belmont, CA: Wadsworth Cengage Learning.

Cooper, E. 2009. "Overloading on Slides: Cognitive Load Theory and Microsoft's Slide Program PowerPoint." *AACE Journal* 17, no. 2: 127–135.

Dodge, B. 1995. "Some Thoughts about WebQuests." WebQuest.org. Updated May 5, 1997. http://webquest.sdsu.edu/about_webquests.html.

DuFour, R. 2004. "What Is a Professional Learning Community?" *Educational Leadership* 61, no. 8: 6–11.

Dyrli, O. 2002. "Does Your Web Policy Cover Student Sites?" *District Administration* 38, no. 12: 46.

Ertmer, P. A., and A. Ottenbreit-Leftwich. 2010. "Teacher Technology Change: How Knowledge, Confidence, Beliefs, and Culture Intersect." *Journal of Research on Technology in Education* 42, no. 3: 255–284.

Foa, L., R. Schwab, and M. Johnson. 1996. "Upgrading School Technology." *Education Week* 15 (May): 52+.

Hall, G. E., and S. M. Hord. 2000. *Implementing Change: Patterns, Principles, and Potholes.* Boston: Allyn and Bacon.

Hohlfeld, T. N., A. D. Ritzhaupt, A. E. Barron, and K. Kemker. 2008. "Examining the Digital Divide in K–12 Public Schools: Four-Year Trends for Supporting ICT Literacy in Florida." *Computers and Education* 51, no. 4: 1648–1663.

Holcomb, L. B. 2009. "Results and Lessons Learned from 1:1 Laptop Initiatives: A Collective Review." *TechTrends* 53, no. 6: 49–55.

Johnson, D. 2003. "Maslow and Motherboards: Taking a Hierarchical View of Technology Planning." *MultiMedia Schools* 10, no. 1: 26–33.

Jukes, I. 1996. "The Essential Steps of Technology Planning." *School Administrator* 53, no. 4: 8–14.

Knezevich, S. 1984. *Administration of Public Education.* New York: Harper and Row.

McKenzie, J. 2002. "Tech Smart: Making Discerning Technology Choices." *Multimedia Schools* 9, no. 2: 34–39.

Miller, J. 2004. "Intellectual Freedom and the Internet: Developing Acceptable Use Policies." *School Libraries in Canada* 23, no. 3: 25–30.

Roblyer, M. D., and A. H. Doering. 2010. *Integrating Educational Technology into Teaching.* 5th ed. Upper Saddle River, NJ: Prentice Hall.

SETDA (State Educational Technology Directors Association). 2008. *High-Speed Broadband Access for All Kids: Breaking through the Barriers.* State Educational Technology Directors Association. www.setda.org/c/document _library/get_file?folderId=270&name=DLFE-211.pdf.

Smith, S. J., and C. Okolo. 2010. "Response to Intervention and Evidence-Based Practices: Where Does Technology Fit?" *Learning Disability Quarterly* 33, no. 4: 257–272.

US Department of Commerce, National Telecommunications and Information Administration. 2011. *Digital Nation: Expanding Internet Usage.* US Department of Commerce. www.ntia.doc.gov/files/ntia/publications/ ntia_internet_use_report_february_2011.pdf.

12

Inquiry-Based Learning

This chapter:

- examines inquiry-based learning in the library curriculum;
- explores mental models of the inquiry process as they influence students' performance;
- introduces concept-based learning;
- considers responsibilities and dispositions as aspects of inquiry;
- proposes self-assessment as a significant component of the inquiry process;
- proposes college standards for inquiry for high school librarians; and
- identifies leadership strategies related to inquiry-based learning.

There was a time when a canon of content constituted a curriculum. However, the learning environment of the twenty-first century is vastly different and demands a more process-oriented curriculum. Students must leave our schools with skills that prepare them to access, evaluate, and use information with efficiency and sophistication. The modes for information delivery are changing in scope, media, and organization. New tools for managing and communicating information emerge with ever-increasing frequency. Succeeding in an environment of rapid change demands skills to function effectively. In addition, it will be essential that students leave our schools with the appropriate dispositions for continuing to learn—dispositions of curiosity, open-mindedness, persistence, and investigative enthusiasm, accompanied by a critical stance. Also, they must accept responsibilities. In eras long past, information belonged to the few, the elite. Now information is broadly accessible, but it must be used in a framework of ethics and responsibility. Finally, the ability to self-assess one's information work is inherent in independent learning. All these dimensions must be considered in designing instruction in the library program.

Inquiry

In the process of inquiry-based learning, students are involved in cycles of questioning, investigation, verification, and generation of new questions (Harada and Yoshina, 2004a). Inquiry-based learning "provokes deeper thinking and investigation and greater student motivation to learn" (Harada and Yoshina, 2004b: 22). But what does it look like? Inquiry-based learning begins with accessing and building background knowledge about a topic. Unfortunately, this collection of knowledge is often the end of a research process when students simply gather facts. For example, they collect information about an animal, say the Canada goose—what it eats, where it lives, what threats for survival it faces, and so on. The outcome is a report of factual learning. However, in an inquiry approach, the result of that background knowledge is the generation of questions about which students are curious now that they know something about the subject; it is from this point that they *begin* inquiry. What if migrating geese stop migrating southward because of climate changes and remain in more northerly habits? How would the stay affect the geese? How would the change affect the new habitat? The generation of these research questions growing out of background knowledge distinguishes inquiry-based learning. These are authentic questions to which students have no answers and for which answers may be difficult to locate. These questions will require investigation into many subquestions and the use of many sources. Students may need to investigate more deeply: Why do geese migrate? What are they seeking and will they find it in one steady location? What resources do they consume and what is their impact on an environment? What are their nesting patterns and how might staying put affect those behaviors? Similarly, secondary school students might gather factual information about a country in Africa and then based on those facts pose a question such as, "What would it take for [Chad, Senegal, Nigeria, etc.] to become a significant participant in the world economy?" In short, inquiry does not end with a collection of facts. Factual findings lead to questions of interpretation, exploration, speculation—all of which require deeper, more complex investigation.

According to Chu and colleagues (2008), the implementation of an inquiry-based learning approach in schools includes the following key components:

- Students are provided with rich information sources.
- Students are equipped with information skills.
- A climate of inquiry is created.
- Scaffolding support is provided to students in developing inquiry-driven questions.
- Students follow an information-seeking process.
- Students learn to present their findings.

The school library is key to ensuring these components, whether it is the availability of resources, the teaching of skills, the nurturing of inquiry, the adoption of an information process model, or the technology for presentation of findings.

Inquiry Skills and Knowledge

The skills and knowledge dimensions of the AASL (2007) *Standards for the 21st-Century Learner* outline the competencies necessary to engage effectively in the inquiry process. These are delineated in 29 discrete skills, 18 of which are summarized in Figure 12.1. For the complete list of skills, see www.ala.org/aasl/guidelinesandstandards/learningstandards/standards.

The curriculum for the library program should address these skills, defining appropriate benchmarks at grade levels, identifying points of integration with content area curriculum to ensure teaching in a meaningful context, and methods of assessment. Figure 12.2 identifies examples of published curricula that may serve as models for such curriculum development.

Inquiry Process Models

A mental model is an intellectual framework created by integrating what one knows or has experienced within a given concept or task. Pitts (1995) investigated the effects of mental models on students' information work. Her findings offer insight into students' library use. She classified learners, based on their mental models of information processing, as either novices or experts. She describes the novice as one who has little prior knowledge of a topic and

FIGURE 12.1

Summary of Information Literacy Skills
from *Standards for the 21st-Century Learner*

Standard	Summary of Skills
Inquire, think critically, and gain knowledge.	• Follow an inquiry process. • Develop and refine research questions. • Find, evaluate, and select appropriate sources. • Evaluate information. • Make sense of information gathered. • Make use of technology tools. • Collaborate with others to broaden and deepen understanding.
Draw conclusions, make informed decisions, apply knowledge to new situations, and create new knowledge.	• Apply critical thinking skills to construct new understandings, draw conclusions, and create new knowledge. • Analyze and organize knowledge, making use of technology tools (e.g., spreadsheets, concept maps). • Collaborate with others to exchange ideas.
Share knowledge and participate ethically and productively as members of our democratic society.	• Use the writing process, visual literacy, and technology tools to express new understandings. • Use information and technology ethically and responsibly.
Pursue personal and aesthetic growth.	• Read, view, and listen for pleasure and personal growth. • Respond to creative expression of ideas. • Seek information for personal learning. • Organize personal knowledge. • Use social networks to gather and share information. • Use creative formats for expression.

whose personal understandings are fragmentary and based on a limited perspective. The expert has more connected understandings and a more global perspective. Pitts examined the work of student groups in a high school assigned to create video documentaries on topics in marine biology. For this project, there was no direct instruction related to either the process or the content of the assignment. Pitts's assessment of the students' work was that they used very little information from libraries and that they were often unsuccessful in their search for information. She identified several reasons for their lack of success. First, she suggested that students had incomplete subject-matter

FIGURE 12.2

Examples of School Library Curricula Online

Entity	Description	URL
Baltimore County School District (MD)	• Grades 1–5 • Curriculum crosswalk with Science and Social Studies • Crosswalk with AASL *Standards for the 21st-Century Learner* • Interactive online research process model	http://www.bcps.org/offices/lis/elmc/index.html
Iowa City (IA)	• Emphasizes both literature and information • Includes grade-span benchmarks • Includes lessons	http://www.iowa-city.k12.ia.us/library/Curriculum.htm See also *Developing 21st Century Literacies: A K–12 School Library Curriculum Blueprint with Sample Lessons* by Mary Jo Langhorne, Denise Rehmke, and Iowa City Community School District (Neal-Schuman, 2011).
New York City Schools	• Based on Stripling inquiry model • Graded by grade benchmarks • Aligned with Common Core Curriculum • Grounded in AASL Standards for 21st-Century Learner • Includes lessons	http://schools.nyc.gov/Academics/LibraryServices/StandardsandCurriculum/default.htm See also *Teaching for Inquiry: Engaging the Learner Within*, by Ruth V. Small, Marilyn P. Arnone, Barbara K. Stripling, and Pam Berger (Neal-Schuman, 2011).
St. Michael-Albertville District (MN)	• Grade-level and grade-span skills • High school skills in context of content areas	http://www.stma.k12.mn.us/curriculum/content_area/information_literacy.php

mental models and that this led to incomplete identification of their information needs. Her analysis of student searching revealed that most searches were very general in nature. In addition, she observed that students had limited mental models for information seeking and information use. They nearly always looked in only one place—the online catalog. If they did go beyond the catalog, they showed little understanding of which other resources would be likely to provide what they sought. A final problem she identified was the inaccurate mental models that adults had of the students' subject expertise or of their information-seeking prowess. Adults tended to provide only locational advice, either assuming that the student could identify the most appropriate resource or overestimating the student's expertise in the topic.

Pitts's findings have some powerful implications for schools. First, school librarians can help students develop a framework for inquiry by giving students a mental model of the process and the tasks associated with it, as well as a framework for the organization of information. Models like this can help students approach information work with an appropriate frame of reference. In addition, teachers can provide students with a framework for the discipline within which they are working. Finally, adult support throughout the inquiry process—not just at the beginning or at the end—will help students maintain a sense of direction. Various strategies can guide students throughout the process (Stripling, 1995):

> *Encapsulation.* At the end of a work session, students briefly record their understanding of the information they gathered.

> *Research log.* Students maintain a research log throughout the process, recording each day what they have learned, what questions they now have, and what they need to do next.

> *Conferencing.* Librarians and teachers confer with individuals or small groups at the end of a work session to discuss their reflections on their work so far.

> *Reflection.* Teachers and librarians pose questions for students to ask themselves along the way: "Am I really interested in this topic? Do my research questions go beyond collecting information to interpreting or evaluating? Do I have support for all of my conclusions?"

> *Rubrics.* Librarians and teachers develop rubrics for the information-processing tasks and refer students to them during each work session.

Overall, the instructional goals of the library program link directly to the work students bring to the library from the classroom. Collaboration between librarian and teacher is essential to achieve library instructional goals. Librarians bring to that collaboration a set of processes and strategies for students to learn, while the classroom teacher has instructional goals related to the content area. By creating challenging assignments and providing instruction, support, and adequate time, this team can provide students with the tools needed to be critical information consumers.

Several models of inquiry are available in the literature, including those of Eisenberg and Berkowitz (1990), Pappas and Tepe (Zimmerman, Pappas, and Tepe, 2002), Kuhlthau (2004), Stripling (Small et al., 2011), and others. All incorporate these basic elements: posing an information question, locating potential sources of information, examining and selecting relevant information, synthesizing, and communicating results. All models acknowledge that information processing is not a simple linear task but is instead recursive in nature; as students explore a topic, their research question may change. As they examine information and identify gaps, they return to the task of locating information. A school does well to adopt an information search model to provide a theoretical substructure to its information literacy curriculum. According to Donham and colleagues (2001: 16), adoption of an information process model serves to:

- break down the research process so that educators can design lessons to teach that process;
- provide a common lexicon for communication among library media specialists, teachers, and students;
- guide students in the research process; and
- help educators monitor what is taught and determine how well students are learning.

Inquiry/The Affective Domain

Foremost among researchers who have examined information processes is Carol Kuhlthau, who has closely monitored students working in libraries and has analyzed her observations in an effort to understand the process and appreciate students' needs. Only when the information process is explicitly considered can school librarians know what students need in order to be successful. After extensive research, Kuhlthau (2004) identified common patterns in students' information work. She describes that process in six stages (initiation, selection, exploration, formulation, collection, and presentation), each with its own typical tasks as well as feelings (see Figure 12.3).

Throughout her work, Kuhlthau emphasizes that movement from task to task is not necessarily a sequential process, but rather one of moving forward

FIGURE 12.3
Kuhlthau's Stages

Stage	Intellectual Tasks	Feelings
Initiation	Recognize the need for information.	Anxiety Uncertainty
Selection	Decide on a topic for study.	Optimism
Exploration	Search for information to become familiar with the topic.	Confusion Frustration Doubt
Formulation	Focus the perspective on the topic.	Clarity Interest
Collection	Gather information.	Confidence
Presentation	Organize information communicate results.	Satisfaction Relief Disappointment

and backward as the results of one part of the process require the student to clarify or expand on a previous task. Kuhlthau's information process model reminds students, teachers, and school librarians that a range of feelings characterizes the inquiry process. Students can begin to appreciate the range of feelings when teachers and school librarians explicitly acknowledge and emphasize the normalcy of anxiety that accompanies true inquiry at the beginning, doubt that occurs in early stages, and increasing confidence that emerges as the inquirer progresses.

At initiation, the student must recognize the need for information; this stage is often characterized by some feeling of anxiety. Too often, because the topic decision is rushed, students pose a rather low-level, fact-based research question. One activity often overlooked in this presearch stage is background building. Students need to spend time just gaining background about a topic before they begin to generate their research question. This may involve watching a video, reading general reference sources, taking a field trip, or browsing on the web. Whatever the medium, the task is to become knowledgeable enough about the topic to be able to pose significant questions. In this way, the research question can go beyond simple fact finding, because students will have already accomplished that during their background building work. Giving more time to the presearch stage may make the difference between a research question that asks, "What is chemical warfare?" and one that asks, "What are the technical, social, and political barriers to controlling chemical warfare and how can they be overcome?" Crucial overall is the importance of accepting uncertainty—knowing that the beginning of learning is wondering and not knowing.

The KWL strategy (What do I *know*, what do I *want* to find out, and what have I *learned*?) encourages inquiry. Activities such as background reading without detailed note taking (a good time for reading general reference resources such as encyclopedias and web browsing) and brainstorming will provide the foundation needed for students to enter into the next stages adequately prepared. Browsing is useful to help students move toward a personally interesting, focused investigation (Pappas, 1995). Students can browse by using an electronic encyclopedia, choosing a broad topic such as baseball, and examining the article titles that emerge. (For example, a student might find a specific personality like George Steinbrenner or Connie Mack of interest, or the National Baseball Hall of Fame, gambling in baseball, or the Negro Baseball Leagues may emerge as potential topics after browsing such a list.) Students can browse topics and subtopics in an online catalog or an electronic database to generate ideas for focusing their topic. All this background work is aimed at stimulating curiosity in the student so that an authentic question can emerge. More authentic yet is observing in real life. Field trips, interviews with experts (in person or online), and observations in the field are examples of experiences that can spark curiosity and wonder.

Curiosity and Wonder in Inquiry

Stripling (Small et al., 2011) presents for school librarians a model of the inquiry process that creates a powerful mental model for students, teachers, and librarians (see Figure 12.4).

This model is of particular note because it uses language accessible by students. School librarians do well to adopt an inquiry process model for the school or district and ensure that teachers know the model as well as students. The language of the model should be used consistently so that students learn to articulate the research process well and establish their mental model of the process. Consider, for example, the word *wonder* from the model. It is natural to begin an inquiry experience by asking, "What do you wonder about [topic] . . . ?" Another strength of this model is the explicit acknowledgment that the inquiry process is not linear; we move forward and backward in the process and eventually come back around to wondering again. As

FIGURE 12.4

Stripling Inquiry Process Model

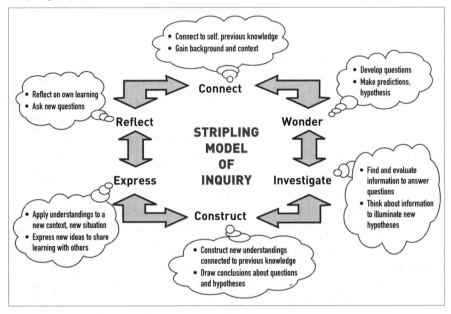

SOURCE: Ruth V. Small, Marilyn P. Arnone, Barbara K. Stripling, and Pam Berger, *Teaching for Inquiry: Engaging the Learner Within* (New York: Neal-Schuman, 2011). Used with permission.

we learn more, we arrive at more things we want to learn. Too often, inquiry is perceived as a closed-ended process where we arrive at *the answer*. True inquiry should propel us into further learning.

Deep Learning

In today's information universe, it takes little effort to locate factual information online. However, once those facts are discovered, the next question needs to be, So what? It is time for school librarians to lead the movement toward deep learning, toward authentic inquiry into problems and questions that are complex, if we are indeed to prepare students for the complex problems they will face.

Concept-Based Inquiry

Taba (1962) proposed an approach to the teaching of social studies of moving away from topical or chronological, fact-seeking tasks to deep, conceptual understanding. Her approach to deepening the learning experience was to refocus student explorations away from topical inquiry toward concept-based inquiry. More recently, Erickson (2008) described a "conceptual lens" as a way of looking at how we frame learning experiences. She suggested that when students engage in a study, they should apply a conceptual lens. She defined concepts as having these attributes:

Broad and abstract. Because concepts are broad, they have potential for transfer across settings; if students study the Pilgrims of the 1600s, they learn about them as a concrete and specific topic; if they study immigration, they learn about an abstract idea that has endurance across a variety of specific examples.

Universal in application. Because concepts are universal, students construct understandings that apply in other settings, and ways of seeing their world that will apply not only in school but also in life beyond school. If, for example, students study the Pilgrims, they take away factual knowledge about the 1600s. If they study the Pilgrims as one example of immigrants along with the Irish, Swedish, Chinese, Mexican, and Hmong, the conceptual lens of immigration affords the opportunity to see the universality of the immigrant experience and the ensuing insights that can come from the comparisons across exemplars. What new attitudes and understandings might arise here that would not have arisen if they studied only the Pilgrims? Consider the universality of civil discourse, civil disobedience, extinction, and culture.

Timeless through the ages. In social studies, for example, when students examine a concept rather than a specific event, the lessons of history become clearer. Consider such concepts as revolution, colonialism, or leadership as lenses for understanding history across eras and nations. What enduring understandings could emerge?

Represented by different examples that share common attributes. By examining the characteristics of exemplars, students derive meaning of the concept. In immigration, for example, as students consider various immigrant examples, new insights and understandings are likely to emerge when they consider the attributes of all migrating groups— reasons for migrating, skills and knowledge the groups bring, and things they leave behind.

Consider a middle school class studying Latin America. Each student investigates a country in Latin America. What questions do they pursue?

- What is the capital?
- What is the population?
- What natural resources does the country have?
- What are the major industries?
- What is the typical level of education of the people?

In addition, they likely try to find a picture of the national flag or a recording of the national anthem in order to dress up a poster or PowerPoint presentation.

Taba (1962) suggested that moving from this topical focus to a conceptual focus would yield a different kind of thinking and questioning. She posed the question, "How would learning change if the *topic* focus were replaced with a *conceptual* focus?" For example, economic development could be a conceptual focus. When students consider sample Latin American countries around the concept of economic development, several shifts occur. The level of complexity of their investigation increases beyond knowing or understanding toward analyzing; with this conceptual focus, student now engage in comparison and contrast among the samples—an analytical process. Students construct the meaning of economic development when they analyze the elements that constitute economic development and how they relate to one another.

The questions students pose immediately change. Now students are not only gathering facts but also *interpreting* how their factual information relates to the concept of economic development. Now when they gather factual information, they are not merely preparing to report the facts but also are applying factual information for the purpose of analyzing economic development. An example of the change in inquiry that results from a conceptual lens is shown in Figure 12.5.

The school librarian can play an important role in moving toward more authentic inquiry and away from fact gathering by suggesting a slight shift when teachers propose to bring classes to the library to do research. By reminding teachers that facts are easy to come by on the web, the school librarian can think with the teacher about designing deeper inquiry. Figure 12.6

FIGURE 12.5

Conceptual Lens Yields Deeper Questions

Colombia (Topic)	Economic Development (Concept)
What are the natural resources of the country?	How are natural resources managed? What is the role of government? What regulations are in place? What is the nature of ownership of property? What is the nature of access to resources? What conservation practices are in place to manage resources?
What kind of government does the country have?	How much freedom do people have? What are the labor conditions?
What are the primary industries?	What is the relationship of the government with other nations around the world? To what extent does industry participate in international markets?
What is the literacy rate?	How difficult is it for young people to participate in the educational system? How up-to-date is the educational system? What languages are taught in the schools and how much access to language learning is there?
What is the average life expectancy?	How readily available is quality health care? Where are medical professionals educated? How up-to-date are medical services?

shows examples of such small shifts accomplished by applying a conceptual lens.

Such a shift also affords opportunities for students to chart and graph their results and observe patterns in their findings in order to construct conceptual understanding. An opportunity here invites school librarians to collaborate with teachers in designing ways to analyze and represent findings that will enhance understanding with graphic organizers, charts, and tables.

The most likely resistance comes from teachers worrying that the investigations will lead into the unknown, which for some will create anxiety. The school librarian needs to step up as the information adventurer who supports genuine inquiry and is willing to assert that sometimes research does not lead to answers, but rather to further questions. Boredom and disengagement in school are often attributed to the current generation's infatuation with media and technology, and we sometimes believe these students need fast-paced experiences as we observe them zip around the Internet. However, another, perhaps more accurate diagnosis is that they want more engaging, more interesting, and deeper work in school.

FIGURE 12.6

Shifts to Conceptual Lenses

Topic	Topical Questions		Concept	Conceptual Questions
Japanese internment	When were the Japanese interred? What provoked this internment? How long were they kept in internment camps? Were they the only people interred?	→	National security	How have nations attempted to ensure security? How does national security divide peoples within a nation? How does it unite them?
American Revolution	Who were the leaders? What battles were fought? What were the conditions under which the soldiers fought? What event(s) provoked the revolution?	→	Revolution	How does a government provoke revolutionary sentiment in its people? How are revolutions organized?
States	What is the capital? What are the natural resources? What is the state flower? Bird? Mammal? Reptile? What is the basis of the state's economy?	→	Adaptation	How have people adapted the land to meet their needs and wants? What have been the consequences of these adaptations?
Polar Bears	How many young do they have? How big are they? What do they eat? Who are their enemies?	→	Migration	Why do animals migrate? How do they know when to begin their migration? Have migration routes changed over time?

Deep Questions

A particularly crucial aspect of inquiry is generating a research question that will lead to new understandings and insights and not merely to a summary of what the published literature says. Dahlgren and Öberg (2001) provide a taxonomy of questions that may be useful in encouraging students to generate a promising research query. They suggest five categories of questions:

Encyclopedic. These are the general factual questions student might pose that would lead them to write a report analogous to an encyclopedia article; for example: What is feminism? What is causing global warming? Too often, this is the kind of question students imagine as they begin an assignment. This kind of question will yield a report but not a research paper; it will yield information but rarely insight.

Meaning-oriented. These questions require students to construct meaning of a concept or phenomenon, often within a given context of time or place or events; for example: What is the significance of feminism in the context of today's increasing emphasis on family values? What are the sources and issues surrounding acid rain?

Relational. These questions require the researcher to explore the relationship between or among phenomena; for example: What factors have influenced women's opportunities from before the women's movement of the 1960s to today? What is the effect of climate change on polar bears?

Value-oriented. These questions require the researcher to interpret events or phenomena in the context of a value system that may be religious, political, social, gender-related, or racial; for example: What has been the impact of the women's movement on men's family roles? What is the importance of animals being identified as endangered species?

Solution-oriented. These questions require the researcher to examine a problem and seek solutions to that problem; for example: How can the remaining barriers that continue to impose a glass ceiling for professional women be removed? How can coral reefs be protected from further loss?

School librarians can give students a taxonomy of questions or recommend a specific type of question for a particular assignment. These categories of questions help articulate the purpose of the inquiry and help students set direction for their work. Teaching these categories to students can help them understand the nature of inquiry.

Managing Found Information

Seemingly traditional skills like note taking (using "notepad" features of electronic resources as well as paper-based note taking and highlighting) and organizing findings (creating charts, graphic organizers, and data-rich spreadsheets) are skills to be taught so that students can see patterns in their findings that will help them analyze, synthesize, and interpret findings. Often, students move from collecting to reporting too quickly. Activities that stimulate students to process include substantive conversation with others about their findings or reflection on their findings. For example, after reviewing information they have found, students can be asked to engage in a free-writing exercise to describe what information they discovered that surprised them or what questions remain unanswered. Or, students can be grouped together to share their findings with others and challenged to pose questions to each other to stimulate personal responses to their findings. For young people, it is important to provide intentional opportunities for them to think about their findings, to engage intellectually, and to challenge themselves to think critically. These are not intuitive behaviors for young students, and so it is important to structure opportunities for them.

Presenting Results

Finally, students begin to apply their findings to the research question. As they work at this stage, it is not uncommon for them to return to earlier stages to collect additional information or even adjust their focus. Here students will need skill in creating a product or presentation to communicate what they have discovered. The specific media they use will determine what presentation skills they need. School librarians can advocate for various forms for presentation, such as debates, letters and journals, multimedia projects, speeches, posters, printed brochures, case studies, or video. Whatever the format, the library program needs to provide the resources and guidance for students to create quality products.

Information work takes time. Quality work demands that teachers allocate enough time for students to move methodically through all stages of the inquiry process, to reflect on what they are learning as they collect information, and to create an effective way to present what they have learned.

Advocacy for time—particularly time in the library—is an important responsibility for the school librarian. Another critical concern is teaching. The inquiry process grows complex as more information is available and as search tools expand in number and versatility. It is never appropriate to say that students no longer need direct instruction or one-on-one help. Minilessons such as demonstrating the idiosyncrasies of a specific search tool, introducing specialized print sources on a relevant topic, or presenting ways to determine a resource's authority will be appropriate through high school. Such lessons at all grade levels are best taught at the point of need when students are engaged in a task that will require use of these sources.

Dispositions for Inquiry

The AASL (2007) *Standards for the 21st-Century Learner* goes beyond skills. Dispositions constitute another dimension of these standards—the habits of mind that students bring to the inquiry process. By underscoring the importance of dispositions, the standards acknowledge that information work requires a stance characterized by readiness to learn. We might expect that students who bring the disposition of a learner to the inquiry process will engage more deeply, be more likely to generate authentic questions, and ultimately arrive at new understandings or insights—the purpose of inquiry.

When Ritchhart (2001) explored an alternative view of intelligence, he synthesized the dispositions of learning. The library program must remain mindful of these learner dispositions:

> *Being open-minded.* A foundational principle for library collections is the provision of multiple perspectives. A school library is an environment that fosters acceptance of diverse viewpoints.

> *Being curious.* By providing an array of resources that can pique interests of students, the school library can serve as the stimulus for curiosity. While essential, a collection of current and high-quality resources alone will not be enough to engender curiosity. School librarians can serve as mediators between students and the collection. In that role, they model curiosity as they help students consider what questions they could pursue and guide them to resources in that pursuit.

Being metacognitive. When students engage in any sort of library re-search, it is important for them to learn to ask and answer the ques-tions "When do I have enough information? Is my information of high enough quality? Am I pursuing a worthwhile question? Have I investigated various perspectives?" A disposition of self-assessment can readily be taught in the context of the library program. Think-alouds should be commonplace among school librarians as a tech-nique for modeling what one is thinking if one is truly engaging in inquiry.

Being strategic. The library provides an excellent laboratory for strategic thinking. To begin, students must have an appropriate mental model of the inquiry process—they must see it as a process of authentic inquiry, not a process of assembly or transfer of information from a source to their end product. The library program needs to help stu-dents learn to be planful as they pursue interests of their own.

Being investigative. School librarians can help students focus their investigations narrowly enough that they can examine questions in depth and arrive at findings and insights of significance. Too often students are rushed through this early stage of their work out of eager-ness to move on to the subsequent stages of their research.

Developing reason. The library offers a reasoning playground. When a teacher librarian and a classroom teacher plan together, they can cre-ate meaningful opportunities for students to develop their abilities to reason. The role for the school librarian is to challenge students' assumptions, question their assertions, point out fallacious reason-ing, and insist on adequate evidence and evaluation of sources of information. Engaging students in conversations—whether informal or scheduled—is productive and gratifying.

Using evidence. By searching for information in the library, students can develop an appreciation for the use of evidence to support an argu-ment or to make a decision. Teaching students to seek verification and to reconcile differences between sources of information are the kinds of critical thinking skills that can be taught when students are work-ing with information from an array of resources.

Responsibilities in the Inquiry Process

Citizens in a free society appreciate the opportunities to access information freely. As with any right or freedom, this opportunity is accompanied by responsibilities, and the AASL (2007) *Standards for the 21st-Century Learner* explicates responsibilities that emerge from central principles of the information professions:

- Respect copyright and intellectual property.
- Seek divergent perspectives.
- Contribute to the exchange of ideas in a community.
- Use information technology responsibly.
- Use valid information and reasoned conclusions.

School librarians can model and encourage students in these responsibilities. Indeed, librarians can encourage teachers to expect students' adherence to copyright law and guidelines. Direct instruction can guide students in appropriate attribution and citation as well as how to determine what is valid information and how to make logical arguments. Collections in libraries should encourage divergent perspectives. Policies must support the responsible use of information technology. While these responsibilities may not be as concrete or measurable as information literacy skills, they constitute as important a place in the information literacy program as citizenship responsibilities hold in the government curriculum.

Self-Assessment in Inquiry

Lifelong learning is the heart of the mission of the library curriculum. The long-term intent is for students to leave school knowing how to continue to learn. To achieve independence as a learner, students must develop the ability to self-assess or self-monitor as they are seeking new knowledge. Critical in self-assessment in this context is the ability to monitor one's information seeking. To develop students' independence, school librarians and teachers can work together to develop habits that cause students to reflect on their work. Repeatedly asking students to pose questions of themselves is one way to develop a habit of self-assessment. Questions to help students develop appropriate self-monitoring habits might include the following:

- Do I have enough information to meet my needs?
- Are the sources of my information authoritative?
- What other points of view should I consider?
- Have I critiqued findings to differentiate between fact and opinion and to examine evidence and conclusions for faulty reasoning?
- Have I accurately represented facts in my expression of findings?

Using Information Technology as a Tool for Inquiry

Information technologies support all aspects of information literacy. A prominent technology role is access to information—whether the information appears in physical resources within the library or is delivered online. Clearly, the Internet provides information across a wide range of authority and quality, and demands that students learn to be astute consumers of information. To evaluate information critically, students should apply the following criteria:

Relevance. Is this source of information directly relevant to my focused topic? If not, how can I change my search strategy to find more relevant sources? Is the information too specific or too general?

Suitability. Does the information make sense to me? Can I easily paraphrase what I am reading?

Currency. How important is copyright date for my topic? Is it likely that newer information would affect accuracy?

Authority. Is the author knowledgeable and the source reputable? Is there an authoritative organization sponsoring this information? Is there potential for bias?

Reliability. Is the information based on fact or is it simply opinion? Can I find sources to verify information?

Information technology extends beyond sources of information. Other information technologies include tools for the following:

Information management. Technology can assist students in keeping track of information they have gathered. For example, Bookmarklets (http://delicious.com) is a web-based tool for managing web links, allowing the user to create tags for entries to develop a scheme for categorizing saved links.

Concept mapping. Webspiration (www.webspirationpro.com) is an example of a highly intuitive software application for generating graphic organizers and concept maps to help students organize ideas and information.

Collaboration. Google Docs, for example, affords students the opportunity to share files for group work, including word processing and spreadsheets. Stixy (http://stixy.com) functions like an online bulletin board, allowing users to post notes, photos, calendars, or lists just as one would use a bulletin board.

Citation. For citing information sources, students can use an application like the Citation Machine (http://citationmachine.net). Ready availability of a tool to generate citations following conventions of a specific style affords students a convenient way to be responsible users of information.

Communication. A wide array of tools facilitate communication, including wikis, blogs, and presentation tools such as Prezi (www.prezi.com), an open source tool for creating online sharable/portable presentations, or GoogleSites (www.sites.google.com) for creation of websites.

Students should develop competency in using information technologies for all stages of the inquiry process, not just the search for information.

Authenticity in Inquiry

Students need to develop information literacy competency not only to be successful in school but also to be capable lifelong learners. An intended outcome for learning is the discovery of new insights as one processes information by interpreting and integrating findings from a variety of sources, including one's prior knowledge. An insight is a clear and deep understanding of a complicated problem, phenomenon, or situation. An important word in that definition is the word *deep*. Deep understanding calls for students to "own" the ideas and information they take from their information searching. Wiggins and McTighe (1998: 10) use the term *enduring understanding* to describe the important "big ideas" that educators want students to retain after they have forgotten many of the details. Burke (2010) applies similar thinking in his proposal that learning needs to be driven by questions, and that teachers need to guide students toward "big questions" that call for interpretation, inference, or analysis. Students must have engaged themselves fully enough in their research to be conversant with the ideas and facts they have uncovered, and be able to apply those ideas to situations, problems, or decisions. This is the way adult information seekers work—they seek and gather information in order to apply it to situations or problems. These big ideas often result from insightful thinking.

For students to develop the ability to arrive at insights in a way that will be useful for lifelong learning, schools must provide experiences that challenge students not only to collect and report information but also to go beyond reporting to analyze, evaluate, and synthesize. Five attributes of an information literacy program can take students beyond collecting information to reaching insight. These are summarized in Figure 12.7.

When teachers direct the questions that students will explore, students take on the role of answer seeker. They look for information to respond to the teacher's query and nothing more. However, they do not own the inquiry, nor are they likely to reflect on their findings in ways that will lead them to insights. When students can direct their inquiry themselves, they are likely to be more vested in their quest and subsequently more likely to push themselves to ask so-what questions that can lead to insight. Similarly, when students respond to fact-oriented assignments, they are again collecting information to respond to largely closed-ended rather than open-ended queries. To the extent that assignments expect students to respond at the conceptual rather than factual level or to address issues rather than information, students are more likely to arrive at insights. Authenticity is an important attribute for tasks that will engage students and lead them to be reflective and insightful. When students perceive that their work is aimed only at communicating with the teacher or pleasing the teacher, the likelihood of that engagement diminishes. When students can identify a more authentic audience for their work, it takes on new meaning and encourages them to think insightfully. Finally, when the assessment of student work is collaborative, students feel more ownership in

FIGURE 12.7
Information Literacy for Insight

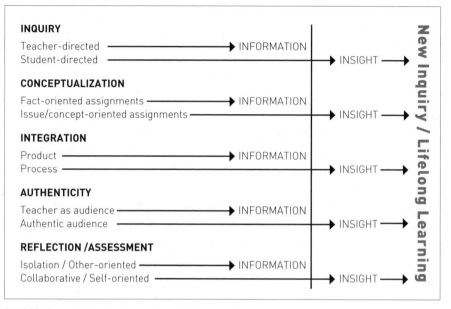

SOURCE: © Jean Donham and June Gross 2001.

the results. If at the end of an information quest students turn in a product to the teacher and the teacher does nothing more than return it to them with a score or grade, the work is merely an exercise. When teacher and students review the work together, that discussion is likely to bring students to a level of insight that might have been lost without the interchange of a collaborative assessment process. The teacher can pose questions that give students opportunities to think reflectively and to consider what they might pursue further to enhance the work they have just completed. These five attributes of information literacy programs—student-directed inquiry, concept-oriented assignments, integration of the research process (as well as the end product) into the instruction, an authentic audience, and collaborative assessment—increase the meaningfulness of the research experience for students and help them develop the intellectual processes that will make them insightful information consumers as adults.

Inquiry and College Readiness

The transition from high school to higher education presents many challenges. High school librarians can alleviate one of set of concerns by preparing students to meet the academic expectations they will encounter when expected to write research-based papers. Owen (2010) offers a set of suggestions for school librarians to consider in preparing students for this transition. She suggests that students need to understand the research process and have a mental model of inquiry. Too often, students arrive at college envisioning research as a process of assembly, of gathering quotations or generating paraphrases from texts and assembling them together. This mental model tends to lead to disappointment and sometimes failure. She further suggests that students need to understand the nature of scholarly literature and how it differs from popular works. Practically speaking, it is disheartening to see college freshmen unable to distinguish between what they can find using the college library catalog and what they can find using databases, in particular as they fruitlessly search the catalog for journal articles. Such basic errors are discouraging for students at a time when they may feel very vulnerable in a new, somewhat daunting circumstance. School librarians can prevent that situation. Adapting to the Library of Congress Classification System is yet another example of a transition that catches the incoming freshman unaware. Citing appropriately is also a surprise to many high school students, who often arrive at college knowing, for example, only MLA and come to find out that the social sciences expect them to use APA or the fine arts are inclined toward Chicago. Learning to use direct quotations and paraphrasing well is another skill set for preparation for the transition. Gordon (2002) suggests that students can anticipate the expectations that await them if they view examples of college assignments. It might be appropriate for high school librarians working with college-bound seniors to introduce students to examples of collegiate syllabi for institutions where local students tend to go. Assignments are often available on web-published college syllabi. Examination of assignments may raise questions such as the following:

- Do students appreciate fully the difference between the Internet and subscription databases?
- Do they apply criteria to assess the authority of information from websites?

- Does the term *peer-reviewed* have meaning for them?
- Do they know how to integrate cited information into their own writing?
- Do they know what a hypothesis is? A thesis?
- Can they formulate a researchable question?
- Do they know how to analyze and present data?

While academic librarians are increasing their efforts teaching information skills, college faculty are still likely to make assumptions about the abilities of their incoming students and may or may not anticipate the need to arrange for library instruction for them. As students arrive at college, they will benefit from having developed a sound foundation for inquiry in high school. Since college librarians are not consistently brought into the classroom as students engage in research, one aspect of that foundation is knowing the value of seeking help from a librarian.

Conclusion

Today's education environment is demanding much of educators. Increased societal concern for schools to graduate students who are college- and career-ready calls for deep learning. Inquiry-based learning that engages students in complex and abstract thinking creates opportunities for students to engage in the kind of intellectual work that our complex world demands. The school library curriculum sets standards for critical evaluation of information, integration of ideas from a variety of perspectives, and persistent investigation. Offering instruction in the library to meet such expectations provides opportunities for rigor in the academic program.

Leadership Strategies

Teacher and Partner

Review models of information processing skills and select or adapt one to be the basis for your library curriculum, and work to ensure that teachers are aware of the model and use consistent language in describing stages of the inquiry process.

As teachers approach with research projects to be accomplished in the library, consider ways to shift work toward a concept-based rather than topical project.

Develop a library curriculum that is based on the AASL *Standards for the 21st-Century Learner* and that has specific benchmarks for grades or grade spans.

Collaborate with teachers of senior high school students to create a high school to higher education unit that provides students with practice in meeting expectations they will face.

Information Specialist

Work with classroom teachers to develop a map or matrix to organize where inquiry fits for each grade level. Skills can be matched to specific classroom assignments. Be certain that specific skills appear more than once so that students apply them in different contexts and at increasing levels of sophistication.

Program Administrator

Reach out to community college, college, or university librarians to exchange teaching strategies and resources for preparing students for the transition from high school to higher education.

Analyze how best to schedule library access so that students have access to expertise and resources when they have the need.

Scenarios for Discussion

Scenario 1

The fourth-grade states unit is coming up at Suzette's elementary school library. Children will come with their worksheet, and each will have an assigned state. Their task will be to locate an image of the state flag, the name of the state bird, the state flower, the state's primary natural resources, the primary industries, major rivers, most important landmarks, and population. Once information is collected, children will learn to create a Glogster poster and report their findings using Glogster. Suzette wonders whether this project could be made more meaningful, since she knows that students will quickly find all their information online. What might you suggest she consider?

Scenario 2

Mary Ellen's high school is troubled by the fact that data show that a high percentage of their high school graduates start into higher education and drop out by the end of their first year. The principal has scheduled a meeting with the entire faculty to discuss what steps they might take to try to improve the success rate of their graduates. She hopes to emerge from the meeting with an action plan that she can then present to the school board, which has expressed considerable concern about this issue. How might Mary Ellen prepare for this meeting? What might you encourage her to consider being ready to propose? Is there a role for the library in improving students' success after graduation?

REFERENCES

AASL (American Association of School Librarians). 2007. *Standards for the 21st-Century Learner.* American Library Association. www.ala.org/aasl/guidelinesandstandards/learningstandards/standards.

Burke, J. 2010. *What's the Big Idea? Units to Motivate Reading, Writing and Thinking.* Portsmouth, NH: Heinemann.

Chu, S., K. Chow, S. Tse, and C. Kuhlthau. 2008. "Grade 4 Students' Development of Research Skills Through Inquiry-Based Learning Projects." *School Libraries Worldwide* 14, no. 1: 10–37.

Dahlgren, A., and Öberg, G. 2001. "Questioning to Learn and Learning to Question: Structure and Function of Problem-based Learning Scenarios in Environmental Science Education." *Higher Education* 41, no. 3: 263–282.

Donham, J., K. Bishop, C. C. Kuhlthau, and D. Oberg. 2001. *Inquiry-based Learning: Lessons from Library Power.* Worthington, OH: Linworth.

Eisenberg, M. B., and R. E. Berkowitz. 1990. *Information Problem-Solving: The Big Six Skills Approach to Library and Information Skills Instruction.* Norwood, NJ: Ablex.

Erickson, H. 2008. *Stirring the Head, Heart, and Soul.* Thousand Oaks, CA: Corwin.

Gordon, C. 2002. "A Room with a View: Looking at School Library Instruction from a Higher Education Perspective." *Knowledge Quest* 30, no. 4: 16–21.

Harada, V. H., and J. M. Yoshina. 2004a. *Inquiry Learning Through Librarian-Teacher Partnerships.* Worthington, OH: Linworth.

———. 2004b. "Moving from Rote to Inquiry: Creating Learning that Counts." *Library Media Connection* 23, no. 2: 22–24.

Kuhlthau, C. C. 2004. *Seeking Meaning: A Process Approach to Library and Information Services.* Westport, CT: Libraries Unlimited.

Owen, Patricia. 2010. "A Transition Checklist for High School Seniors." *School Library Monthly* 26, no. 8: 20–23.

Pappas M. 1995. "Information Skills for Electronic Resources." *School Library Media Activities Monthly* 11, no. 8: 39–40.

Pitts, J. M. 1995. "Mental Models of Information: The 1993–94 AASL/Highsmith Research Award Study." Edited by Joy H. McGregor and Barbara Stripling. *School Library Media Research* 23, no. 3: 177–184.

Ritchhart, R. 2001. "From IQ to IC: A Dispositional View of Intelligence." *Roeper Review* 23, no. 3: 143–150.

Small, R. V., M. P. Arnone, B. K. Stripling, and P. Berger. 2011. *Teaching for Inquiry: Engaging the Learner Within.* New York: Neal-Schuman.

Stripling, B. 1995. "Learning-Centered Libraries: Implications from Research." *School Library Media Quarterly* 23, no. 3: 163–170.

Taba, H. 1962. *Curriculum Development: Theory and Practice.* New York: Harcourt, Brace.

Wiggins, G., and J. McTighe. 1998. *Understanding by Design.* Alexandria, VA: Association for Supervision and Curriculum Development.

Zimmerman, M., M. Pappas, and A. Tepe. 2002. "Pappas and Tepe's Pathways to Knowledge Model." *School Library Media Activities Monthly* 19, no. 3: 24–27.

13

Assessment of Student Learning

This chapter:

- defines assessment and clarifies its purposes;
- applies performance assessment to inquiry processes;
- discusses rubrics and the benefits they offer in defining and assessing the inquiry curriculum;
- examines self-assessment;
- describes other assessment tools and procedures; and
- identifies leadership strategies for assessment.

Assessment Defined

Assessment and evaluation are easily confused. Examining their etymologies helps to clarify the critical differences between them. *Assess(us)* is the past participle of the Latin verb *assidere*; the prefix is the preposition *ad,* meaning near, and the root is the verb *sidere,* meaning to sit. The visual image of assessment then is sitting down beside someone. It is a cooperative task. Assess has come to mean careful examination based on the close observation that comes from sitting together. Evaluation, on the other hand, carries a connotation of judgment, as it means ascribing value to something. The visual image is of something being done to, rather than with, someone. Nothing in the etymology of *evaluation* suggests that it is a collaborative process. Its meaning suggests that its primary purpose is to make a judgment about the value of something.

Assessment serves four purposes, two for teachers and two for students (Donham, 1998), and are illustrated in Figure 13.1. First and perhaps most important for students, assessment is a means of monitoring progress in order to improve their performance. The basic question is, How is the student

FIGURE 13.1

Four Purposes of Assessment

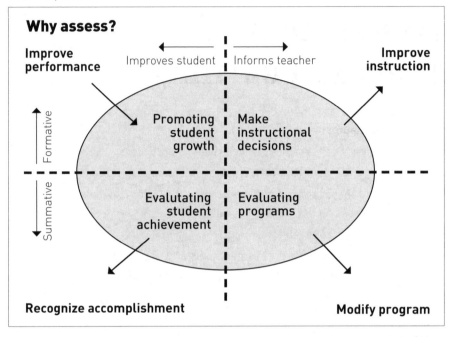

progressing on the established criteria? When students know how their work compares to a standard, they can then set appropriate goals for themselves and focus on what needs to be improved. Assessment contributes to student evaluation—its second purpose. Periodically, at conference time, report card time, or the end of a school year, student progress is synthesized into a grade or a narrative. The purpose is to recognize accomplishment, and this feedback also informs the student.

Assessment provides information for the teacher as well, and thus contributes to instructional decisions. The basic question here is, How can I use the evidence provided by assessment to improve my teaching so that my students do better? Finally, the results of assessment can inform the teacher about how well the instructional program is working and what needs to be modified so that future students will perform more successfully.

In summary, assessment serves these four purposes, two of which are formative (i.e., they provide information that informs the teaching and learning process and suggest ways to correct the course) and two summative (i.e., they indicate the degree of success in both learning and teaching):

Formative

- Improve student achievement by giving feedback on student progress.
- Improve the instruction by giving feedback on its effectiveness.

Summative

- Evaluate student performance.
- Redesign instructional programs by monitoring student achievement.

Assessment is not a single event, but rather a part of the learning experience. Some would say that observers should not be able to distinguish immediately between teaching and assessing because the two processes are so integrated.

Formative and Summative Assessment

Stripling (2007: 16) describes formative assessment as "measurement of knowledge and skills during the process of learning." By assessing student progress as a project or task is under way, the school librarian can know whether certain lessons need to be retaught or can identify a gap in student knowledge that can be remedied before the project proceeds toward completion. Formative assessment is success oriented in that its purpose is to know whether corrections in instruction need to occur before the student continues and then is not successful in meeting expectations. Formative assessment can be accomplished in various ways. As a class is working in the school library, the librarian and the teacher can check in with individual students and examine their progress. Corrective instruction can be given on the spot, or if there is a consistent misunderstanding among several students, a minilesson can be taught. Exit slips are another method of formative assessment. At the end of a work period, students can be asked to respond on a slip of paper to a brief question such as "What did I accomplish today?" or "What will I plan to do first in tomorrow's session?" or "What resource did I find today that is most promising for my project?" The exit question can be tailored to the activity of the day, but it provides information about the student's progress or frustrations. Checklists can also be used for formative assessment. By creating a checklist of tasks to be accomplished at the beginning of work on the assignment, the school librarian provides students a way of self-monitoring as well as a way for the teacher and school librarian to check on progress

FIGURE 13.2

Formative Assessment Checklist

Approval	Date	Task
		Developed an open-ended research question
		Developed an introductory narrative to introduce the research question
		Listed possible sources of information
		Located at least six authoritative and timely sources of information
		Took two-column notes on found information, organized by subtopics
		Outlined the paper
		Drafted the paper
		Shared draft of paper with peer writing partner
		Responded to feedback from peer writing partner and followed up on suggestions
		Rewrote paper
		Created works cited page for paper
		Submitted paper (all drafts)

(see Figure 13.2). Depending on the circumstances, the checklist can require signing off by the teacher or school librarian for each task. Formative assessment can be as simple as providing students a note-taking template and then requiring a sign-off on students' note taking before they proceed to producing their final product.

Since the classroom teacher typically has responsibility for summative assessment, school librarians are wise to collaborate with teachers to ensure that aspects of the inquiry process are considered at the end of a project or assignment. Summative assessments tend to be designed from the standards and benchmarks that define expectations. Hence, teachers will develop their summative assessment criteria from their content standards and benchmarks. The school librarian will need to introduce the teacher to the standards and benchmarks of the library curriculum so that these inquiry process expectations are included in the summative assessments. For example, if the library curriculum for ninth grade has set as a benchmark that students will be able to takes notes from an online resource using a two-column note-taking strategy, then this benchmark should be a part of the summative assessment criteria for a ninth-grade project.

FIGURE 13.3

3-2-1 Summative Self-Assessment

3 tips about information searching that I learned
1.
2.
3.
2 aspects of my inquiry work that make me proud
1.
2.
1 mistake I made that I will try not to make again
1.

Students can self-assess at the end of an experience to provide a summative view of their learning. One simple and quick framework for such a self-assessment is a 3-2-1 form as shown in Figure 13.3. The prompts can be composed to match the assignment and expectations of the particular learning experience, or they can generically feature aspects of the inquiry process.

Self-Assessment

Independent lifelong learning is the ultimate goal of the school library instructional program. For such independence to be realized, students must develop a sense of agency, an ability to self-manage their learning characterized by metacognition and reflection. Such reflective behavior calls for intentionally reviewing one's own performance based on internalized criteria. Independent learners are aware of what they know and what they don't know. In order for behaviors of metacognition and self-reflection to become student habits, educators need to intentionally build these capacities and automate these behaviors by continuous practice so that students can become self-directed learners who know for themselves what they don't know and can self-correct.

We live in an other-directed era in education, according to Costa and Kallick (2004), where learning is measured by scores on tests externally designed and scored. However, lifelong learning is a personal, self-directed process that begins with self-generated questions and curiosity, includes self-directed exploration, and concludes with self-measured success. Imposed other-directed experiences alone will not be adequate to prepare students to continue to learn effectively beyond school.

Students recognize this sense of other-directedness. For them, their teacher directs their learning. Speaking of other-directed learning, Gordon (1999: 167) opines in *Education for Health*:

> An auditor checks on the banker's ledgers. A building inspector signs off on the engineer's drawings. But who signs off on the physician's orders? Typically no one. Physicians [and many other professionals] operate under the social contract for legitimate autonomy. In exchange for this privilege they are expected to self-regulate; to keep abreast of fast-moving advances that affect the health of patients and communities. Meeting these expectations depends not only on their willingness but also on their ability to assess their professional knowledge and skills and to act constructively on these assessments throughout their long careers.

Gordon argues for developing skills of self-assessment he considers crucial to effective professional performance in a world of change. The ability of physicians to self-assess can be a matter of life and death. It is important to believe that even with the other-directed and externally imposed agenda in K–12 education today, individual teachers and individual teacher librarians can help students develop habits of self-assessment—habits that will lead them to be self-reliant learners for life. Self-assessment can give students a sense of ownership of their learning—and thereby responsibility for it.

Too often students complete an assignment, get the grade, and move on without looking back. When we allow this, we pass up on one of the most important reasons for assessment—to use it as a learning opportunity. Students need to review their work as it progresses through formative assessment and then to look back on finished work in order to look forward to the next task with strategies for improvement. This requires self-assessment and reflection to be regular components of each lesson or session in the school library throughout a unit or project. Students' final assessment of their own work affords the opportunity to think about the so-what of the learning experience to answer the questions "I finished the assignment—so what? What did I learn about the content, and what can I learn from the process I used to accomplish the task?" Without intentionally engaging in the self-examination inherent in these questions, process learning may be lost, and there is less likelihood that the next experience will be better.

This brings into focus an important disposition inherent in self-assessment—a disposition toward excellence. Such a disposition needs to be oriented toward the long term, not only toward satisfying the teacher. Self-assessment affords students the opportunity to cultivate both the strength and humility to continue to learn. Likewise throughout life, the ability to self-assess will be the mark of a lifelong learner in any walk of life—the disposition to pose and the ability to answer such fundamental questions as these:

- Do I have enough information?
- Do I have the right information?
- Are these sources of information I trust?
- Have I interpreted and applied the information appropriately?
- How will I improve my use of information next time?

Self-assessment means developing internal standards and comparing performance to those standards. While teachers can assess students' products as manifestations of their learning, it is the student who can assess his or her thinking, attitudes, motivations, and learning processes. Only the student can know how he or she chose when to stop seeking information. Only the student can assess how he or she reconciled differences among sources. Only the student can assess the ways in which information was interpreted to serve his or her purpose. Only the student can assess the degree of willingness to live with ambiguity or uncertainty versus the desire for certainty or finality.

Self-assessment requires looking in three directions: back at completed work, down at present work to determine next steps, and forward to the

FIGURE 13.4

Three Directions of Self-Assessment

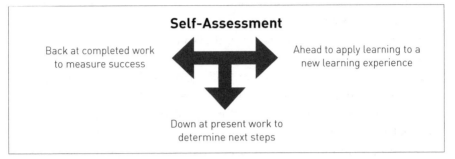

SOURCE: J. Donham, "Creating Personal Learning through Self-Assessment," *Teacher Librarian* 37, no. 3 (2010): 14–21.

future to apply what has been learned to the next learning opportunity (see Figure 13.4). Self-assessment is essential to learning as the learner reflects on what is known, what remains to be known, and what will be required to fill the gap.

Assessment Tools

Rubrics

Rubric derives from the Latin adjective for red. Rubrics in a liturgical context are directions for conduct of religious services, written in prayer books in red ink. In education, rubrics are intended to direct students. An assessment rubric is an ordered set of criteria that clearly describes for the student and the teacher what the range of acceptable and unacceptable performance looks like. This definition has several key words, the first of which is *ordered*. A rubric sets out to describe a continuum of performance from expert to novice. Descriptions occur at points along the continuum, and these descriptions are ordered from high to low. Each rubric describes levels or degrees of performance. *Criteria* is the next key word in the definition. A rubric provides criteria for excellence in performance in order to compare a student's performance to criteria, not to the performance of other students. The next key word is *describes*, for a rubric creates a visual image of what excellent performance looks like, as well as a description of the degrees of excellence along the continuum. Descriptive language is a key to the rubric. For example, we can say that a student took notes effectively. This does not describe the note taking; it labels it as effective. In a well-written rubric we might instead say, "A student paraphrased the essential relevant information from the source." Or, to describe delivery in public speaking, one might state: "The rate of speaking varied so that major points were emphasized." Such a description creates a mental model for the student because the performance is described, not merely labeled as "rate: excellent."

The range of performance portrayed by a rubric is another key idea in the definition. A rubric describes a range of performance descriptions, so that students can gauge themselves along a performance continuum. Most often, students improve their performance incrementally. Descriptions of stages toward excellence guide such incremental growth. Usually rubrics have three or four levels of performance. Sometimes each of these levels of performance is assigned a score (4 = highest level, 1 = lowest level). Using words rather than numbers to identify those levels of performance helps give students a sense of the progressive nature of rubrics:

- Novice
- Apprentice
- Competent
- Expert

These identifiers suggest that the student can progress toward the expert level, whereas assigning numbers suggests that they have attained a score that has permanence. The words *novice* and *apprentice* suggest that the student is on the path toward expert, but simply isn't there yet. Such language connotes more optimism for the student's ability to succeed than does the label of a 0 or F. Rubrics should offer a guide so that students know what it takes to be an expert. Reducing the rubric's information to a number nullifies it.

Another way to envision a rubric is to consider it a road map to success for students. Of course, road maps are examined at the beginning of trips, and so with rubrics it is crucial that they be given to students in advance and then used throughout the task to gauge where they are and nudge them along the performance continuum. For example, when students get lost in a project spending too much time creating a beautiful report cover, the rubric is useful to refocus their efforts. Students can know how to be successful when they know at the outset what success looks like.

Rubrics represent a carefully articulated description of performance across a continuum of quality or sophistication—a continuum from novice to exemplary performance. To create such a description requires careful analysis of the desired performance. One of the best ways to design rubrics is to begin by observing closely a range of products or performances. If the task is to generate a thesis statement for a research paper, then observing products created by a variety of students will yield a range of quality and sophistication. Consider, for example, a high school research paper assignment where students write a thesis statement that represents a position taken on an issue. These examples might emerge from students:

- This paper is about chemical warfare.
- There are many examples of the use of chemical warfare in twentieth-century history.
- Control of chemical warfare is complex.
- It is impossible to control chemical warfare today because of scientific, tactical, and political factors.

By analyzing examples of students' thesis statements, the critical attributes of an exemplary statement become clearer: the thesis statement reveals what the student believes about a topic. The thesis statement includes the topic and a debatable position statement. Three critical attributes are sought: statement of topic, statement of position, and the potential for the position to be argued.

A common error in designing rubrics is to describe performance with such adverbs as *frequently, sometimes,* or *always.* Rubrics are more often used to assess a single performance. These modifiers suggest that the assessment relates to multiple performances; as such they are appropriate for summative, but not formative evaluation. Other adverbs to avoid are such words as *effectively, well,* and *poorly.* These words judge but don't describe. Be aware that rubrics are intended to describe quality, not quantity, in performance. Avoid developing rubrics where better performance is only more; for example, instead of "uses more library resources," the description should be "uses more relevant resources." Figure 13.5 provides an example of a rubric for a high school research paper. The language is intended to be descriptive so that students can examine their own work and assess whether they are on the road to success based on this road map.

Rubrics can provide a point of departure as a school librarian checks in on students' progress when they are working in the library. Often, a school librarian might approach a table where students are working and say, "How

FIGURE 13.5

Sample Research Paper Rubric

Criterion	Expert	Proficient	Apprentice	Novice
Transfer of Knowledge	The paper demonstrates that the writer fully understands the content and interprets ideas without excessive direct quotations.	The paper demonstrates that the writer, for the most part, understands concepts but relies somewhat on sources to convey ideas.	The paper demonstrates that the author, to a limited extent, understands the concepts but relies heavily on source material.	The paper does not include any interpretation beyond the ideas provided in the sources.
Depth of Discussion	Details and examples provide elaboration in all sections.	Details and examples provide elaboration in most sections.	Brief explanation is included in all the sections of the paper.	Brief explanation and/or limited support is provided for ideas.
Cohesion	Ties together information from all sources. Paper flows from one issue to the next. Author demonstrates understanding of the relationship among ideas obtained from all sources.	For the most part, ties together information from sources. Paper flows with only some disjointedness. Author demonstrates understanding of the relationship among ideas obtained from all sources.	Sometimes ties together information from all sources. Paper does not flow and disjointedness is apparent. Author does not relate ideas or information from various sources.	Does not tie together information. Paper does not flow and appears created from disparate sources. Writing does not explain relationships between "chunks" of information.

SOURCE: J. Donham, "Creating Personal Learning through Self-Assessment," *Teacher Librarian* 37, no. 3 (2010): 14–21.

are you doing?" and receive a response like "Okay" and then proceed to the next table. Instead, using a rubric to guide assessment as teaching, the librarian would say, "Let's look at how you are doing. Look at the rubric for note taking and look at your notes. Where are you on the continuum?" Assessing where students are while the work is in progress may result in a correction of their information seeking that will save them time and improve the quality of their process and end product, which is after all the intention of assessment.

In addition to being a guide to student work, rubrics can be useful for end-of-term or end-of-unit assessment of student work. At the summative stage, assessment becomes evaluative, yet the rubric format can still be useful for describing to students the qualities of their work and the qualities of exemplary work, so that they can see how close or far they are from where they want to be. A grade labels student achievement but provides no specific information to help the student improve performance; it says "good enough" or "not good enough," when what is needed is a specific description of what "good enough" represents and how to get there. In this way, the rubric justifies the grade. While students may argue with a B, it is harder to argue when the B is supported by a rubric that describes the student's performance. Finally, using rubrics in summative assessment can contribute to consistency; the more defined the criteria are, the easier it becomes to apply the criteria evenly among students and across performances.

Some people find rubrics too constraining for the student or the teacher. At times it seems that the highest level of performance is not high enough for some students. One solution to that concern is to add a column at the high end of the rubric, label it "Legendary Performance," and ask the student to write the description of what he or she does beyond the highest level (Lockett, 1996). Another concern is that students may work hard at moving to the next level of performance on a rubric but narrowly fail to reach it. Again, the consultant suggests simply adding "skinny columns," that is, lines drawn between labeled points where a performance falls between levels to indicate to a student that he or she is progressing and is almost there.

A final concern about rubrics is that librarians might focus too tightly on details and lose sight of the overall information process. Writing a rubric about finding the index at the back of a book is probably unnecessary. More important is using the index to access the needed information, so the rubrics for index use need to be related to choosing search terms, using pagination information, and using cross references and subheadings. The point is that rubric development can be taken to an unnecessary extreme. Consider the processes that need teaching, reteaching, and repeated practice, and then consider the processes for which there are levels of sophistication in performance—these are the processes for which rubrics can be helpful. A key question may be, Is this something one either does or does not do, or are there degrees of quality? If there are degrees of quality, then a rubric may help students move to higher and higher levels of performance.

Other Assessment Tools

Performance assessment is based on observable activity. Clearly, some intellectual processes cannot be observed directly. One can only make assumptions about those processes based on outward actions by the student. Other assessment strategies are available to help students analyze their work. Two examples of narrative methods are the I-Search process, advocated by Macrorie (1988) and described by Joyce and Tallman (1996), and student research journaling.

In the I-Search process, students report their research as a personal narrative describing not only what information they have found but also how they found it. By explicitly describing their process, students reveal their research strategies and assess what worked and what didn't. When their self-assessment is coupled with feedback from teachers, students gain further insight into what works and what doesn't.

Student journaling is another strategy for student's self-analysis in the research process. Here, students step back from their work periodically and make journal entries about their progress, their frustrations, and their successes. Careful monitoring of the journal can inform teachers of what students need to learn. In one case study, Tallman (1998) found that through journaling, educators can challenge students to reexamine their research and engage in higher-order thinking as they make judgments about their work. Harada (2002) describes the use of journaling with elementary school students and emphasizes that in the early stages of journaling, students made a high proportion of nonspecific comments. Later, however, their entries exhibited more specificity and depth as they described both their activities and their feelings at each stage of research. Such progress speaks for the power of journaling as a strategy for helping students gain understanding of the research process.

Both journaling and the I-Search process engage students and teachers in dialogue about their information work. These strategies are open-ended; therefore, they demand some sophistication about the inquiry process in students, or they require some specific prompting from teachers to focus students' remarks. Prompts such as "Write an entry in your journal today about organizing your note cards" or "Write an entry in your journal today about the problems with searching in the EBSCO database" may give students enough of a cue to reflect on what they know about the process and may reveal enough about their frustrations to cue the school librarian about what they need to learn. Such information becomes a point of departure for either individual conversation with students or microteaching. A comprehensive program will use various assessment strategies over time, based at least in part on the sophistication of students' understanding, their propensity for writing, the preferences of the teacher, and the character of the information work.

End-of-unit interviews are another way to assess students. Brief, structured interviews can provide insight into what students know about the research process. The teacher and school librarian can share responsibility for brief interviews with students at the end of a unit involving intensive research. Questions to ask might be the following:

- What can you tell me about your project?
- How did you find your information?
- Did you ever get stuck? What did you do then? What was hard about doing research?
- How could you tell when you were done with research? How could you tell if you did a good job?
- What did you learn from this research?

Collecting responses to these interview questions can provide data to determine what worked and what did not work in the instruction.

Conventional testing is a long-standing method for collecting data about what students know and can do. Stiggins (2002) cites a study by Black and William, who conclude that classroom formative assessment increased students' scores on standardized achievement tests; in fact, they reported effect sizes of one-half to a full standard deviation. Stiggins explained that increases of this magnitude can yield gains of 30 percentile points, two grade equivalents, or 100 points on the SAT scale. Such results suggest that if the purpose of testing is to document student achievement for accountability, then schools do well to make use of other assessment strategies between high-stakes tests since such interim assessment appears to produce better standardized test performance.

In testing, it is crucial to ensure that the test measures what matters. In today's environment of high accountability, most schools use standardized tests, and many standardized tests have a subtest on using reference sources. School librarians do well to examine tests to know what is being asked. With this knowledge, they can either ensure that they are teaching the skills tested, or they can point out to administrators, teachers, and parents the discrepancy between what is being taught and what is being tested. Boolean logic, truncation, and evaluating sources are all topics emphasized in curricula; standardized tests currently place heavy emphasis on identifying keywords, alphabetizing, and choosing an appropriate resource for a given question.

Testing services struggle to update their tests to match existing curricula; however, they tend to be conservative out of concern for equity across the nation. One possible side effect of the higher levels of accountability is less attention to process learning (e.g., inquiry) and more emphasis on content learning (e.g., reading, mathematics, or science). Such a resurgence of emphasis on content can threaten to draw resources away from library programs unless their impact on students' overall achievement can be conveyed. In such an environment, the need for advocating for the importance of information literacy as a life skill—as well as the impact of the library program on reading and other disciplines—cannot be understated. School librarians will want to share results of research that shows relationships between effective library media programs and student achievement as measured by these achievement tests. Keith Curry Lance is associated with substantial efforts at measuring the association between library programs and achievement. In analyzing the results of research in eight states, Lance and Loertscher (2002) found consistently that levels of student performance on standardized tests were better where the school librarian directly taught information literacy to students. The library program can naively be considered a fringe or nonessential program under pressure for test performance in content areas, especially in settings where test results are highly valued. Therefore, these findings need to be shared with administrators and teachers to support continued library program development.

Where testing is highly valued, the school librarian may consider a nationally standardized test to measure students' knowledge of the processes taught in the library program. Funded initially by a grant from the Institute of Museum and Library Services, the TRAILS (Tool for Real-time Assessment of Information Literacy Skills) battery of tests available at www.trails-9.org is worthy of careful consideration. Incorporating this test into the library program and reporting results to teachers and administrators provides objective data about student performance. Again, with the notion of "what matters gets measured," school librarians may need to board the testing bandwagon if information literacy is to remain an important part of the instructional program in the school. As long as tests are important, the school librarian needs to join the conversation by:

- studying the items on standardized tests to determine how well they fit what is being taught;

- informing colleagues about research that shows relationships between library programs and test performance;
- encouraging the use of alternative methods of formative assessment (e.g., rubrics, checklists, and journals) to improve learning and teaching and emphasizing the positive effect that such assessments have on summative assessment in testing; and
- considering tests as one assessment method for demonstrating students' learning in the library curriculum.

Conclusion

Rubrics, I-Search, journaling, checklists, interviews, and tests are all assessment strategies that provide information for student evaluation and that will help educators know what needs to be taught in the future. While the summative measurement of student achievement is important for accountability, formative assessment informs teaching and gives students a description of their performance and the target performances. In fact, research supports implementing both testing and formative assessment for the best student achievement. Matching the assessment tool to the purpose calls for judgment by the school librarian and the teacher. If the processes and skills of the library curriculum are to be valued, the program must include assessment strategies, both formative and summative, and these strategies are best implemented in collaboration with classroom teachers.

Leadership Strategies

Teacher and Partner

Consider a variety of methods for assessment (including checklists, interviews, rubrics, journaling, testing, and the I-Search process) in order to focus students' attention on the inquiry process, not just the end product.

Examine standardized test items to determine what is being asked of students. Provide information to teachers to help them interpret the match between items on the test and what is being taught.

Align summative assessments with benchmarks in the library curriculum to ensure accountability for meeting the standards of the program.

Review the TRAILS tests to determine feasibility of administering them periodically, and develop a plan for disseminating results to key stakeholders to demonstrate both the need and the effects of the library program.

Program Manager

Share results of research studies that show the relationship between student performances on standardized tests and school library programs.

Scenarios for Discussion

Scenario 1

In Hill City, national standardized tests are administered in October each year to students in grades 3 through 6. The school librarian works with students—sometimes in collaboration with teachers, sometimes in isolation—throughout the year to help them learn strategies for locating and using information. However, he has been unable to persuade teachers to integrate synthesis and evaluation of information into classroom work on a regular basis. The results of the current year's standardized tests have arrived in the building. The principal makes it a point to come to the library and comment on how well the students performed on the test regarding use of sources of information. The school librarian, however, regards the test as invalid for testing what he is teaching because many items on the test do not reflect the modern school library online information resources. How should he respond to the principal?

Scenario 2

Sarah enjoys the fact that teachers in her high school regularly arrange to bring classes to the library to find information resources for their projects and course work. However, locating the sources is as far as it goes for these classes. Sarah is allowed very little time for teaching, as teachers are pressed for time in this high-performing academic high school and feel they cannot spend additional time in the library. However, Sarah observes students copying and pasting information from sources without appropriate attribution or citation. She also sees students accepting at face value information from websites that may not be the most authoritative. While she is pleased that teachers are using the library, she is concerned about what students are really learning. How could Sarah use assessment as a way to help teachers identify the need for additional instruction?

REFERENCES

Costa, A., and B. Kallick. 2004. "Launching Self-Directed Learners." *Educational Leadership* 62, no. 1: 51–55.

Donham, J. 1998. *Assessment of Information Processes and Products.* Professional Development Series. McHenry, IL: Follett Software.

———. 2010. "Creating Personal Learning through Self-Assessment." *Teacher Librarian* 37, no. 3: 14–21.

Gordon, M. 1999. "Commentary: Self-Assessment Skills Are Essential." *Education for Health* 12, no. 2: 167–168.

Harada, V. 2002. "Personalizing the Information Search Process: A Case Study of Journal Writing with Elementary-Age Students." *School Library Media Research* 5. www.ala.org/aasl/aaslpubsandjournals/slmrb/schoollibrary.

Joyce, M., and J. I. Tallman. 1996. *Making the Writing and Research Connection with the I-Search Process: A How-to-Do-It Manual for Teachers and School Librarians.* New York: Neal-Schuman.

Lance, K. C., and D. V. Loertscher. 2002. *Powering Achievement: School Library Media Programs Make a Difference.* San Jose, CA: Hi Willow Research.

Lockett, N. 1996. "Rubrics in the Classroom." Handout distributed at Iowa Success Network workshop, January 11–12, Cedar Rapids, IA.

Macrorie, K. 1988. *The I-Search Process.* Portsmouth, NH: Heinemann.

Stiggins, R. J. 2002. "Assessment Crisis: The Absence of Assessment for Learning." *Phi Delta Kappan* 83, no. 10: 758–765.

Stripling, B. 2007. "Assessment of Information Fluency." In *Assessing Student Learning in the School Library Media Center,* edited by A. L. Vance and R. Nickel, 15–26.. Chicago: American Association of School Librarians.

Tallman, J. 1998. "I-Search: An Inquiry-Based, Student-Centered, Research and Writing Process." *Knowledge Quest* 27, no. 1: 20–27.

14

Library Program Evaluation

This chapter:

- discusses the importance and purpose of program evaluation;
- contextualizes program evaluation as a process of continuous improvement;
- examines the importance of data collection and analysis;
- details a rubric for assessment of program components; and
- identifies leadership strategies for program evaluation.

Purpose of Evaluation

Systematic program evaluation is necessary most importantly to provide guidance for improvement. No system, organization, or program is static but is always improving or declining. Systematically examining performance provides an accurate way to determine which direction it is heading. Besides maintaining and improving program quality, systematic evaluation provides an opportunity to educate stakeholders about the program and its effects on learning and on the school's culture. To accomplish a systematic process of evaluation, a school librarian needs to begin with creating a plan that considers how program evaluation will be carried out, who will be the participants in the process, when program evaluation work will be done, and how the outcomes from the process will be used for program improvement.

Library programs often suffer from a degree of invisibility; because librarians tend to work in partnership and often work behind the scenes to organize and provide resources, it is easy to go somewhat unnoticed by administrators and other educators. By engaging stakeholders in formal and systematic program evaluation, school librarians shine the spotlight—even if only temporarily—on what is happening in this program and what additional potential may lie there. Parents, teachers, administrators, and voters are not likely to extend resources to a program they don't understand.

Continuous Improvement

Continuous improvement assumes that evaluation is an ongoing cyclical process wherein expectations or goals in each cycle are based on current performance, with an expectation that programs improve continually (Gilmore, 2009). Figure 14.1 shows the continuous improvement cycle.

FIGURE 14.1
Continuous Improvement Model

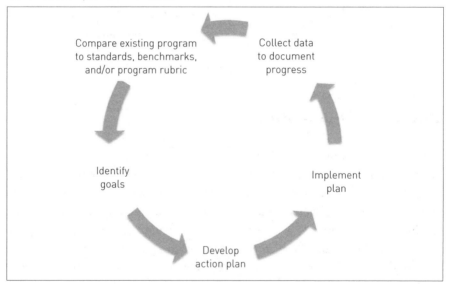

Compare existing program to standards, benchmarks, and/or program rubric

Collect data to document progress

Identify goals

Implement plan

Develop action plan

Measuring a Program's Current Status

To enter the cycle initially, one begins by comparing the existing program to a set of standards, expectations, or a program rubric. The American Association of School Librarians (AASL) guidelines, published under the title *Empowering Learners: Guidelines for School Library Programs*, define a set of expectations against which a library program can be measured. AASL offers an online rubric to assist in applying these standards as a measurement of a program's progress toward implementing the guidelines. This tool is available as a subscription at www.ala.org/aasl/guidelinesandstandards/planningguide/planningguide.

Alternatively, Figure 14.2 offers a program evaluation rubric that integrates dimensions of a library program as portrayed throughout this book with descriptions of degrees of implementation to serve as a road map for program growth and improvement. Rubrics provide an excellent form for such a purpose because they describe a range of levels of quality in a performance. By providing rubrics on the various program dimensions, the strengths and shortcomings of the program become visible. More important, because of their descriptive nature, rubrics communicate a program's quality to those outside the library profession. Far too many teachers, parents, and administrators have not had experience from which to learn what to expect of a library program. A program rubric can help extend their vision so that they can understand more clearly what the goals of the library professional might be for the program.

A school library program may employ benchmarking to measure its current status. Benchmarking is a process of examining a program internally, then searching for best practices in other organizations and adapting practices that promise to improve performance (Epper, 1999). This strategy is grounded in the total quality management movement and fits into the mode of continuous improvement. Here evaluation is not an event scheduled to occur periodically, but rather a way of operating all the time. The other organizations considered in benchmarking may be other similarly situated school library programs, or they might be organizations that share some aspect of the work of school library programs. For example, Epper mentions Southwest Airlines comparing notes with a pit crew of an Indy 500 race car team to improve on-time departures. School librarians might look, for example, at college libraries for website design practices or at retail training programs for customer service excellence. Finding best practices within school library programs may also be an effective approach to benchmarking. The AASL annually names National School Library Programs of the Year. These programs exhibit best practices in school librarianship. Winners are announced each year at the American Library Association annual meeting, and information about the winners is available at the AASL website. Comparing the practices of these acclaimed programs to a local library program can provide new targets or programming ideas.

FIGURE 14.2

Rubric for Program Evaluation

INQUIRY-BASED LEARNING			
Library Curriculum	*Comprehensive.* A written curriculum guide, based on an information process model, contains a sequence of information seeking and using strategies, model lessons, and assessment strategies.	*In progress.* A written curriculum guide contains a sequence of information seeking and using strategies.	*Under development.* Plans exist for developing a formal curriculum guide.
Conceptual Learning	*Concept-based.* Learning focuses on concepts, and students use their findings to make interpretations or propose solutions to problems.	*Topical.* Research in the library is topical and students generate reports.	*Fact-oriented.* Students typically gather discrete facts to be reported in response to scaffolded or prescribed teacher-generated questions.
Authenticity	*Authentic.* Students engage in research to answer authentic questions for which answers are truly unknown. Questions evolve after development of background knowledge.	*Guided.* Students generate questions within parameters set by a teacher or librarian.	*Other-directed.* Students find answers to questions generated by a teacher, a textbook, or other external source.
Integration	*Integrated.* A matrix or map identifies where inquiry skills fit into classroom activities for introduction, elaboration, and reinforcement; lessons are taught in collaboration with classroom teachers.	*Ad hoc.* As teachers make assignments, information seeking and using strategies are taught in relation to the assignment.	*Isolated.* Information skills are taught sequentially without regard to classroom activities.
Assessment	*Formative and summative.* The school librarian has developed and implemented an assessment plan for measuring student performance, including formative assessments to assist in the learning process and summative assessments for accountability.	*Classroom-based.* Assessment of student work in inquiry occurs in the classrooms only.	*Not yet developed.* Assessment of students' understanding of inquiry and their research skills is not a part of the library program yet.
READING			
Materials Support	*Selective.* The school librarian provides materials that meet exact specifications for the instructional goals at appropriate levels of difficulty with high-quality standards.	*Expansive.* The school librarian delivers to teachers whatever materials are available on the general topic of their units.	*Self-help.* The school librarian encourages teachers to visit the library and explore available materials.

Promotion	Initiating. The school librarian promotes reading by initiating booktalks and individualized reading guidance.	Responsive. The school librarian supports students' interest in reading when asked.	Passive. The library features displays and book lists to support existing interest in reading.
	Continuous. Reading promotion is ongoing and involves sustained support as well as feature events.	Periodic. Special short-term reading promotion activities occur throughout the year.	Intermittent. Reading promotion primarily occurs as special events.
	Intrinsic. Activities to promote reading are grounded in intrinsic motivation (i.e., reading for the sake of enjoyment or information).	Neutral. Effort focuses on students continuing to read.	Extrinsic. Special reading promotions feature extrinsic rewards for students who read.

COLLECTION

Collaboration	Collaborative. Decisions about collection priorities set collaboratively by the school librarian and teachers.	Consultative. Teachers' suggestions for collection enhancement are sought.	Autocratic. The school librarian makes collection decisions independently.
Curriculum Support	Curriculum-based. Curriculum support is a high priority for collection additions.	Curriculum-related. Curricular topics are considered in collection development but are not a high priority.	Balanced. Balance is the highest priority in collection development.
Levels of Difficulty	Client-based. Level of difficulty responds to assessment of the local student clientele.	Balanced. A balance among easy and challenging materials is sought.	Unheeded. Criteria other than level of difficulty are considered.
Diversity	Multicultural. Cultural diversity is considered in collection development, including but not limited to cultural groups represented in the local population.	Client-based. Materials are selected to match those cultures represented in the school's population.	Spontaneous. Multicultural materials are selected as they are requested but without specific planning.
Currency	Current. Collection is kept current by additions and weeding according to a regular schedule of review.	Mixed. Some parts of the collection, particularly time-sensitive topics, are maintained by additions and weeding.	Outdated. Collection shows evidence of little or no weeding.
Adequacy	Ample. Collection has ample materials to meet the needs of its clientele and is supported by a budget to accommodate both replacement and growth.	Adequate. Collection can usually meet the basic needs of clientele.	Inadequate. Collection lacks materials for topics commonly investigated.

(cont.)

FIGURE 14.2

Rubric for Program Evaluation

COLLECTION (cont.)			
Quality	*Criteria-based.* Selection of materials is based on explicit criteria based on quality, learning goals, and beliefs.	*Quality-based.* Selection is based on standards of quality defined by reviewing media.	*Demand-based.* Selection is based on what teachers and/or students request exclusively.
Multiple Formats	*Interdependent.* Virtual resources provide substantial content for information and personal interest and complement the physical collection.	*Supplementary.* Virtual resources are provided as subscriptions are made available by state purchasing and websites are featured on the library webpage.	*Single format.* The physical collection of resources dominates the shape of the collection.
TECHNOLOGY			
Technology Use	*High cognitive level.* Uses of technology cause students to work at Bloom's application level or higher.	*Low cognitive level.* Uses of technology require students to work at the knowledge or comprehension level.	*No cognitive criteria.* No criteria are applied for selection of technology uses based on cognitive level.
Planning Process	*Formalized.* Planning for technology integration is ongoing and includes broad-based participation.	*Ad hoc.* When money is available, a planning committee convenes to decide how to spend it.	*Unilateral.* A single individual or a select few make decisions about technology.
Staff Development	*Comprehensive.* All staff members must meet a set of competencies for using technology.	*Adaptable.* Staff development includes use of applications that can be adapted to meet individual needs.	*Elective.* Staff members choose from a menu of technology training based on their own self-assessment or personal interest.
	Relevant. Staff development has direct application to the work of the staff members who participate.	*Need-driven.* Staff members seek out technology-related training as they identify a specific need.	*Basic.* Staff development focuses on the basics of how to operate equipment.
	Ongoing. Support is readily available as staff members integrate new skills into their work.	*Intermittent.* Review sessions are offered periodically.	*One-time.* Training occurs at scheduled times and no ongoing assistance is conveniently available.
Budget	*Comprehensive.* The annual budget includes specific line items for training, new hardware, replacement hardware, hardware upgrades, repair, new software, software upgrades, supplies, and technical support staff.	*Basic.* Line items are included in the annual budget for hardware and software.	*Ad hoc.* As money becomes available, it is spent on technology.

Hardware	**Focused critical mass.** As each technology application is recommended, the necessary critical mass of hardware is purchased.	**Scattered deployment.** Hardware is deployed to spread available resources throughout the school fairly rather than considering what critical mass is needed to effectively meet a specific need.	**Underequipped.** Too little hardware is available to accomplish an identified goal.
Applications (purchased and accessed)	**Criteria-based.** Applications are selected based on explicit criteria related to learning goals and beliefs.	**Quality-based.** Applications are selected based on standards of quality as defined by reviewing media.	**Demand-based.** Application selection is based on what teachers and/or students request exclusively.
Policy	**Formalized.** Written policy exists for copyright, intellectual freedom in electronic environments, equity, privacy, and other technology-related concerns. These policies have board approval and are reviewed systematically. They are intentionally communicated to all appropriate constituencies.	**Informal.** Policy decisions about technology-related issues have been discussed and agreed to but are not formalized.	**In progress.** Policy for technology-related issues is under discussion.
COLLABORATION			
Team	**Defined.** Members of the planning team, including the librarian, accept clearly defined roles and expectations.	**Informal.** When a task needs to be done, whoever volunteers does it.	**Unassigned.** Conversations do not lead to assignment of tasks.
Level of Professional Complexity	**Professional.** The school librarian collaborates with teachers to design instructional objectives, activities, and/or assessment and to identify resources.	**Supportive.** The school librarian recommends and provides resources.	**"Go-fer."** The school librarian provides resources requested by teachers.
ACCESS			
Integrated Instruction	**Integrated.** Based on collaborative planning, classes are scheduled when activities require lessons on seeking or using information.	**Reserved.** Each class has a block of time reserved for its use as needed.	**Fixed.** Each class comes to the library on a regular basis; lessons may or may not be aligned with classroom activities.

(cont.)

FIGURE 14.2
Rubric for Program Evaluation

ACCESS (cont.)			
Access	**Open access.** Both library and classroom policies allow students to access the library at their point of need.	**Controlled.** Students have regularly scheduled opportunities to access the library.	**Limited.** Students can access the library when their class is scheduled there.
Policies	**High access.** Circulation policies regarding loan periods, loan limits, and overdues aim to maximize opportunities to use library resources.	**Controlled.** Circulation policies include provisions for limiting access when circumstances so indicate—excessive losses, overdues, etc.	**Limited.** Circulation policies limit use of the collection with ceilings on the number of resources to be borrowed, number of renewals allowed, etc.
24/7	**High access.** The library website offers 24/7 off-campus access to such resources as subscription databases, e-books, and research guides, and provides well-organized links to curriculum-relevant or student-interest websites that have been vetted for quality.	**Controlled access.** The library website offers 24/7 off-campus access to the library's online catalog only.	**Limited.** Free resources on the library webpage are accessible off-campus, but subscription databases or other fee-based resources are accessible only within the school's network.
CLIMATE			
Friendliness	**Inviting.** Students and staff feel welcome to use the library and show no hesitation to ask questions.	**Neutral.** The library elicits no affect—it is neither friendly nor unfriendly.	**Austere.** Students and teachers use the library only when necessary; they are reluctant to seek assistance.
Productivity	**Productive.** Students are working productively at worthwhile tasks; a buzz of activity is evident as groups converse about their work.	**Silent.** Students work quietly and in isolation.	**Distracting.** Too much social activity distracts from work.
User Orientation	**Assistive.** Library staff behaviors indicate to students and teachers that the library is a place for assistance and that they are important "customers."	**Passive.** Library staff will answer questions when asked but do not initiate assistance.	**Supervisory.** Library staff supervise behavior rather than provide information assistance.
COMMUNICATION			
Principal	**Shared vision.** The principal envisions the library program as an integral part of the school.	**Supportive.** The principal supports the library program with resources and communications to constituencies.	**Passive.** The principal takes no action to support the library program.

Parents	**Involved.** Parents participate in the library through volunteerism, committees, and programs.	**One-way.** Parents receive information from the library through newsletters and other communication media.	**Indirect.** Parents learn about the library program through their children or classroom teachers.
Business	**Involved.** The library program has active partnerships with businesses.	**Informative.** The library program targets relevant information to local businesses such as bookstores or technology vendors.	**Indirect.** Businesses know about the library program only from general school district communication.
Public Library	**Collaborative.** The school librarian and the public librarian communicate frequently about programs and resources.	**Informative.** The school library notifies the public library about specific programs or activities on an ad hoc basis.	**Indirect.** Libraries only know about each other's programs and resources through publicly disseminated communication.
LEADERSHIP			
Engagement	**Involved.** The librarian takes initiative to identify and promote new projects, technologies, and ideas grounded in research and professional best practice.	**Available.** The librarian is willing to participate in new initiatives in the school.	**Supportive.** The librarian envisions the library as a supportive resource for initiatives.
Change	**Initiating.** The librarian takes ownership of new initiatives and works to engage others.	**Partnering.** The librarian cooperates with teachers and administrators in implementing change.	**Accepting.** The librarian is accepting of new ideas.
Professional Learning Communities	**Leader.** The librarian is ready to lead professional learning community initiatives and accepts responsibility for organizing and coordinating professional activities at the school and/or district level.	**Participant.** The librarian participates in professional learning communities in the school or district.	**Supporter.** The librarian provides resources for professional learning communities.

Another type of comparison for benchmarking is to look at data on school library programs as represented in survey results and compare those findings to the local program to measure status or progress. The National Center for Education Statistics provides data from its Schools and Staffing Survey at its website (www.nces.ed.gov/surveys/libraries/school.asp). Tables in this report break out data by state to provide comparable settings for benchmarking. In some parts of the country, data are available from state departments of education and thus offer opportunities to benchmark a program. An advantage of state data is the comparability of budgeting methods and constraints within each state. Benchmarking involves looking for best practices, comparing the local program to those best practices, and identifying ways to improve local practice. The results of benchmarking should be shared with stakeholders to help prioritize goals and gain advocacy for program growth and development.

Whether through benchmarking, the examination of a set of standards, or the use of a rubric, the result of the comparison of the program at hand to the measure selected will reveal gaps between where the program is in its development and where it could be. This identification of gaps lays the foundation for setting and prioritizing goals.

Goal Setting

Once gaps between a standard and current program status are identified, it is important to prioritize and select high-priority goals for attention. The idea of continuous improvement ensures that the opportunity to tackle goals next in priority will come around. Goal setting needs to be realistic; setting a few goals and focusing time and resources to meet those is far better than setting many goals and finding it impossible to make progress on them all. Three to five goals may be appropriate for a year.

Action Planning and Implementation

Once priority goals are identified, an action plan is developed. An action plan identifies goals, outlines a list of steps to be taken to meet each goal, establishes who will be responsible and what the cost will be, and sets a target date for completion. Once the action plan is created, it must be carried out and its provisions implemented. Figure 14.3 shows a segment of an action plan. For each goal, assessment of progress needs to be considered. Evidence of progress is key to the continuous improvement model. This will require identifying data to collect to document progress.

FIGURE 14.3

Action Plan: School Library Program Development

Expectation from Rubric	Goal	Action Steps	Responsibility	Budget Needs	Target Date	Evidence
Cultural diversity is considered in collection development, including but not limited to cultural groups represented in the local population.	Improve representation in the collection of various cultures—especially Muslims and Latin Americans.	Identify recommended texts in Wilson Children's Core Collection. Identify texts not currently held and tag for consideration for purchase. Create list of texts with annotations. Share with teachers at relevant grade levels for input. Finalize selections. Purchase and add to collection. Market to students and teachers. Identify age-appropriate websites for a variety of cultures and create a virtual culture center on the library website.	School librarian with consultation from classroom teaches	$1,000	Sept. 2013	Use of resources in classroom units and student feedback regarding books; webpage hits
Uses of technology are chosen to expand existing curriculum goals.	Expand use of tablet technology in classrooms.	Meet with teacher teams to share exemplary applications for their curriculum and level. Arrive at consensus on at least two applications per team. Work as professional learning communities to adapt applications to meet instructional needs. Assess student engagement and student learning using the technology.	School librarian and teachers	-0-	May 2013	Student end-of-unit assessments and student interviews regarding tablet apps

327

Data Collection and Analysis

Data can be classified as direct measures or indirect measures. In addition, data can constitute inputs, outputs, and outcomes. Direct measures are just that—actual measures, such as measures of student learning through testing or performance appraisal. Direct measures can be simple counts of hits on webpages or numbers of classes in the library in a week. Indirect measures are often gathered through surveys, questionnaires, or interviews. Indirect measures often reveal people's perceptions of progress or accomplishment, and as such they may or may not be accurate. Students can respond to a questionnaire at the end of a unit indicating that their inquiry project was excellent and that they used outstanding resources. A direct measure would be derived when the librarian or teachers examine their resources against a set of standards like authority, relevance, timeliness, or lack of bias.

Inputs are measures of resources of the library such as number of online database subscriptions, seating capacity, or staffing full-time equivalency. In some instances such measures can be useful. However, more frequently output measures can indicate how the inputs are being used. Output measures include such data as circulation counts, number of classes taught per month, or number of teacher–librarian collaborative planning sessions in a week. Output measures reveal productivity and demonstrate how busy the library and its staff are. Outcome measures are the most significant measures for most key stakeholders. These are measures of the effect of the library program's activity on teaching and learning. Outcome measures are the product of the student assessment activities discussed in Chapter 13. Outcome measures can be as simple as reading logs that indicate what books children in a class are reading and whether their reading is varied, if engaging students in reading in diverse genres is a goal. For example, outcome measures can be scores measuring performance on TRAILS (Tool for Real-time Assessment of Information Literacy Skills), or they can be indirect measures such as teacher perceptions of student performance at the end of an inquiry-based unit where the library was engaged. While not a direct measure, a brief student or teacher survey at the end of an inquiry-based unit can provide some indication of how well the library program is performing. Following are examples of survey questions:

- Were your students frustrated in searching for information for their assignment?
- What topics/questions went underserved?

- Did your students have all the necessary inquiry skills to meet your standards for their assignment?
- Did students have enough time in the library to complete their work?

The data sources need to be identified during the action planning process to ensure a clear planful approach for determining the impact of activity from the action plan. By being involved in the evaluation of the library program, stakeholders increase their understanding and ownership of the program. As results are analyzed, it is important that stakeholders participate in identifying accomplishments to be recognized and in setting goals for continued improvement of the program. Participation in the analysis really provides a feeling of ownership. Finally, when stakeholders help report the results to constituents (e.g., parent organizations, faculty, and staff), they develop a sense of pride in their findings and enthusiasm for the next steps—and are more ready to support allocating the resources needed to continue improvement.

Conclusion

A teacher's perspective of the library program is reminiscent of the fable of "The Blind Man and the Elephant"—each sees the program only through the lens of his or her interaction with it. As data are collected, it is instructive to share the big picture with faculty as well as administrators, boards, and parent groups. As others learn about the totality of the program, they are more able to become advocates to help it gain the resources it needs for development. In addition, they bring perspectives that can be constructive. In the end, program evaluation is aimed at helping the program become better at supporting the mission of the school—teaching and learning. Data collection and analysis followed by sharing and gathering observations from stakeholders represent a process that can deliver the opportunity for the program to have an impact on students today and in the future.

Leadership Strategies

Teacher and Partner
   Implement data collection practices to ensure that there are data to document the impact of the school library program; for example:

- Survey teachers and/or students at the end of inquiry-based units to gather indirect measures of student learning.
- Use TRAILS consistently for assessment of student learning and to track progress over years.
- Maintain a file of units developed collaboratively by teachers and the school librarian to document contributions to teaching and learning.
- Use a matrix or curriculum map to monitor teaching of the inquiry process in the context of classroom curriculum.

Program Administrator

Advocate for a formal planning process for the library program and involve representatives of key stakeholder groups to enter the continuous improvement cycle and assess the program against a state measure (e.g., benchmark, rubric, or standards).

Report on progress in the continuous improvement model to key stakeholders.

Collect data to profile the status of the program based on inputs (e.g., staff, facilities, access, resource collection, and equipment) and outputs (e.g., circulation, classes, staff development, and teacher collaboration) and compare them to data from other programs in the state or nation.

Identify and seek resources for inputs needed for accomplishment of new goals.

Scenarios for Discussion

Scenario 1

In LouAnn's school district, each curricular area has a place on a seven-year cycle for systematic district-level program review. LouAnn is a high school librarian and has served as a committee member for the review of the social studies program. The review process includes a self-study by teachers in the program in which the department compares its curriculum and resources to national standards and to peer school districts in the state. An outside panel came to the district and performed an external audit of the program based on the self-study and then made recommendations for future enhancement of the program. As she worked with the social studies review process, it occurred to LouAnn that the library program is not included in the cycle. How might LouAnn proceed to make a case for adding the library program to the district cycle?

Scenario 2

Joan has been the school librarian at Harrison Middle School for four years. While she has worked hard to collaborate with teachers and is able to point to several individual successes in these collaborations, her principal still shows little interest in the library and has tended to reduce the library budget each year by approximately 5 percent. He is very interested in data and likes to share information about programs with parents and the central office. So, he touts the percentage of students who participate in at least one sport and the percentage of students on the honor roll. He has also publicized the small number of detentions given in the school and the attendance record of the student body. He recently published the percentage of students involved in nonathletic extracurricular activities. Joan needs to figure out how to reach her principal and educate him about the library. Is there a way that the process of program evaluation could help her? What would you suggest to her?

REFERENCES

Epper, R. M. 1999. "Applying Benchmarking to Higher Education; Some Lessons from Experience." *Change* 31, no. 6: 224–231.

Gilmore, S. L. 2009. "Evidence-Based Practice for Lifelong Learning." *Leadership* 38, no. 2: 30–31.

Kent State University Libraries. 2012. *TRAILS: Tool for Real-time Assessment of Information Literacy Skills.* Kent State University Libraries. www.trails -9.org.

NCES (National Center for Education Statistics). 2012. *Schools and Staffing Survey.* National Center for Education Statistics. www.nces.ed.gov/surveys/ libraries/school.asp.

15

Leadership

This chapter:

- describes expectations for leadership for school librarians;
- defines leadership attributes for school librarians;
- explores principle-centered leadership;
- defines the concept of influence in the context of "leading from the middle";
- considers strategic leadership;
- explores strategies for leaders to succeed as advocates; and
- identifies leadership responsibilities of the school librarian as a professional.

Throughout this book, school librarians are encouraged to play leadership roles in their schools. They bring to the school a vision for the ways in which the library program intersects with all aspects of the school community and curriculum. They work collegially with teachers, administrators, staff, and parents. They bring expertise in literacy, the inquiry process, and applications of technology appropriate for their settings. It is fitting to end this book with a chapter that explicitly profiles the leadership characteristics of the library profession.

Unfortunately, other educators tend to hold no such expectations for school librarians. Shannon (2009) investigated principals' perceptions of librarians by investigating criteria considered for hiring and competencies principals valued. Leadership related to integrating technology into teaching and learning was rated as "highly important" by 82 percent of respondents. However, when asked to rate the competence of their current librarians as curricular leaders in the same study, most principals tended not to rate them highly in this category—only 28 percent rated their school librarian highly on this competency. In Shannon's open-ended query, only 5 of the 189 respondents proposed leadership with respect to the school librarian. Such findings suggest that stereotypes die slowly, and that the notion of the librarian as a responder but not a leader persists.

Attributes of Leaders

Bennis (1999) promulgates a set of traits for successful leaders in business. These characteristics can apply also to school librarians:

Technical competence. School librarians have knowledge of information organization, teaching, management, technology, and learning resources. Their set of skills and knowledge are unique in their schools, and as potential leaders they need to make those skills visible to their colleagues.

Conceptual skill. School librarians have considerable procedural knowledge, but they also think in terms of principles and concepts. Principles of organization, access, confidentiality, and ethical use of information guide their policy making, while conceptual understanding of information systems informs their resource management and information dissemination.

People skills. School librarians know they cannot be successful in isolation. They communicate, inspire, and delegate. They establish collaborative networks within their local learning community.

Judgment. As managers of substantial space and resources, school librarians are called on to make decisions promptly, even with imperfect data. They make daily decisions regarding purchasing, resource allocation, technology, scheduling, work assignments, and instruction. To the extent possible, these decisions are informed by data, but in the real world it is rare that data are so clear and comprehensive as to remove the need for judgment calls.

Character. Grounded in the foundations of librarianship, school librarians are inspired by a set of principles that guide behavior.

Principle-Centered Leadership

The library profession is grounded in powerful overarching principles. These principles commit librarians to intellectual freedom and the right to privacy, equity of access and respect for diversity, and respect for intellectual property. The profession's principles are manifest in the American Library Association Code of Ethics.

Code of Ethics of the American Library Association

I. We provide the highest level of service to all library users through appropriate and usefully organized resources; equitable service policies; equitable access; and accurate, unbiased, and courteous responses to all requests.

II. We uphold the principles of intellectual freedom and resist all efforts to censor library resources.

III. We protect each library user's right to privacy and confidentiality with respect to information sought or received and resources consulted, borrowed, acquired, or transmitted.

IV. We respect intellectual property rights and advocate balance between the interests of information users and rights holders.

V. We treat co-workers and other colleagues with respect, fairness, and good faith, and advocate conditions of employment that safeguard the rights and welfare of all employees of our institutions.

VI. We do not advance private interests at the expense of library users, colleagues, or our employing institutions.

VII. We distinguish between our personal convictions and professional duties and do not allow our personal beliefs to interfere with fair representation of the aims of our institutions or the provision of access to their information resources.

VIII. We strive for excellence in the profession by maintaining and enhancing our own knowledge and skills, by encouraging the professional development of co-workers, and by fostering the aspirations of potential members of the profession.

Source: Office for Intellectual Freedom, "Code of Ethics of the American Library Association," part IV in *Intellectual Freedom Manual,* 8th ed. (Chicago: ALA Editions, 2010), www.ifmanual.org/codeethics.

As leaders, school librarians are guided by these principles; they apply them in decision making and policy discussions. For example, decisions regarding circulation policies are guided by a commitment to "equitable access." Collection development is guided by the professional distinction "between our personal convictions and professional duties." School librarians "respect intellectual property rights and advocate balance between the interests of information users and rights holders" in developing and implementing policies regarding the ethical use of information. The commitment to these principles affords librarians the status of a profession. While these principles complement the educational context in which school libraries reside, they define librarianship. Moreover, they demand a leadership stance for librarians to advocate for beliefs that may be tested from time to time in the school setting. Langhorne (2010: 60) asserts that leaders must have the courage to "do the right thing." Indeed, school librarians who remind themselves of their professional code of ethics are likely to have opportunities to do the right thing on behalf of the learners they respect and cherish.

Influence or "Leading from the Middle"

School librarians live in a world where they wield little authority. Even the support staff who work with them, in most settings, officially report to a school principal. This leaves librarians with a challenge to lead from the middle where they use influence rather than authority to lead change or to advance the library program. Cialdini (2001: 73) asserts, "No leader can succeed without mastering the art of persuasion." Cialdini suggests that influence depends on unwritten social rules. He identifies six principles of behavior likely to increase support and cooperation from others:

> *Liking (people like those who like them).* Cialdini cites a variety of sales research that suggests that people are more likely to make purchases from salespeople with whom they have something in common—for example, age, religion, politics, or hobbies. He suggests that a way to be liked by your colleagues is to engage in informal conversations that help you identify common ground that creates a sense of "liking" between you. Another strategy for being liked is to praise others. Again, he points to research that indicates that positive remarks about

another person's attitude or performance or other traits tend to generate "liking." Cialdini then suggests that by being liked we position ourselves to have influence.

Reciprocity (people repay in kind). The notion here is simple: do a favor for someone else and it is likely it will be repaid—whether volunteering for a committee or taking a recess duty when the principal is in a bind. While leverage may be too strong a word, in fact this is a matter of gaining a bit of it.

Social proof (people follow the lead of similar others). Testimonials from satisfied customers work best when the satisfied customer is someone people know. So, a testimonial from a teacher to other teachers in the school about a successful collaborative experience may influence your opportunities for additional collaborative partners.

Consistency (people align with their clear commitments). People tend to adhere to a commitment once they make one. This principle may underscore the value of a written collaboration plan with roles formally identified—something like a contract that implies commitment. Or, when making plans for collaboration, either the teacher or the librarian can provide a follow-up e-mail outlining what has been decided. The commitment is "sealed."

Authority (people defer to experts). Too often people have the idea that it takes no special training or special skills and knowledge to be a school librarian. If a school librarian wants to have influence and wants to be a leader, it is imperative that people know that this person has expertise. Displaying one's credentials is a start, but more important is demonstrating knowledge and expertise—whether it is in searching skills, knowledge of resources, pedagogy, or technology tools.

Scarcity (people want more of what they can have less of). This principle is one to use with caution, but it does suggest that the school librarian's time is finite. For example, when encouraging teachers to take advantage of opportunities for team teaching, there are limits, and occasionally it may be appropriate to demonstrate that with a calendar that shows how many time slots are available.

These principles suggest ways to develop relationships that open the door for influence and leadership from the middle. Chinese Taoist philosopher Lao-tzu said, "When the best leader's work is done, the people say, 'We did it ourselves.'" School librarians can succeed only when they work collegially with the other educators in their organizations. A principal holds a position of ex officio leadership in the school. The position innately holds authority and demands followership among the rest of the school community. However, a school librarian leads more often through influence; the position he or she holds, while likely to be unique in the building, is collegial and not superior to the rest of the faculty.

Leaders act from an internal locus of control. This orientation suggests that a person has the power to control the outcome of his or her own actions. By contrast, people whose orientation is an external locus of control frequently look outside themselves to explain their situation. Externally oriented school librarians might contend, for example, that they cannot teach inquiry skills because the teachers will not cooperate, or the principal does not give adequate support, or the facility does not accommodate instruction, or some other external barrier prevents their success. Internally oriented school librarians, on the other hand, will listen to teachers' concerns and find alternative ways to schedule the teaching or organize lessons to make it work for the students' sake. They embrace the responsibility to make good things happen in their schools. Locus-of-control orientation is the difference between saying, "I can find alternatives or compromises" and "There is nothing I can do." Leaders are can-do people who look to themselves to make programs great and inspire others to join in the enterprise.

Hartzell (2000) considers this can-do mind-set through the idea of being proactive. He acknowledges that one's work environment can influence the maximal level of job performance, but he quotes psychologist J. M. Crant: "The notion of proactivity argues that we can intentionally and directly influence these and other elements and by doing so influence and enhance our chances of being successful in our jobs" (Hartzell, 2000: 15). Hartzell suggests that proactive people look for change opportunities; they anticipate and prevent problems; and they take action and tend to persevere. All of these behaviors imply an internal locus of control—a belief that the power to make things work lies within and the external environment can be influenced.

In *Good to Great*, Collins (2001) analyzes why some companies "make the leap" from good companies to great companies. School librarians who aspire to lead great programs can benefit from keeping in mind two bits of advice resulting from Collins's analysis:

Understand what you can and cannot be best at. The library profession calls for diverse skill sets that include knowledge of the literature appropriate for the ages of students served, skill in technology applications, knowledge of information organization systems, and teaching aptitude. Clearly, each school librarian has special strengths in some areas of expertise. Leaders will work to be the best at those areas and will strive to be as good in other areas as is reasonable. Rare is the school librarian who is a true expert in all dimensions of the field. The challenge is to pursue to the maximum what one has aptitude for and strive for acceptable performance in the other aspects of the field.

Pursue what you are deeply passionate about. Passion is a word often associated with leadership. Soul-searching to determine where one's passion lies is a first step toward becoming a leader—whether that passion is the gratifying feeling of seeing a student learn something new, the effect of a literary work, the power of technology to communicate information, or any other aspect of the profession. While the library program is comprehensive and embraces many dimensions, the passion for one aspect of the field will generate the intense enthusiasm to invigorate and inspire students and to keep oneself energized. This is not to say that all other aspects can be ignored, but acknowledging and pursuing one's passion can help sustain one's own energy as a leader.

Strategic Leadership

Strategic is a word often used to describe military operations where the key steps are anticipating what needs to happen, devising a plan to set the course of action, and organizing resources to carry out the plan for success. Critical attributes include looking to a desirable future (vision), planning the steps for attaining that future (action planning), and assessing progress (benchmarks and outcomes). Effective library programs are ever-changing, and setting the course for change requires strategic thinking and strategic leadership. Reeves (2002) defines strategic leadership as the simultaneous act of executing, evaluating, and reformulating strategies, and focusing organizational energy and resources on the most effective strategies. Since it is likely that teachers and administrators have not personally experienced the kind of library program called for in national guidelines, the school librarian must be proactive in articulating a vision for the library media program.

A vision is a clear mental picture of a desired future. A vision needs to be easily perceived and clearly communicated. A library might be a learning commons. Such a vision is quite different from a storehouse of educational resources. What image does the library bring to mind?

Libraries as Learning Commons

"Our Library Learning Commons is a place where groups of students investigate and problem-solve in self-defined directions, limited only by the creativity of their questioning." (Newton North High School, Newton, MA)

"The Library Commons in Newman Library brings together library, technology, campus services and refreshment in an environment that fosters informal, collaborative and creative work, and social interaction." (Virginia Tech, Blacksburg, VA)

"At any hour of the day and throughout much of the night, we are a place where great thinking and learning happens." (Cornell College, Mount Vernon, IA)

"The learning commons is a place of teaching and learning, group work, collaboration, professional development, creativity, change, inquiry, communication, and community." (Chelmsford High School, Chelmsford, MA)

"Belmonte Middle School's learning commons is a center for information, knowledge and enjoyment. The environment is one of inquiry and creativity, not just skill-building and fact-gathering." (Saugus, MA)

Close behind development of a vision is the need to articulate a mission statement for the library program. While this statement can be developed collaboratively with other educators in the school, the leadership for its development comes from the school librarian. The mission statement will provide a focus for developing the goals and objectives of the program aligned with the school's mission and goals.

Another aspect of strategic leadership is opportunism. A strategic leader is in a state of readiness—ready to seize opportunities as they arise. Davies (2003) describes strategic leaders as having the ability to define the critical

Learning Commons Mission Statements

"The Learning Commons is a nexus of student, faculty and staff collaboration devoted to promoting positive conditions for student learning inside and outside the classroom." (Tallahassee Community College, Tallahassee, FL)

"The Learning Commons fosters a collaborative approach to learning by integrating informational materials, technological resources and support services into a comfortable and accessible space in order to provide students, faculty and staff with an environment for instruction, interaction and inspiration." (University of North Carolina–Wilmington, Wilmington, NC)

"The mission of the Lawrence High School Campus Learning Commons is to enable students to become educated, self-confident, lifelong learners and responsible citizens." (Lawrence High School, Lawrence, MA)

"Our ongoing mission . . . to boldly search where no one has searched before!" (Watertown Middle School, Watertown, MA)

"The Learning Commons creates and cultivates a vibrant, welcoming and integrated learner-centered environment." (University of Massachusetts–Dartmouth, Dartmouth, MA)

moment for new directions or interventions. When a school staff begins discussion of a new curriculum initiative—character education or integrated mathematics, for example—the strategic leader is ready to assert how the library program fits into that initiative. This requires a strategic mind-set, calling for the librarian to be active in committees, task forces, brainstorming sessions, leadership teams, or whatever forms idea-generating groups take within the school. In football parlance, the winning coach or the effective leader is not bound to the playbook but is ready to go with the "audible" play or formation when the situation arises. Some people attribute success to luck or serendipity (Blanchard and Shula, 2002). The school of strategic leadership says, however, that people create their own luck or seize the opportunities that serendipity offers.

Effective leaders reflect periodically on progress made and goals yet to be met. At least once a year it is worthwhile to ask three questions:

- What will I do differently from what I did last year?
- What will I stop doing that I did last year?
- How and when will I know that I am making progress?

Meanwhile, each day for a leader ends with questions like these:

- What did I learn today?
- Who did I nurture today?
- What challenge did I confront today?
- How did I make a positive difference today?

Advocacy

Advocacy is a key responsibility of a library leader. The lack of understanding of the school library profession across all educational professions as well as among parents and other stakeholders demands that school librarians advocate for their programs. Key audiences are the teachers and students for whom the library program exists, and people of influence such as school administrators and boards and parents. Effective advocacy begins with getting the facts. Data that indicate students are learning significant skills and dispositions through the library program underpin advocacy efforts, because for most constituents student learning is the bottom line. Data from assessment of student work in inquiry projects, from standardized testing that reveals learning in the library, or from student self-reporting are examples. A most important strategy for advocacy is to embed the intended audience's agenda into the message. When speaking to a parent group, a savvy school librarian will imagine what is on their minds—literacy, technology skills, critical thinking skills, affinity for reading—and weave the library message into what matters to them. Similarly, when standing before a board of education, the question in mind needs to be, What matters to them—Internet safety, efficient use of resources, or confidence of the community in the school? Again, the school librarian must consider the audience carefully. Advocacy cannot be successful if it sounds like complaining or has a negative spin. Jargon also has no place when advocating for the school library program. Somehow, the message must be framed in positive language. For example, a narrative can be very effective in helping nonlibrarians envision what is and what can be happening in a school library. Storytelling can be powerful and personal. In short, advocacy requires careful planning, positive demeanor, and clarity.

The American Association of School Librarians (AASL) offers substantial advice for advocacy in its toolkit (www.ala.org/aasl/aaslissues/toolkits/slmhealthandwellness). Among the AASL recommendations is a planning outline for advocacy that includes these steps:

Identify the school library program's stakeholders and their agendas. For each stakeholder group, list their issues, concerns, priorities, and needs. Too often, school librarians focus on the library and their own positions, when effective advocacy will focus on the people the library program affects.

Analyze stakeholder goals and issues for potential alignment with library activities and resources. Identify ways in which the library program addresses the agendas of each stakeholder group. Adjust current programs to be more responsive to stakeholder priorities. Develop new library programs and resources to address stakeholder needs.

Build promotional efforts around stakeholder needs. Leverage the library program through messages that reveal how the library serves and meets the needs of stakeholders. Position the library as a solution.

Collect and analyze relevant data about library programs and resources. One of the primary things to be measured is student learning and the impact on student achievement. Use data to identify ways to improve practice and make library programs and resources more responsive to stakeholder needs.

Organize and utilize the data that show contributions to educational goals. Make positive messages and evidence of student learning part of the culture of the library program. Take the initiative to report data about how the library impacts students' information, technology, and reading skills. Be prepared to share building- and district-level library program data. Write articles and regular reports giving concrete evidence of what the library does to prepare students to be successful in the twenty-first century.

Of particular importance is understanding that advocacy begins before a crisis—before a program is challenged. Advocacy begins by building support among key stakeholders every day by making visible what the library program does to enhance learning and teaching, and what the teacher librarian does to help parents and teachers.

Professional Leadership Responsibilities

To belong to a profession brings expectations of leadership. A profession is composed of persons who share a special set of qualifications, an ethical code, a distinctive body of knowledge grounded in scholarship and principles, a set of standards of performance, and a shared commitment to continuous improvement. School librarianship is a profession unto its own within the educational community, and as members of that profession school librarians have responsibilities to uphold the ethical code of the library profession and to engage in professional activity that will sustain and advance the profession.

Professional Associations

National and state professional associations are partners in advocacy, scholarship, and continuous professional improvement. In a world of multiple demands on one's time, school librarians may think that devoting time and money for active participation in professional associations is not a high priority. However, a profession is marked by commitment to its professional association, and these entities maintain the standards that guide the profession. They lobby on behalf of the profession to garner resources and commitment and provide professional development and networking opportunities. These benefits are easy to take for granted, but they cannot continue without leadership. Associations do their substantive work through their members who volunteer for leadership positions, accept invitations to contribute to shared professional work, and support the association through their participation in events. To appreciate the importance of associations, school librarians might wonder what if they had no association; for example:

- Who would support the profession in Washington, DC?
- Where would school librarians turn for questions regarding censorship?
- Who would develop student standards for inquiry-based learning?
- Who would recognize outstanding performances in our profession?
- Who would support and advance research to inform our practice?
- Who would provide venues for sharing new insights and ideas?
- How would professionals develop networks with other professionals to create learning communities that inform practice and advance professional growth?

Yet, professional associations accomplish these and many other activities only when leaders step forward to be actively engaged. This is one responsibility that comes with being a professional and seeking respect as such.

Similarly, school librarians as leaders have a responsibility to nurture newcomers to the field. School librarians can mentor their own students toward the information professions by showing enthusiasm for what they do and by encouraging students to consider the career opportunities the field offers in schools and in other settings. For the field to flourish, it must attract bright newcomers, and those working in the profession are best positioned to encourage them.

Action Research

While scholarship is a central responsibility of the faculty who populate the institutions of higher education, practitioners can also contribute to the advancement of our understanding of the profession and its manifestation in teaching and learning. Action research is a process of systematic inquiry into one's own practice (Diana, 2011). Howard and Eckhardt (2005) propose a set of steps that describe the action research process for school librarians. While there is not a standard protocol for action research, it generally follows this pattern:

Identify a problem to investigate. A reflective school librarian resides in a mode of reflective self-assessment, continually observing and wondering. What went well today? How might I have improved on a lesson? How might the school library be situated to better assist? What gaps in student learning do I observe and how could the library fill them? Once a problem is identified, the school librarian sets out to learn about it by investigating what is in the professional and scholarly literature and by carefully observing phenomena within the real school setting.

Review the literature. The next step is to investigate the professional literature (journals and books) to determine whether others have examined your topic already and with what results.

Examine the school context. It is important to make visible any aspects of the school culture or environment that may influence the solution to a problem, such as the proportion of English language learners, rate of poverty, degree of family engagement in student learning, and so on.

Implement response/collect data. Grounded in the findings from observation and literature review, the school librarian lays out a plan for implementing a response (e.g., a program, design, or set of activities) and a design for collecting data to monitor the effects of the response. Diana (2011) recommends that the plan for data collection consider triangulation, that is, use multiple sources of data to verify the findings. Action research usually lacks the size of population to be subjected to statistical analysis to confirm significance; however, by triangulating the data, the credibility of the findings is enhanced. Examples of data sources might be interviews, surveys, student work samples, structured observational notes, or recordings.

Analyze data and synthesize results. Once data are collected, the school librarian then investigates the findings and looks for patterns or themes in the data, seeking a conclusion as to the effectiveness of the response to the problem. It is as important to find that a response to a problem did not produce the desired result as it is to find a successful solution. Action research is, after all, a never-ending cycle where the outcome typically leads to the next question or problem for either taking a new approach to a problem or refining and improving one. It is this very cyclical nature that makes action research an important professional responsibility, if we are indeed committed to the professional principle of continuous improvement.

Gordon (2008) describes an example of action research in a high school where the problem identified was low participation in summer reading among high school students. The action research involved implementation of a web-based summer reading program. The outcome of the first cycle resulted in ideas for improvement of the program in the subsequent summer. Because of the systematic collection of data from one year, it was evident to the action researcher what kinds of changes should be attempted in the second season. By continuously adhering to an action research model, the program could be refined and improved each year. School librarians can engage in action research independently, in partnership with other teachers in the school, or in partnership with faculty in higher education. Results can be shared locally with teachers in the building, within the state through the state professional organization conferences or publications, or in national publications or conferences. In this way, action research can add to the understanding of professional practice.

National Board for Professional Teaching Standards

Established in 1987, the National Board for Professional Teaching Standards (National Board) offers National Board certification that attests to a teacher's high-level skills and ability to satisfy rigorous professional teaching standards. The National Board has established a set of standards for certification as a Library Media specialist. The standards are organized around what school librarians know, what they do, and how they grow as professionals. Candidates are required to provide evidence of their work within each of these areas of the standards. The process is rigorous, but the result is certification as a professional leader in a context well respected throughout the education profession. Details are available at www.nbpts.org/for_candidates/certificate_areas1?ID=19&x=43&y=12.

Although board certification is holistically aimed at leadership, the standards also have a focus area in Standard X related to leadership in the Library Media certificate area. Here, school librarians are described as "instructional leaders who forge greater opportunities for learners" (National Board, 2001: 43). School librarians carry out that role by taking initiative, partnering with other educators, reflecting on professional practices, assessing, and evaluating. They communicate with stakeholders in their community, manage staff and resources, and use research to support programs for which they advocate. The specific standards (National Board, 2009: 2) state that "accomplished library media specialists . . .

- have knowledge of learning styles and of human growth and development.
- know the principles of teaching and learning that contribute to an active learning environment.
- know the principles of library and information studies needed to create effective, integrated library programs.
- integrate information literacy through collaboration, planning, implementation, and assessment of learning.
- lead in providing equitable access to and effective use of technologies and innovations.
- plan, develop, implement, manage, and evaluate library programs to ensure that students and staff use ideas and information effectively.
- engage in reflective practice to increase their effectiveness.
- model a strong commitment to lifelong learning and to their profession.
- uphold professional ethics and promote equity and diversity.
- advocate for the library program, involving the greater community."

These are the behaviors of leaders in the school library profession. The National Board certification process is a voluntary opportunity for an experienced school librarian to take the challenge of examining his or her professional practice, measuring it against rigorous standards, and attaining affirmation as a professional leader.

Conclusion

The courage to do the right thing—this is the mark of a leader. School librarians can look to a set of professional principles that guide the profession and challenge librarians to be leaders as they advocate for what is best for creating a learning environment likely to develop the skills and dispositions for lifelong learning. Library leadership calls for specific abilities and dispositions to envision and then articulate what the library program can become for all of its constituencies. Further, leadership calls for behaviors that help the librarian garner the influence needed to lead from the middle. The profession's future depends on school librarians accepting their responsibility to lead.

Leadership Strategies

Teacher and Partner

Identify your special expertise (e.g., literature, technology, or information searching) and play to that strength in developing the library program and establishing your relationship with teachers. Develop your skills in other areas as required to meet the needs of your constituencies.

Apply Cialdini's (2001) principles to build relationships with colleagues so that you can influence their work and encourage collaboration with you.

Information Specialist

Increase the visibility of the library with an easily navigable library home page. Include the library program's vision and mission statement on the page. Advocate high-profile linking from the school's home page to the library page.

Make careful observations of the library program with an intention to identify problems to be addressed through the systematic inquiry of action research.

Pay attention to the work of your professional associations—state and national—and use information you glean there to inform your constituencies about school libraries.

Program Administrator

Add information about careers in librarianship to the library's home page.

Review the work occurring in the school library and answer the question, How is the library affecting student learning? Share the answers with constituents.

Volunteer to be on building-wide committees (e.g., the school improvement plan team, the faculty council, the technology team, the parent advisory committee, and the curriculum council) and then be an active participant. Listen well and volunteer to be the note taker/reporter. Write up and distribute the minutes promptly. Whatever the actual work of the committee (drafting/writing goals, conducting surveys, or putting together slides), volunteer to do it. Thoughtfully offer up your viewpoint, which is slightly more global than that of most classroom teachers.

Scenarios for Discussion

Scenario 1

Joan's principal has invited her to be the speaker for the program meeting of the parent organization at her elementary school in November, because he heard that National Library Week occurs during that month and though this might be a topic of interest. The school has been working hard to improve its performance on standardized tests in literacy especially. There also are parents who are curious about technology and its place in the elementary school, mostly from community concerns about the money being spent equipping schools and the need for accountability and understanding how technology investment benefits students. As often occurs, there have been parent rumblings about Internet safety and stories of some cyberbullying that have cast a shadow over technology implementation. What should Joan focus her presentation on? What advice would you give her for taking best advantage of this opportunity?

Scenario 2

David has been in his high school library position for two years now. He arrived at a rather traditional quiet library and is determined to liven it up. However, in this academically ambitious school the expectation of students, teachers, administrators, and parents is that a library is a quiet place for individual work. This is not to say that the library lacks technology or electronic resources of connectivity. It has excellent high-speed Internet access, Wi-Fi, 75 individual desktop workstations, and a wealth of print and online resources including e-books and subscription databases. It is the atmosphere that concerns David. Because of the expectation for a quiet space for individual work, the library clientele is made up of perhaps 20 percent of the student body—the highest-achieving, most ambitious students in the school. The rest of the student body tends not to approach this space. Teachers, meanwhile, have shown great reluctance to bring their classes to the library for fear of disrupting the quiet study environment they believe a library represents. How does David proceed to attract more students to the library and to embolden teachers to bring their classes there for instruction, group work, and access to rich resources?

REFERENCES

Bennis, W. 1999. "The Leadership Advantage." *Leader to Leader* 12. www.hr-newcorp.com/articles/bennis_Leaders.pdf.

Blanchard, K., and D. Shula. 2002. *The Little Book of Coaching.* New York: HarperBusiness.

Cialdini, R. B. 2001. "Harnessing the Science of Persuasion." *Harvard Business Review* 79, no. 9: 72–79.

Collins, J. 2001. *Good to Great: Why Some Companies Make the Leap . . . and Others Don't.* New York: HarperBusiness.

Davies, B. 2003. "Rethinking Strategy and Strategic Leadership in Schools." *Educational Management and Administration* 31, no. 3: 295–312.

Diana, T. J. 2011. "Becoming a Teacher Leader through Action Research." *Kappa Delta Pi Record* 47, no. 4: 170–173.

Gordon, C. A. 2008. "A Never-Ending Story: Action Research Meets Summer Reading." *Knowledge Quest* 37, no. 2: 34–41.

Hartzell, G. 2000. "Being Proactive." *Book Report* 18, no. 5: 14–19.

Howard, J. K., and S. A. Eckhardt. 2005. "Why Action Research? The Leadership Role of the Library Media Specialist." *Library Media Connection* 24, no. 2: 32–34.

Langhorne, J. 2010. *Beyond Luck: Practical Steps to Navigate the Path from Manager to Leader.* Coralville, IA: Corridor Media Group.

National Board (National Board for Professional Teaching Standards). 2001. *Library Media Standards.* National Board for Professional Teaching Standards. www.nbpts.org/userfiles/File/ecya_lm_standards.pdf.

———. 2009. *Early Childhood through Young Adulthood: Library Media.* National Board for Professional Teaching Standards. www.nbpts.org/userfiles/File/ECYA_LM_AssessAtaGlance.pdf.

Office for Intellectual Freedom. 2010. "Code of Ethics of the American Library Association." Part IV in *Intellectual Freedom Manual.* 8th ed. Chicago: ALA Editions. www.ifmanual.org/codeethics.

Reeves, D. B. 2002. *The Daily Discipline of Leadership: How to Improve Students' Achievement, Staff Motivation, and Personal Organization.* San Francisco: Jossey-Bass.

Shannon, D. 2009. "Principals' Perspectives of School Librarians." *School Libraries Worldwide* 15, no. 2: 1–22.

For Further Reading

This selective compilation of books can enrich the professional collection of the school library. The resources were selected specifically to facilitate the connection between the library program and its educational community. For school librarians who are collaborators in book study or professional learning communities, these titles may be worthy of consideration.

Students

Kohn, A. 1993. *Punished by Rewards: The Trouble with Gold Stars, Incentive Plans, A's, Praise, and Other Bribes.* Boston: Houghton Mifflin. This classic work discusses the dangers of reliance on extrinsic rewards.

Monteil-Overton, P., and D. C. Adcock, eds. 2008. *School Library Services in a Multicultural Society.* Chicago: American Association of School Librarians. A collection of nine articles from issues of *Knowledge Quest* provides insight into various aspects of library programming in a multicultural context.

Munk, D. D. 2010. *Leadership Strategies for Successful Schoolwide Inclusion: The STAR Approach.* Baltimore, MD: Paul Brooks. A practical guide to inclusion, emphasizing collaboration among professionals.

Sousa, D. A., and C. A. Tomlinson. 2011. *Differentiation and the Brain: How Neuroscience Supports the Learner-Friendly Classroom.* Bloomington, IN: Solution Tree Press. Covers a variety of aspects of differentiation, of which one particularly interesting topic is the effect of the teacher's mind-set on students.

Curriculum

Erickson, H. L. 2007. *Stirring the Head, Heart, and Soul: Redefining Curriculum and Instruction.* 3rd ed. Thousand Oaks, CA: Corwin. Offers planning tools and specific classroom examples of effective teaching strategies. The author focuses on the need for curriculum and instruction that allow students to move beyond factual learning to a level of understanding where knowledge transfers readily to new situations.

Wiggins, G., and J. McTighe. 1998. *Understanding by Design.* Alexandria, VA: Association for Supervision and Curriculum Development. Raises important questions about the design of curriculum; for example, How do we pose essential questions that lead to deep learning? How can we design curriculum to engage students in the facets of understanding (i.e., explanation, interpretation, application, perspective, empathy, and self-knowledge)?

Zmuda, A., and V. H. Harada. 2008. *Librarians as Learning Specialists: Meeting the Learning Imperative for the 21st Century.* Westport, CT: Libraries Unlimited. Examines the role of school librarians in the context of the school curriculum.

The Principal

Farmer, L. S. J. 2007. *Collaborating with Administrators and Educational Support Staff.* New York: Neal-Schuman. Provides strategies and justification for working with school administrators and also addresses working with other staff in the school context.

McGhee, M. W., and B. A. Jansen. 2010. *The Principal's Guide to a Powerful Library Media Program: A School Library for the 21st Century.* Santa Barbara, CA: Linworth. As a practical handbook for principals, supports working with the school librarian; includes several appendices that offer worksheets for personnel and budget tasks.

Community

Doll, C., and B. Doll. 2010. *The Resilient School Library.* Santa Barbara, CA: Libraries Un-limited. Offers advice on how school libraries can support children at risk.

Feinberg, S., et al. 2007. *The Family-Centered Library Handbook.* New York: Neal-Schuman. Aimed at public libraries, offers ideas for how any library program can reach out to families, particularly in support of literacy.

Collaboration

Buzzeo, T. 2007. *Collaborating to Meet Standards: Teacher/Librarian Partner-ships for K–6.* Worthington, OH: Linworth. Describes the ideals of collabora-tion and some of the variations found in schools. Includes a template for use in planning collaborative units, with samples of task analysis activities for students, interviewing guides, and rubrics.

Rosenfeld, E., and D. Loertscher. 2007. *Toward a 21st-Century School Library Media Program.* Lanham, MD: Scarecrow Press. Covers a wide range of topics associated with collaboration and integration of the library program across the curriculum.

Wallace, V., and W. N. Husid. 2011. *Collaborating for Inquiry-Based Learning: School Librarians and Teachers Partner for Student Achievement.* Santa Barbara, CA: Libraries Unlimited. Outlines best practices for collaboration between teachers and school librarians.

Access for Learning and Teaching

Adams, H. 2008. *Ensuring Intellectual Freedom and Access to Information in the School Library Media Program.* Westport, CT: Libraries Unlimited. Defines intellectual freedom in the context of the school library; also discusses privacy and First Amendment rights.

Everhart, N. 2003. *Controversial Issues in School Librarianship: Divergent Perspectives* (Managing the 21st Century Library Media Center). Worthington, OH: Linworth. Provides various perspectives on scheduling for teaching in the library as well as flexible access, in particular in the chapter on scheduling.

Collection

Bishop, K. 2007. *The Collection Program in Schools.* Westport, CT: Libraries Unlimited. Discusses needs assessment, selection policies and criteria, maintenance, circulation, and promotion.

Gregory, V. L. 2011. *Collection Development and Management for 21st Century Library Collections.* New York: Neal-Schuman. As a practical guide, includes policy issues as well as specific procedures for collection development and management.

Johnson, P. 2009. *Fundamentals of Collection Development and Management.* Chicago: American Library Association. Covers all aspects of collection development, maintenance, and marketing for all types of libraries, including school libraries.

Lowe, K. 2001. *Resource Alignment: Providing Curriculum Support in the School Library Media Center.* Millers Creek, NC: Beacon Consulting. Includes steps and strategies for honing a collection that is aligned with curriculum standards.

Literacy

Daniels, H. 2002. *Literature Circles: Voice and Choice in Book Clubs and Reading Groups.* Portland, ME: Stenhouse. Addresses common pitfalls in implementing student-led discussion groups and discusses mature or "advanced" literature circles, as well as provides strategies, structures, tools, and stories to support literature circles.

Gallagher, K. 2004. *Deeper Reading: Comprehending Challenging Texts, 4–12.* Portland, ME: Stenhouse. Provides strategies to teach students to successfully read a broad range of challenging and difficult texts with deeper levels of comprehension.

Gear, A. 2008. *Nonfiction Reading Power.* Portland, ME: Stenhouse. Grounded in the use of nonfiction trade books, provides strategies for teaching students to comprehend and extract information from informational texts.

Szymusiak, L., F. Sibberson, and L. Koch. 2008. *Beyond Leveled Books: Supporting Early and Transitional Readers in Grades K–5.* 2nd ed.

Portland, ME: Stenhouse. Guides young children in transitioning to independent reading.

The Virtual Library

Berger, P., and S. Trexler. 2010. *Choosing Web 2.0 Tools for Learning and Teaching in a Digital World*. Santa Barbara, CA: Libraries Unlimited. Offers strategies and examples for integrating Web 2.0 tools into instruction in the school and the school library.

Scheeren, W. O. 2010. *Technology for the School Librarian: Theory and Practice*. Santa Barbara, CA: Libraries Unlimited. Describes technology applications for the school library context; of particular note are chapters on the library website and Web 2.0 tools.

Technology Leadership

Farmer, L. S. J., and M. E. McPhee. 2010. *Neal-Schuman Technology Management Handbook for School Library Media Centers*. New York: Neal-Schuman. Includes all aspects of technology planning, maintenance, and policy.

Inquiry-Based Learning

Harvey, S., and H. Daniels. 2009. *Comprehension and Collaboration: Inquiry Circles in Action*. Portland, ME: Stenhouse. Integrates reading comprehension, student collaboration, and inquiry into ideas for working together to act on curiosity.

Langhorne, M. J., and D. Rehmke. 2011. *Developing 21st Century Literacies: A K–12 School Library Curriculum Blueprint with Sample Lessons*. New York: Neal-Schuman. Provides principles of developing a library curriculum that includes information literacy and literature strands. Sample lessons add practicality.

Small, R. V., M. Arnone, B. K. Stripling, and P. Berger. 2012. *Teaching for Inquiry: Engaging the Learner Within*. New York: Neal-Schuman. Addresses the AASL *Standards for the 21st-Century Learner* call for inquiry-based learning and includes planning tools and models for implementation of an inquiry model.

Thomas, N. P., S. Crow, and L. L. Franklin. 2011. *Information Literacy and Information Skills Instruction: Applying Research to Practice in the 21st Century School Library.* Santa Barbara, CA: Libraries Unlimited. Provides a comprehensive review of research on teaching information literacy skills.

Assessment of Student Learning

Church, A. P. 2003. *Leverage Your Libraries to Raise Test Scores: A Guide for Library Media Specialists, Principals, Teachers, and Parents.* Worthington, OH: Linworth. Explains the finding of major testing studies and discusses the implications for instruction; also examines elements of successful media programs.

Harada, V., and J. Yoshina. 2005. *Assessing Learning: Librarians and Teachers as Partners.* Westport, CT: Libraries Unlimited. Covers purposes of assessment, essential elements of assessment, knowing what to assess, multiple methods for assessment, and management and communication of assessment results.

Tallman, J. I., and M. Z. Joyce. 2006. *Making the Writing Connection with the I-Search Process: A How-to-Do-It Manual.* 2nd ed. New York: Neal-Schuman. Explains the I-Search process, in which students write in the first person and invest themselves in describing both their search process and their findings.

Library Program Evaluation

Adcock, D., ed. 2010. *A Planning Guide for Empowering Learners with Assessment Rubric.* Chicago: American Association of School Librarians/American Library Association. Serves as a planning guide for implementation of the library programs laid out in Adcock's *A Planning Guide for Information Power* (AASL/ALA, 1999) and includes a set of rubrics to assist in evaluating library media programs.

Nebraska Educational Media Association. 2010. *Guide for Developing and Evaluating School Library Programs.* Santa Barbara, CA: ABC-CLIO. Includes surveys, checklists, and other practical tools for evaluating programs, collection, and facility.

Leadership

Andrews, S. 2012. *The Power of Data: An Introduction to Using Local, State, and National Data to Support School Library Programs.* Chicago: ALA Editions. Advises on ways to use data to advocate for the school library program for a variety of audiences, including school administrators, teachers, parents, and other key stakeholders.

Bush, G., and J. J. Jones. 2010. *Tales Out of the School Library: Developing Professional Dispositions.* Santa Barbara, CA: Libraries Unlimited. Discusses a variety of issues of disposition for library leaders, including ethics, communication, and advocacy.

Crowley, J. D. 2011. *Developing a Vision: Strategic Planning for the School Librarian in the 21st Century.* 2nd ed. Santa Barbara, CA: ABC-CLIO. Presents a model for applying strategic planning steps to the library program.

Langhorne, J. E. 2010. *Beyond Luck.* Coralville, IA: Corridor Media Group. Offers practical guidance in principle-centered leadership.

Levitov, D., ed. 2012. *Activism and the School Librarian: Tools for Advocacy and Survival.* Santa Barbara, CA: ABC-CLIO. Provides a step-by-step approach to developing an advocacy program, with emphasis on the proactive stance of the school librarian.

Toor, R., and H. Weisburg. 2011. *Being Indispensable: A School Librarian's Guide to Becoming an Invaluable Leader.* Chicago: ALA Editions. Guides school librarians in being strategic and applying marketing techniques to communicate the value of the library program.

Index